Developing Corporate Social Responsibility

This book is dedicated to Italy

......Non semper ea sunt quae videntur: decipit
frons prima multos, rara mens intellegit
quod interiore condidit cura angulo......

Phaedrus (20 B.C. – A.D. 50)
Phaedri Augusti liberti fabulae Aesopiae, Liber Quartus

Developing Corporate Social Responsibility

A European Perspective

Francesco Perrini

Stefano Pogutz

Antonio Tencati

Bocconi University, Milan, Italy

Edward Elgar
Cheltenham, UK • Northampton, MA, USA

Published by
Edward Elgar Publishing Limited
Glensanda House
Montpellier Parade
Cheltenham
Glos GL50 1UA
UK

Edward Elgar Publishing, Inc.
136 West Street
Suite 202
Northampton
Massachusetts 01060
USA

A catalogue record for this book
is available from the British Library

Library of Congress Cataloguing in Publication Data

Perrini, Francesco.
   Developing corporate social responsibility / Francesco Perrini, Stefano
Pogutz, Antonio Tencati.
      p. cm.
   Includes bibliographical references and index.
1.   Social responsibility of business. I. Pogutz, Stefano. II. Tencati,
Antonio. III. Title.
   HD60.P4258 2006
   658.4'08–dc22

                                              2006012799

ISBN-13: 978 1 84542 782 5
ISBN-10: 1 84542 782 3

Printed and bound in Great Britain by MPG Books Ltd, Bodmin, Cornwall

Contents

Figures

Tables

Boxes

Contributors

Francesco Perrini
Associate Professor of Management and CSR, 'G. Pivato' Department of Management (IEGI) and Senior Professor of Corporate Finance and Real Estate, SDA Bocconi School of Management, Bocconi University. Board member and Coordinator of the Academic Committee of I-CSR, the Italian Centre for Social Responsibility, Milan, Italy.
Email: francesco.perrini@unibocconi.it

Stefano Pogutz
Assistant Professor of Management and CSR, 'G. Pivato' Department of Management (IEGI) and Senior Researcher at SPACE, the European Research Centre on Risk, Security, Occupational Health and Safety, Environment and Crisis Management, Bocconi University. Coordinator of Bocconi University 1st Level Master's Program in Environmental Economics and Management.
Email: stefano.pogutz@unibocconi.it

Carlo Secchi
Professor of European Economic Policy at Bocconi University in Milan, where he was Rector in the period 2000-2004. He is currently the Director of the Institute of Latin American Studies and on Transition Economies and Special Advisor for International Activities. He was a member of the European Parliament in the IV Legislature (1994-99), where he was Vice-President of the Economic and Monetary Affairs Committee. He is the Chairman of the Italian Group of the Trilateral Commission and of the Italian Centre for Social Responsibility (I-CSR).
Email: carlo.secchi@unibocconi.it

Antonio Tencati
Assistant Professor of Management and CSR, 'G. Pivato' Department of Management (IEGI) and Senior Researcher at SPACE, the European Research Centre on Risk, Security, Occupational Health and Safety, Environment and Crisis Management, Bocconi University. Vice-Coordinator of the Academic Committee of I-CSR, the Italian Centre for Social Responsibility, Milan, Italy.
   Email: antonio.tencati@unibocconi.it

David Vogel
Solomon Lee Professor of Business Ethics at the Haas School of Business and Professor of Political Science at the University of California, Berkeley, USA. Member of Academic Committee of I-CSR, the Italian Centre for Social Responsibility, Milan, Italy. His most recent book is *The Market for Virtue. The Potential and Limits of Corporate Social Responsibility.*
   Email: vogel@haas.berkeley.edu

Clodia Vurro
PhD student of Business Administration and Management at Bocconi University. Research Assistant at SPACE, the European Research Centre on Risk, Security, Occupational Health and Safety, Environment and Crisis Management, and the 'G. Pivato' Department of Management (IEGI), Bocconi University, Milan, Italy.
   Email: clodia.vurro@unibocconi.it

Preface *by David Vogel*

While the concept of corporate social responsibility (henceforth CSR) is more than a century old, the last decade has witnessed an unprecedented explosion of interest in this subject on the part of the business, academic and policy communities. This growth of interest in CSR is notable on several dimensions. These include the number of global firms, as well as global industries that have issued codes of conduct governing various aspects of their social, environmental and human rights policies and practices, the expansion in the number of social or ethical brands, labeling and certification schemes, the increase in the number and size of ethical or social investment funds, the expansion in the number of non-governmental organizations that monitor and assess corporate practices, the growth in the number of firms that issue annual social reports, and the increasing interest in governments in promoting more responsible business practices,

Perhaps most significantly has been the change in global business norms and public expectations. CSR is not longer a marginal or contested ideology. The notion that the social contribution of firms extends beyond maximizing shareholder value and that managers have an affirmative responsibility for both reducing the negative social impacts of their business operations and increasing the supply of various public goods is now widely accepted – by firms, the public and governments.

Perhaps nowhere is the increasing legitimacy of CSR more striking than in Europe. Two decades ago, CSR was largely an American construct, rooted in the distinctive historical role played by business and government in American society capitalism. Specifically, CSR reflected the limited role of the state in the development of American capitalism and the reliance of America on private institutions, such as the corporation, in supplying a wide range of public services that in Europe were traditionally delivered by governments.

The contemporary growth of interest in CSR has taken place on both sides of the Atlantic. Yet it is clear that the global center of gravity of CSR has now switched to Europe. London has replaced New York City and Washington as the intellectual and organizational locus of CSR activity. It is where a disproportionate amount of NGOs engaged in lobbying corporations are headquartered and is the location for a major share of international conferences on CSR. European based multi-nationals are more likely to subscribe to the United Nations Global Compact and to utilize the Global Reporting Initiative in reporting on their social impact. The market share of a number of ethical brands and labels is higher in much of Europe than in the United States.

Perhaps most importantly, European governments, including the European Union, have become much more active in promoting CSR than has the American government. In particular, several European countries have enacted legislation that both requires institutional investors to consider social and ethical criteria in making investment decisions and mandates corporate social and environmental reporting.

The factors underlying the 'Europeanization' of CSR are complex. One has to do with the increased role of markets and market competition due to the reduction of trade barriers both within Europe and globally and the movement toward privatization and deregulation, both of which have focused increased public attention on the social role and responsibilities of firms. A second factor is the increase in public concern with the global dimensions of CSR and in particular with the extent to which the impact of economic globalization has adequately benefited citizens and employees in developing countries. In part because of their heritage of colonialism, citizens and policy-makers in many European countries have had a heightened interest in the social role and responsibilities of European-based global firms. In addition, CSR, with its emphasis on voluntary standards, soft law, and business-government cooperation is consistent with the regulatory style of many European governments. Interest in CSR in Europe also flows from a core mission of the EU, namely to make the development of the single market consistent with the achievement of broader social objectives.

For all these reason, the essays in this volume fill an important, and timely objective: they provide an invaluable window on how CSR is evolving in Europe, at the level of both public policy and corporate policies and practices. They also contribute to helping us understand the complex and dynamic relationships between CSR and long-term business success – an understanding that is central to any appraisal of the potential and limits of CSR to improve corporate social performance.

As the essays in this volume make clear, it is difficult to generalize about the relationship between CSR and profitability. Under some circumstances, CSR can be appropriately understood as *critical* to the long-term financial viability of business. This perspective suggests that CSR has become a business imperative: accordingly, more 'responsible' firms are also more likely to be financially sustainable. Under other circumstance, CSR can: assist in identifying creative ways of reducing costs, opening up new markets, reducing risks, and attracting and retaining the loyalty of consumers, employees and investors. For some firms under some circumstance, CSR is *consistent* with the long-term maximization of shareholder value. Under this scenario, more profitable firms are in a better position to satisfy the needs of multi stakeholders. Finally, CSR can also be viewed as *inconsistent* with the maximization of shareholder value. This perspective emphasizes the extent to which market competitive forces can, under some circumstances, *constrain* the exercise of CSR.

While students of CSR can and do disagree as to the relative importance of each of these relationships of CSR to profitability, it is likely that none hold true for all firms under all circumstances. An important challenge for researchers is to explore the circumstances under which each of these scenarios is likely to hold. For both policy-makers and managers, the challenge is to better understand how and to what extent public policy can contribute to strengthening the positive relationship between CSR and profitability. The essays in this important volume provide an important foundation to help us begin to meet both challenges.

In many important respects, CSR is a matter of trade-offs, just like all the other disciplines on business management. We cannot expect too much, but at the same time it would be short-sighted to ignore the enormous potential of CSR to improve social welfare. In this sense, research and practice on CSR need to engage the specific circumstances under which CSR can and should improve both corporate social and financial performance. Doing so can help provide a richer understanding of the potential and limits of CSR.

The objective of this book is to develop a European perspective on the role and responsibilities of business in society. Its detailed, multi-faceted and sophisticated portrait of the European setting of CSR significantly enriches our understanding and appreciation of the potential contribution of companies to both sustainable development and overall European competitiveness as firms engage the difficult challenge of integrating the values of social justice, environmental sustainability, and social cohesion with economic efficiency and long term success.

The analysis in this book, shifting the focus from the institutional context in which business and society relationships develop to more practical implementation, highlights the importance of a dialogue between companies and their stakeholders. It presents CSR as a strategy of dealing with the social context in which firms function, initiating a process of reciprocal interactions in which being socially responsible – as defined by increased engagement and transparency about what the company stands for, how it creates long-term value for its shareholders, clients and employees, and how it contributes to society – can both improve its social performance and, ideally, contribute to profitable growth.

David Vogel

Foreword *by Carlo Secchi*

Corporate social responsibility has undoubtedly entered our common language, evolving even more quickly than we perceive. Multi-level interests are focused on it, trying to track a new path for future economic development. Regardless of their perspectives, companies, governments, stakeholders and social or political institutions share the belief that CSR is a substantive reality.

The underlying assumption is clear: the kind of commitment CSR entails, focused on a dynamic management of stakeholders' needs and expectations, has a positive impact on the business environment, in that it fosters competitiveness and long-term growth through valuable resources: from qualified employees to a stronger reputation and a broader social consensus. A CSR strategic orientation therefore encompasses a renewed way of *doing business* that combines economic success and value creation with a respectful and proactive attitude towards the network of company stakeholders.

Along with the increasing number of successful case histories and studies that attest the superiority of a stakeholder-based approach, CSR impact is also evident at the macro level: the entire economic system can benefit from socially responsible behavior, in terms of improved social cohesion, stronger environmental protection and higher economic development and competitiveness. In this sense, CSR not only results in strategic differentiation, and leads to more robust company performance; it also contributes to the pursuit of the strategic priorities set up by governments, nations and international organizations. In particular, CSR can create innovative directions for a renewal of traditional welfare state mechanisms, through active participation by companies. Governments increasingly call for their help in configuring welfare policies, through voluntary and strategy-driven interventions. The ferment of ideas and initiatives across all of Europe confirms that CSR will last. Among many others, the Italian Center for Social Responsibility (I-CSR) strongly supports voluntary participation in CSR by companies.

I-CSR is an independent think-tank founded in April 2005 by the Italian Ministry of Labour and Social Affairs, INAIL (Italian Workers' Compensation Authority), Unioncamere (Italian Union of Chambers of Commerce) and the 'Luigi Bocconi' University. It is financed by the founders along with private contributions and the Italian government according to a four-year plan, with a precise mission defined by the following five objectives:

- to promote CSR concepts to new and different stakeholders;
- to spread the culture of CSR, facilitating the exchange of experiences and best practices especially amongst small and medium-sized enterprises (SMEs);
- to develop basic and applied research on social responsibility to strengthen the Italian contribution to national and international academic communities;
- to foster the dialogue among public and private institutions, enterprises, universities and various stakeholders involved in CSR;
- to provide support, help and training to the Italian economic system mainly based on SMEs.

Although it is necessary to start from a clear, shared vision of the main components of CSR and ways in which companies can accomplish it, cultural, social and economic differences should also be taken into account. The I-CSR Foundation has been created to promote a modern culture among companies, consistent with the specific economic, social, and cultural traits typical of the European context; all this relying on the assumption that companies can become more efficient and competitive by assuming an active role in the social system.

Carlo Secchi

Acknowledgments

We would like to acknowledge first of all Clodia Vurro for her extraordinary support to the realization of this book. Many thanks also to David Vogel for his insightful suggestions and fruitful exchange of ideas and to Carlo Secchi for his contribution and comments. We wish to thank Sergio Pivato, Director of the European Research Centre on Risk, Security, Occupational Health and Safety, Environment and Crisis Management (SPACE) for his continuous encouragement and support.

Many thanks to the colleagues of Bocconi University of the 'Giorgio Pivato' Department of Management (IEGI), the European Research Centre on Risk, Security (SPACE), the Centre for Finance and Industry Studies (Findustria), and the Corporate Finance and Real Estate Department of the SDA Bocconi School of Management. We wish to thank also the colleagues of the Legal Studies and Business Ethics Department (Wharton School of Business of the University of Pennsylvania) and, in particular, Thomas W. Dunfee, Thomas Donaldson and Nien-hê Hsieh; and Jane Nelson of the Corporate Social Responsibility Initiative at the Kennedy School of Government of Harvard University.

We would also like to thank the participants in seminars at the European Academy of Business in Society (EABiS) Colloquia, the Academy of Management Annual Conferences, the Strategic Management Society Annual Conferences, the TransAtlantic Business Ethics Conferences, the Legal Studies and Business Ethics Department Faculty Research Program Seminar Series, the Wharton Social Impact Management (SIM) Initiative, and the students of the Wharton MBA classes on 'International Business Ethics', and 'Corporate Responsibility and Ethics'; and all colleagues of the international research groups in which we are involved at the Community of European Management Schools (CEMS), Brunel University, Copenhagen Business School, Corvinus University, Cranfield Business School, Darden School of Business at the University of Virginia, Durham Business School,

ESADE Business School, HEC Genève, IESE Business School, INSEAD, L. K. Academy Warsaw, Michigan Ross School of Business at the University of Michigan, Norwegian School of Management, Vlerick Leuven Gent Management School, and The Copenhagen Centre.

We would like also to express our gratitude to the Italian Ministry of Labour and Social Affairs and the Working Group of the Ministry on CSR for their enthusiasm in following our studies.

All of them have supported us directly in our work on this book, and indirectly over the years that we have known and worked with them.

Finally, we would like to thank the Italian Centre for Social Responsibility (I-CSR) and the Research Committee of Bocconi University for their support of part of this project.

Obviously, we are entirely responsible for the application of the remarks received and for the finished book.

Francesco Perrini
Stefano Pogutz
Antonio Tencati

1. Corporate social responsibility: new equilibria in managing firms[*]

1.1 WHAT'S NEW IN THE DEBATE OVER CSR

After a 2005 that will hardly go down in history as a model of business virtue, 2006 can and must be the year of corporate social responsibility (henceforth CSR), a renewed approach to company management, a new model for sustaining the corporate relationship network based on the integration of economic, social and environmental dimensions and on consistency with the sustainable development paradigm.

To date, the capitalistic model is still better than others, though it is far from perfect. Adjustments are needed, and CSR might concretely contribute to such a renewal process, fostering the search for new equilibria in managing firms.

A well-functioning market economy does not need new rules, but should rather aim at an improved and increased respect for existing rules. The cause of the recent financial crisis has more to do with institutional breakdown than with the inadequacy of current legal systems. Here a shift from shareholder supremacy to stakeholder dominance would more than suffice. The invisible hand of the market does not exist *per se*. To be efficient it needs rules, as Adam Smith argued in 1776 in *The Wealth of Nations*, written after the less acknowledged 1759 work, *The Theory of Moral Sentiments*.

A century later, in 1890, Alfred Marshall in *Principles of Economics* still categorized economics as a moral science rooted in ethics.

[*]   This chapter is a modified version of Francesco Perrini, 'Corporate Social Responsibility: nuovi equilibri nella gestione d'impresa', *Economia & Management*, Milan: Etaslibri, **2**, 7-11, 2006.

The implications for the twenty-first century are that the profit motive is not enough of a goal in itself; economic systems should be based on socially responsible firms.

From another perspective, along with the deterioration of ecological equilibria, the spread of social inequalities throughout the world, and the questionable effects of growth processes, the production and consumption models are increasingly changing. It is in this sense that firms' and organizations' marginal interests should be superseded by a higher goal. The 1987 Nobel Laureate in economics, Amartya Sen, has highlighted the inadequacy of economic decisions guided exclusively by self-interest. More recently, the 2002 Nobel laureate Joseph Stiglitz confirmed the importance of ethics in business along with a deep rethinking of the functioning of existing financial systems.

The steadily evolving debate over CSR can no longer be dismissed as faddishness. However, even if academics, managers and policy makers have firmly supported the ubiquitous relevance of the subject, opponents remain. The *Economist*, for example, has regularly expressed skepticism regarding the effectiveness of CSR. Recall, for example, the January 2005 survey 'The Good Company: A sceptical look at corporate social responsibility', with its criticisms of CSR theory and practice. In the May 26th 2005 issue of the *Economist*, the worldwide managing director of McKinsey & Company, Ian Davis, affirmed the strategic importance of developing systematic responses to the expectations of society as key to competitive advantage for firms. Moreover, Davis objected to companies' adoption of merely defensive or greenwashing policies as an inadequate response to activists' demands. On the contrary, in order for CSR to be effective and in line with economic objectives, companies should shift to a different strategy, based on new social contracts with stakeholders.

Regardless of either the most enthusiastic or critical perspectives on CSR, we cannot analyze current situations apart from it. The debate over the necessity to innovate management models is present and pervasive. Proof of this is the increasing number of researchers, managers and consultants, international organizations, nonprofits, governments, institutions and opinion leaders focused on the necessity to include CSR and sustainability in the corporate agenda, integrating them into the firm's blueprint.

Typing 'Corporate Social Responsibility' into one of the Web search engines brings up more than 10 000 000 references.

Moreover the number of leading world authorities on the academics of CSR is also increasing. For example, Jay Barney, after studying the resource-based theory of the firm for years, is now exploring the relationship between CSR and company performance. The guru of marketing, Philip Kotler, in 2005 wrote a book on CSR in which companies are invited to experience *A Shift from Obligation to Strategy* (Kotler and Lee, 2005). The 2005 Academy of Management Conference was centred on the exploitation of A New Vision of 'Responsible' Management in the 21st Century; while during the most important international conference for economists, at the Annual Meeting of Allied Social Science Associations (Boston, 5 January 2006), the keynote speaker on CSR was Robert Reich, former U.S. Secretary of Labor under President Bill Clinton (1993-1997) and currently professor of Public Policy at Berkeley.

In addition, the relevance of CSR in current debate over the role of firms in society is supported by the commitment of international institutions like the United Nations, the World Bank, the Organization for Economic Cooperation and Development (OECD), the International Labour Organization (ILO), the European Union (EU) and also, increasingly, national governments. The last step of the European debate over CSR is the publication of a new communication entitled 'Implementing the Partnership for Growth and Jobs: Making Europe a Pole of Excellence on Corporate Social Responsibility' (22 March 2006). The European Commission stresses the relationship between CSR, sustainability, globalization and competitiveness.

In March 2000, the government of the United Kingdom was the first of its kind to create a CSR minister in the Department of Trade and Industry. In 2002, the Italian Minister for Labour and Social Affairs launched The Corporate Social Responsibility– Social Commitment (CSR-SC) Project, aimed at spreading CSR culture on a voluntary basis, as suggested in the Green Paper promoted by the EU in 2001. In Germany, Chancellor Angela Merkel recalled the importance of CSR in sustaining long-term economic growth objectives, during the inaugural ceremony of the European School of Management and Technology (3 February 2006).

Finally, CSR is no longer confined to the Western world. China's interest is growing, as shown by the focus on company responsibility in the debate over future paths of Chinese development at the Third Session of the Tenth National People's Congress in March 2005.

To summarize, the debate over CSR is developing simultaneously with a radical rethinking of corporate theory. The progressive strategic integration of social and environmental concerns into the business operations and interactions with firms' stakeholder networks has been contributing to promoting a new model of economic success, based on the ability of firms to interact directly and dynamically with the different categories of stakeholders

This new direction in managerial paths should be centred on a strategic framework in which CSR is integrated across all the corporate functions.

1.2 A MEANING FOR CSR

The public concern with the social responsibilities of business is neither novel nor unusual. It is strictly related to the large amount of literature on corporate theory and the role of companies in society. Consider, for example, stakeholder theory, business ethics, the triple-bottom-line approach, systemic theory, the resource-based view, and so on.

After a time of shared consensus over the dominance of the shareholder-value approach as the objective of the most rational firms, the recent trend towards an alignment of shareholder interests with the interests of the other categories of stakeholders now prevails. However, even if we agree with the idea that, in all, the interests tend to be satisfied in the long run, this process cannot be taken for granted. Managers should consciously and responsibly commit themselves to CSR practices and objectives. In this sense, the ability to effectively manage the increasingly pressing requests from workers, consumers, local communities, suppliers and so on, has become crucial for economic sustainability, in that an unsatisfied stakeholder can interfere with the survival of firms in the long run.

As a result, CSR can be defined as the voluntary integration of economic, social and environmental objectives in the relationship with company stakeholder networks. Freeman, the originator of the stakeholder theory, has recently proposed to redefine the acronym CSR as *corporate stakeholder responsibility* (Freeman and Velamuri, 2006). Other researchers and practitioners prefer corporate sustainability to CSR, in that sustainability refers directly to the triple-bottom-line approach and the integration of social, environmental and economic dimensions into management practices, taking for granted the stakeholder orientation.

Again in this context, the sole dimension of shareholder value cannot provide a complete and accurate picture of the quality of company management and the ability of firms to deal with stakeholders. This fact is confirmed by many negative examples: the failure of many dot.coms, symptoms of a fragile, speculative New Economy, or the cases of Enron, Worldcom, Global Crossing and Tyco in the US, Bipop-Carire, Cirio, Giacomelli, Parmalat in Italy, and so on.

Voluntary adoption of social and environmental standards beyond legal prescriptions, opening companies to stakeholder dialogue and cooperation, addressing operations toward sustainable development, together gain consensus, trust and legitimacy for firms in the globalization era. In other words, adopting a responsible approach means laying the foundation of a long-lasting development in the history of business and economics.

CSR refers to a new governance model based on stakeholder satisfaction beyond not only legal prescription but also individual ethical orientation. CSR involves strategies and company policies, as a consequence interacting with all the areas of corporate management:

- production processes: the reduction of environmental damage, health and safety of workers, quality and safety of products and services exemplify ways in which CSR can be integrated concretely into company production processes;
- marketing policies: efforts toward customer satisfaction or transparency in promotional policies;
- internal organization: support, provided by CSR policies, of career management, training policies and employee turnover;
- financial and economic performance: capability of CSR practices to positively influence company efficiency and reduce the risk profile.

In this sense, CSR becomes an integrative approach to firms' management, like investments that, minimizing risks, represent an innovative source of competitive advantage and do not increase costs. This new management model is characterized by the centrality of stakeholders, by a tendency towards constant improvement and by continuous innovation.

The more integrated the economic, social and environmental dimensions are into company strategies, the more processes will be oriented towards the long run, the better the relationship with stakeholders will be, fostering company legitimacy and the related accumulation of intangibles based on trust and knowledge. As a result, the likelihood of surviving in the long run will increase.

This assumption holds regardless of the adoption of an instrumental approach to CSR (that is, better stakeholder relations are functional to better competitive performance and overall company success), and a normative approach as well (that is, firms must satisfy stakeholder needs because of moral duties and ethical principles).

1.3 COMPANIES BETWEEN MARKET PRESSURE AND CSR

Skeptics and opponents find support in their assertion that beyond good intentions and turns of phrase firms must account for reality. A reality characterized by hypercompetition and strong pressure to cut costs, compelling firms to search desperately for growth opportunities, leaves no room for initiatives consistent with the CSR philosophy.

However, to probe more deeply, along with the increasing competition and the financial markets' pressure toward gains, companies have gradually lost sight of the sustainability of their equilibria, trading in their growth aptitude for opportunistic behaviors and frauds.

Yet, on the contrary, to paraphrase the words of Professor Mario Monti (2003), formerly the European commissioner for competition and now president of Bocconi University, competition can help companies to fulfill their CSR objectives. Different from company and organizational beliefs about competition, CSR and competitiveness are not opposed but rather linked in a synergic relationship. In fact, by pursuing competitive advantages, companies strengthen themselves.

Within this scenario, CSR cannot oppose such objectives, in that it represents a much more advanced behavior for companies engaged in competition. Markets can foster the CSR initiatives, as they do now.

If the invisible hand on its own does not suffice to push companies in the right direction, there are three different supportive mechanisms to resort to (Demattè, 2002).

First, CSR can be promoted through legislation. A number of initiatives are associated with this approach. In general they refer to a system of incentives and punishments that subject companies to external verification by law. But if we accept the assumption that CSR plays a strategic role as the source of competitive advantage for committed firms, it cannot be imposed by law. Moreover, a law on CSR inevitably leads to distortions, new restrictions and a general bureaucratization that could prevent, at least partially, innovations and changes.

Second, CSR can exist based on the complementary social mechanisms able to trigger virtuous cycles and provide market benefits. Relevant examples refer to the gain in productivity brought about by an improved corporate climate, to the preference of customers for CSR-based products and services, to the mushrooming of socially responsible investing and the related possibility for firms to access new sources of financing, and so on.

Third, CSR can derive from the integration of social and environmental objectives into the corporate identity through a shift in the fundamental principles at the core of corporate actions. In other words, the corporation's final objective must reorient away from a shareholder-value approach to the centrality of stakeholders.

The last two approaches are based on a voluntary adoption of CSR practices. Companies engage with CSR consciously and voluntarily, thereby improving their performance. The emphasis on CSR as a crucial driver of competitiveness, for both themselves and the entire systems to which they belong, coheres with the European strategy adopted in March 2000 during the European Council in Lisbon:

To become the most competitive and dynamic knowledge-based economy in the world, capable of sustainable economic growth with more and better jobs and greater social cohesion (CEC, 2001d, p. 3).

While at first sight one could argue that the more competition prevails, the less autonomy managers have in the decision-making process, in reality the opposite is true. This means that the correct interpretation of CSR strategy can generate market advantage for the company, and foster the sustainability of its social and economic development as well. In this sense, CSR necessarily implies costs for firms, but at the same time it is not a self-indulgence that companies can access when everything else goes well. CSR is a competitive strategy for generating profits for firms and positive externalities for the related social context.

The CSR path is certainly not easy. Choices are complex and not yet entirely clear to stakeholders and firms themselves. But, as evidenced by those signals that firms acknowledged in the CSR field are sending to their markets, and through the decisive support by institutions at the local and global levels, CSR has ascended from a concept to a concrete reality that is growing every day.

1.4 AN OVERVIEW OF THE BOOK

The strong belief that CSR is at the forefront in the competitive strengthening of the entire European system drives the bottom line of the book. It represents an attempt to guide readers through the CSR approach in progress at the European level. This is why a double line of reasoning, partly theoretical and partly practitioner-based, characterizes all of the chapters. In this way we attempt a complete portrait of CSR, from principles and theoretical premises to concrete implementation.

In attempting a systematic description of the distinctive traits of the European setting, chapter 2 elaborates on the European perspective on the role and responsibilities of business in society. The potential contribution of companies to sustainable development and to European competitiveness in general appears to be of critical importance, supporting the integration of social cohesion, economic efficiency and long-term success.

Chapter 3 goes over the national public policies and ongoing initiatives in the field of CSR. Different perspectives emerge on the role of governments and public institutions in fostering the debate on CSR, highlighting the variety of solutions and concrete experiences: from the liberal tradition of the UK, characterized by a low degree of legally binding public policies, to the French regulatory approach. Also analyzed are the partnership-oriented strategy typical of the Nordic nations and the multi-stakeholder model in the Mediterranean countries.

The evolution of the concept of CSR is analyzed in chapter 4. A history of perspectives is developed, to highlight how the relationship between business and society has been interpreted throughout recent history. The heterogeneity of theories emerges: from business ethics to corporate citizenship; from the analysis of the determinants of socially responsible behavior to the measurement tools; from stakeholder management to the identification of social, environmental and sustainability indicators.

Chapter 5 explores CSR from the perspective of its contribution to firms' competitiveness. It relies on the assumption that, in terms of sustainable development, CSR actually contributes to the process of value creation and for this reason can positively affect company performance and competitiveness. The emphasis is on the growing strategic importance of the intangible assets. In that CSR activities foster the accumulation of intangibles, they represent a source of competitive advantage for committed firms. Also considered are the importance of cooperation with stakeholders, the engagement of stakeholders in company decision making, and the definition of appropriate systems to measure and control CSR behavior. The effects of CSR are grouped into four areas: internal organization, consumer market, financial market and community relationship.

From the concept of CSR it is possible to derive the complementary concept of accountability, which means that the company is held responsible for its actions. Chapter 6 deals with this perspective, analyzing the most important European and international standards, tools and methodologies regarding CSR. Following the triple bottom line approach, the analysis groups management tools into three main categories: corporate social performance, corporate environmental performance, and corporate sustainability performance.

To face the strategic challenge of managing stakeholder relationships and meet the managerial needs especially of SMEs, what is needed is a clear and modular methodology for a sustainability performance management system. Chapter 7 describes an innovative framework, the SERS model, which is designed to monitor and track both qualitatively and quantitatively the overall corporate performance from a stakeholder perspective and which is based on a flexible structure that can be adapted to different industries, sizes and countries.

Chapter 8 reviews the Italian experience, by means of a wide-ranging examination of the principal initiatives achieved in the last few years, at both the private and public levels, involving firms, institutions and local communities. The chapter is divided into two parts: first, an analysis of the impact of CSR in Italy, and then the models of CSR that typify the Italian context.

Starting from the premises set down in the previous chapter, chapter 9 offers a careful description of the implementation of the European CSR strategy in Italy: the *Corporate Social Responsibility-Social Commitment Project* (CSR-SC). The main steps of the project are analyzed in detail.

Finally, chapter 10 concludes the book by presenting the path ahead for the European debate over CSR. The content of the Communication 'Implementing the Partnership for Growth and Jobs: Making Europe a Pole of Excellence on Corporate Social Responsibility', published by the European Commission on 22 March 2006, is presented. The focus is on the strategic role played by SMEs.

The Appendix describes the core element of the CSR-SC project: the Social Statement. It is a voluntary tool mainly conceived to help firms to report their CSR actions and performance. The core of the Social Statement is a specific set of key performance indicators, covering a wide range of CSR issues (social, environmental and economic) and in agreement with the 'stakeholder management model' and the 'triple bottom line' approach. More important, the Social Statement represents a concrete attempt to translate into practice those indications for CSR implementation and company involvement highlighted in the Green Paper.

2. The EU Strategy: promoting CSR across Europe

In a globalised market economy, CSR is part of a modern business.
Thomas Donaldson
(*Financial Times*, June 2, 2005)

2.1 INTRODUCTION

Throughout the last few decades, the world economic scene has been continuously changing. Such changing refers to several issues, each involving different actors at different levels (i.e., policy makers, governments, organizations, and so on). In this context, a great deal of attention has been paid to the social responsibility and commitment characterizing a firm's strategic mission and behavior. Following government indications as well as developing their own voluntary actions, firms are showing their willingness to adopt socially responsible behavior, in that these might have direct and indirect effects on the socio-economic context in which they operate.

In such a dynamic context, CSR is defined as a new managerial model centred on the voluntary integration of economic, social and environmental responsibilities into the entire value chain and all company functions, and on the relationships with the stakeholder network. CSR is a discipline through which the progressive alignment of shareholder and stakeholder interests is satisfied, along with a shift from short- to long-term objectives.

CSR appears to have become increasingly integrated into corporate strategies. Strategy is what links a company with its market (economic, financial and technological) and non-market (social, political and cultural) environment; and a company is inextricably linked by a dynamic process of interaction with a diverse set of stakeholders in this environment, where the boundaries between market and non-market become increasingly blurred.

Therefore, CSR represents the main driver of *corporate sustainability*, that is, the capability of the firm to generate long-term value through mutually beneficial relationships with its entire network of stakeholders, 'business stakeholders' and 'sociopolitical stakeholders'.

Through the 1980s, CSR was disproportionately if not almost exclusively an American phenomenon. It was primarily associated with the pressures on American-based firms by investors, consumers and activists. And it was American-based firms that pioneered many of CSR's principles and practices, such as corporate philanthropy, social audits, corporate codes of conduct and so on.

This is no longer the case. The United Kingdom is now the country in which CSR is most evident, but it is not alone. More and more European governments are including CSR in their strategic priorities, defining specific objectives and ad hoc organizational structures. In other words, European countries, institutions and European companies are actively contributing to the global debate on CSR, promoting initiatives and formal definitions, proposing approaches and management tools and supporting rules of conduct and promotional campaigns (Tencati, Perrini and Pogutz, 2004).

Notwithstanding the variety of different approaches and the lack of a unique definition of socially responsible behavior, the link among perspectives lies at the nexus of responsibility and accountability, meaning 'social responsibility' in the sense that a company is held accountable for its actions. Therefore, a sustainable and responsible company is one that identifies, measures, monitors and reports all social, environmental and economic effects of its operations on society at large, in order to both increase internal and external dialogue with its constituencies and improve managerial awareness of and control over the social, economic and environmental impacts of corporate activity.

This model, which combines economic prosperity, social cohesion and environmental protection, is functional and in keeping with the company's long-term objective of creating value. The company whose goal is to create wealth and reward the different stakeholders who provide the resources needed to support the company's economic operations must be sustainable and socially responsible.

At a more institutional level, the European Union (EU) has been actively dealing with these issues since 2001, when it presented the Green Paper 'Promoting a European framework for CSR'. This paper was the EU's response to the strategic goal adopted in March 2000 during the European Council in Lisbon: 'to become the most competitive and dynamic knowledge-based economy in the world, capable of sustainable economic growth with more and better jobs and greater social cohesion' (CEC, 2001d, p. 3).

Since the inclusion of CSR in the European political agenda as one of the most relevant sources of competition for the entire economic system, each country's interest, at both the public and private level, has grown exponentially.

The rest of this chapter attempts to construct the traits of European CSR within an institutional setting. In the first part, the two key elements, that generated the interest in stimulating the European economy through the CSR paradigm, are analyzed: the first key element includes the rise of European competitiveness based on social cohesion and knowledge; the second one includes the political belief in the necessity to stimulate CSR in order to pursue sustainable development (CEC, 2002d). For these reasons, the Commission stresses the fact that CSR is not an additional element in the company management, but rather intrinsically linked to the objective of value creation.

In the second part of the chapter, attention is focused on the definition of CSR, in order to establish a common language that will guide the reader through the chapters in this book.

2.2 THE EUROPEAN POLITICAL DEBATE OVER CSR

Accelerating economic liberalization without effective global governance and defective corporate governance practices among some major companies have focused public attention on corporate integrity and attitudes not only toward their shareholders, but also toward society as a whole. Today, as business is expected to be accountable for its impact on society, CSR is increasingly debated in Europe. Table 2.1 provides an overview of the main EU contributions to the CSR development at a European level. As is evident from the brief descriptions, across the years the EU has been clamoring for an increasing awareness among companies of the advantages of responsible behavior from a competitive point of view.

Table 2.1 Political milestones at the European level

March 22, 2006	*Communication on CSR – Implementing the partnerships for growth and jobs: making Europe a pole of excellence on corporate social responsibility*	
March 22-23, 2005	*European Council Brussels*	In order to encourage investment and provide an attractive setting for business and work, the European Union must complete its internal market and make its regulatory environment more business-friendly, while business must in turn develop its sense of social responsibility.
February 9, 2005	*Social Agenda 2005-2010*	In its Social Agenda 2005-2010 for modernizing Europe's social model under the revamped Lisbon Strategy for growth and jobs, the Commission announced that it will continue to promote CSR. In order to contribute to the effectiveness and credibility of these practices, the Commission, in cooperation with the Member States and the parties involved, will put forward initiatives designed to further enhance the development and transparency of CSR.
February 2, 2005	*Working together for growth and jobs: A new start for the Lisbon Strategy*	In its new Growth and Jobs Strategy for the EU, the Commission stressed that CSR practices can play a key role in creating more and better jobs and in contributing to sustainable development while enhancing Europe's innovative potential and competitiveness.
June 29, 2004	*EU Multi-Stakeholder Forum on CSR*	The Final Report was presented to the Commission on June 29, 2004.
November 14, 2003	*The role of Public Policies in promoting CSR*	Italian EU Presidency Conference on CSR, Venice, Italy
May 13, 2003	*European Parliament report on CSR*	
December 2-3, 2002	*Council Resolution on CSR*	
November 21-22, 2002	*Mainstreaming CSR across Europe*	Danish EU Presidency Conference on CSR - Helsingør, Denmark
October 16, 2002	*EU Multi-Stakeholder Forum on CSR*	The European Multi-Stakeholder Forum on Corporate Social Responsibility (CSR EMS Forum), chaired by the Commission, brought together European representative organizations of employers, business networks, trade unions and NGOs to promote innovation, convergence and transparency in existing CSR practices and tools. The Forum's

		mandate was approved at the launch on October 16, 2002.
July 2, 2002	*Communication on CSR - A business contribution to Sustainable Development*	
November 27-28, 2001	*CSR on the EU social policy agenda*	Belgian Presidency Conference on CSR, Brussels
July 18, 2001	*Green Paper Promoting a European framework for CSR*	
March 23-24, 2001	*Stockholm European Summit*	The European Council in Stockholm in March 2001 welcomed the initiatives taken by businesses to promote CSR and referred to the next Green Paper to encourage a wide exchange of ideas with a view to promoting further initiatives in this area.
June 28, 2000	*Social Policy Agenda*	Adopted in June 2000, the Social Policy Agenda stressed the importance of CSR essentially in terms of the employment and social consequences of economic and market integration and the adaptation of working conditions to the new economy. Consequently, the Commission expressed its intention to issue a communication in 2001 to promote CSR at corporate level.
June 19-20, 2000	*Feira European Summit*	The European Council in Feira reiterated the appeal made in Lisbon, applauded the ongoing follow-up and welcomed the initiation of a process to establish a network for European dialogue encouraging companies' sense of social responsibility.
March 23-24, 2000	*Lisbon European Summit*	At the European Council Summit in Lisbon, March 2000, the European Union set itself a new strategic goal for the next decade: to become the most competitive and dynamic knowledge-based economy in the world, capable of sustainable economic growth with more and better jobs and greater social cohesion. For the first time the European Council addressed businesses directly in 'a special appeal to companies' corporate sense of social responsibility regarding best practices on lifelong learning, work organization, equal opportunities, social inclusion and sustainable development'.
1998	*Gyllenhammar report*	At the European level, the High Level Group on the economic and social consequences of industrial change, 'The Gyllenhammar Group' (set up as a result of the Luxembourg Jobs Summit in November 1997), suggested in its final report that 'businesses with more than 1000 employees should publish a report on the management of change' on an annual basis in order 'to give an account of the impact of their social activities'.

2.2.1 CSR in the European Strategy

The Commission defines CSR as 'a business contribution to sustainable development, that is, a management approach enhancing competitiveness, social cohesion and environmental protection.'

More broadly, CSR is an instrument that can contribute to the objectives of EU policies, as well as to development and better global governance, by supplementing existing policy tools such as legislation and social dialogue.

The development of CSR reflects the evolution of corporate governance, with a progressive inclusion of more and more issues and categories of stakeholders. A company's management of social and environmental issues is therefore an important part of corporate governance. It is also important that business integrate all relevant stakeholders, including trade unions and NGOs, into this dialogue.

In political terms, CSR appeared on the European political map during the 1990s. The EU official commitment to CSR came out of the Lisbon Summit in March 2000, which set a new strategic goal for the Union, which was becoming the most inclusive and competitive society in the world. In Lisbon, EU leaders made a specific appeal to companies' sense of CSR. CSR is expected to contribute to the wider process of modernizing and strengthening the European economic and social model.

The Commission defines CSR as (CEC, 2001d; p.6):

A concept whereby companies integrate social and environmental concerns in their business operations and in their interaction with their stakeholders on a voluntary basis.

From the definition above, it appears to be clear how the European interpretation of CSR goes beyond country-specific factors or geographical boundaries. Rather, the concept of CSR calls for the strong involvement of appropriate stakeholders, based on open dialogue among involved parts, and, above all, is intended as a voluntary approach beyond legal requirements. It is in this sense that CSR and legal setting become reciprocally complementary, not different alternatives between which firms can choose their own best way.

Across time, however, the European political contribution to the CSR debate has progressively shifted from clarifying the relevant concepts and motivation underlying that relevance to defining specific ways through which the implementation of CSR philosophy was concretely possible.

What distinguishes today's understanding of CSR from the initiatives of the past is the attempt to manage it strategically and to develop instruments for this. It means a business approach, which puts stakeholder expectations and the principle of continual improvement and innovation at the heart of business strategies. In the current climate, knowledge and innovation are a high priority for companies, and socially responsible practices can help them to recruit and retain skilled staff.

For these reasons, the Commission is now implementing a CSR strategy that pursues three priorities: promotion of CSR practices, credibility of CSR claims and coherence of CSR public policies.

The first priority aims at promoting the uptake of socially responsible practices among enterprises. CSR is about daily management of social and environmental issues in every department of a company. Enterprises are not expected to adopt CSR practices for marketing or philanthropic reasons but because CSR makes sense for their competitiveness. It should not be just a public relations exercise, but should lead companies to reassess and reorganize their core business activities, and ensure that they manage risk and change in a socially responsible way.

CSR is at the same time an instrument for better management of social and environmental risks, a tool for total quality management. It gives enterprises a clear picture of their social and environmental impacts, helping them to manage them well, and a new and wider approach to corporate governance involving more issues and more stakeholders.

CSR is not a new phenomenon. The manifestation of business relationships with society has changed over time from the nineteenth-century paternalism to today's commitments of business to take on new social responsibilities. A common thread that runs through the changing manifestation of CSR, however, is a certain complementarity between government, business and social organizations in addressing society's problems.

In this context, the most challenging area of intervention remains the promotion of the actual adoption of CSR among enterprises, in particular small and medium-sized enterprises

(SMEs). Surveys indicate that lack of awareness, especially of the relevance and benefits of CSR for every business, is a major obstacle to the promotion of CSR. Many issues need to be tackled, to raise general awareness of CSR. There is not enough knowledge regarding the business case for, obstacles to and drivers of CSR, and building a solid body of evidence could be a major contribution to furthering adoption of CSR among businesses. SMEs in particular need to know more about the potential benefits of socially responsible practices. The Commission also supports the analysis and dissemination of information about CSR good practices through social partners, business networks and professional associations.

The second main European strategic priority deals with the credibility of responsible practices. The European approach to CSR is focused on the strong belief that CSR is so effective because it is voluntary. But to be credible and effective it requires measurement and assessment. CSR performance assessment helps businesses to improve their practices and behavior as it facilitates an effective and credible benchmarking of their social and environmental performance. Transparency about CSR performance also enables stakeholders to measure how businesses meet their expectations.

The third area of intervention is the search for coherence of CSR public policies. To ensure that CSR both on the marketplace and in public policies contributes to sustainable development, it is essential to use benchmarks which properly reflect its components; that is, competitiveness, social cohesion and environmental protection. Otherwise there would be a risk of promoting ineffective practices and behavior.

As transparency has become a key element of the CSR debate, the number of codes of conduct, reports, labels, awards, indices and other tools have increased during the last decade. CSR has become a market issue for consumers and investors. Like any information related to the market, CSR claims must be substantiated. When individual consumers or investors are not in a position to verify the information provided to them, a level playing field must be established by public authorities to protect them against unfair practices.

CSR is also becoming an issue for public authorities at all levels, which increasingly include CSR criteria in market regulation, provision of grants or tax incentives, and public procurement. Despite the good intentions of the actors, this development risks introducing new barriers to trade on the EU internal market. These developments were discussed in depth at the CSR conference organized by the Italian Presidency of the EU on 14 November 2003 in Venice.

The growing importance of CSR on the marketplace and in public policies raises a key issue: the legal recognition of CSR benchmarks – labels, marks, certificates, ratings, and so on – and their progressive convergence across the internal market.

This requires the development of a consensus on the scope and contents of CSR benchmarks: what issues are assessed by benchmarks; on benchmarking processes: how performance is measured; and on control procedures: what skills and capabilities are required to properly measure CSR performance.

Since November 2003, several initiatives have been emerging to work towards the convergence of CSR benchmarks, which provide a useful starting point to develop solutions to respond to these challenges. This is why the Commission set up a European multi-stakeholder forum on CSR. The EU CSR forum aimed at facilitating the exchange of experience and good practices in order to establish common guidelines for CSR tools such as codes of conduct, reporting, labeling and socially responsible investment. The Forum drew together business, trade unions and civil society. The Commission believes that the success of CSR in Europe will ultimately depend on its widespread 'ownership', with all stakeholders feeling they have a say in how it is developed and applied.

As an instrument for sustainable development, CSR can be used more widely in all policies, including employment and social affairs, enterprise, environment, development and trade, and so on. National governments are taking various initiatives to promote CSR in their policies, and the Commission is facilitating the exchange of information about national policies in support of CSR. The Commission has also committed itself to integrating CSR principles into all of its policies and published a progress report with regard to the achievement of sustainability objectives in early 2005.

CSR, a management tool for business, is also a powerful policy instrument of the European Union toward the attainment of the objectives adopted by the European Summit of March 2000 in Lisbon for better jobs, a better society and a better world.

2.2.2 Focus on the Green Paper and the Official Communication

On 18 July 2001, the EU presented the Green Paper: *Promoting a European framework for CSR* (CEC, 2001d). The document suggests an approach based on strengthening partnerships among all interested parties (for example, companies, NGOs, social partners and local authorities). After the consultation process on the Green Paper closed on 31 December, 2001, the EU began to work on a new document. The new Official Communication, entitled 'CSR: A business contribution to Sustainable Development', was released on 2 July, 2002 (CEC, 2002b). These two documents are the final outcomes of a long discussion, carried on for years in Europe at both the theoretical and institutional level, about the social implications of business activities and the social role of companies in supporting community development at the local and national levels (Petrella, 1995; Copenhagen Centre, 1998; Hutton, 2002).

According to the Green Paper, 'CSR is essentially a concept whereby companies decide voluntarily to contribute to a better society and a cleaner environment' (CEC, 2001d, p. 4) and 'a concept whereby companies integrate social and environmental concerns in their business operations and in their interaction with their stakeholders on a voluntary basis' (CEC, 2001d, p. 6). An increasing number of companies recognize social responsibility as part of their identity. This responsibility affects employees and more generally all stakeholders (amongst others shareholders, customers, suppliers, banks and insurance companies, retailers, competitors, state and local authorities, civil society at large and media), and this in turn can influence corporate success. The Green Paper identifies four factors behind the growing success of the CSR concept:

- the new concerns and expectations of citizens, consumers, public authorities and investors in the context of globalization and large-scale industrial change;
- social criteria, which increasingly influence the investment decisions of individuals and institutions both as consumers and as investors;
- increased concern about the damage caused by economic activity to the environment;

- transparency of business activities brought about by media and modern information and communication technologies.

The EU also proposes a framework to better understand the different elements of CSR: according to this approach, CSR has an internal and an external dimension. The internal dimension of CSR encompasses human resources management; occupational health and safety management; business restructuring; management of environmental impact and natural resources. The external dimension of CSR, which goes beyond the doors of the firm and involves many stakeholders, affects local communities; business partners and suppliers; customers and consumers; protection of human rights along the whole supply chain; global environmental concerns.

Therefore, in order to respond adequately to the pressures coming from the society of which companies form an integral part, firms should co-ordinate their economic, social and environmental goals. They should integrate social and environmental concerns into their business strategies, their management tools and their activities. That means going beyond compliance and investing more in human, social and environmental capital. Finally, the EU underlines the need for a holistic approach towards CSR-integrated management in order to include social and environmental considerations into corporate planning, measuring and controlling of processes and to define a long-term strategy that minimizes the risks linked to uncertainty.

While the Green Paper is more centered on defining CSR boundaries and intersections, the Commission Communication of July 2002 forms the basis for the European Strategy on CSR. The Communication sets up a European Multi-stakeholder Forum on CSR, as a platform to promote transparency and convergence of CSR practices and instruments. The Forum, launched on 16 October 2002, presented its conclusions and recommendations to the European Commission at its final High Level meeting on 29 June 2004. The Forum's final report was established on the basis of the presentations and discussions carried out in four thematic Round Tables that examined the following issues:

- improving knowledge about CSR and facilitating the exchange of experience and advice on good practice;
- fostering CSR among SMEs;

- encouraging the diversity convergence and transparency of CSR practices and tools;
- anticipating the developmental aspects of CSR.

In other words, the Forum provides a platform for discussions among the main stakeholder groups at the European level – employers, trade unions, business organizations/networks and civil society organizations – with the Commission playing a facilitating role based on two main themes. The first theme focused more on raising awareness of the relationship between CSR and sustainable development (including its impact on competitiveness, social cohesion and environmental protection) by facilitating the exchange of experience and good practices and bringing together existing CSR instruments and initiatives. Special emphasis is given to specific aspects of SMEs. The second theme explored the importance of establishing a common starting base, in terms of guiding principles, for CSR practices and instruments.

The political interest in CSR promotion across Europe was again confirmed during the Third European Conference on CSR 'The role of Public Policies in promoting CSR' (Venice, 14 November 2003). There the Italian Ministry of Labour and Social Affairs presented its Corporate Social Responsibility – Social Commitment (CSR-SC) Project, a two-level framework aimed at fulfilling company needs and reconciling different positions. Specifically, it represents a concrete attempt to actualize those suggestions highlighted in the Green Paper on CSR implementation and companies' involvement. It aims to address the credibility gaps concerning responsible practices and overcome all the undesired effects caused by the current proliferation in Europe of suggested tools for management and evaluation of corporate social and environmental performance.

2.2.3 Some Other Relevant Institutional and Public Contributions

In any case, policy makers, citizens and companies are paying increasing attention to CSR. According to the U.S.-based global business organization Business for Social Responsibility (BSR), corporate responsibility (or corporate citizenship) means 'operating a business enterprise in a manner that consistently meets or exceeds the ethical, legal, commercial, and public expectations society has of business'.

The World Business Council for Sustainable Development (WBCSD, 1999) proposed another definition of CSR:

CSR is the continuing commitment by business to behave ethically and contribute to economic development while improving the quality of life of the workforce and their families as well as of the local community and society at large.

Another interesting definition of CSR comes from the Prince of Wales International Business Leaders Forum:

CSR means open and transparent business practices that are based on ethical values and respect for employees, communities, and the environment. It is designed to deliver sustainable value to society at large, as well as to shareholders.

In order to promote the idea of corporate citizenship and socially responsible behavior, at the World Economic Forum in Davos on 31 January 1999, United Nations Secretary-General Kofi Annan challenged world business leaders to embrace and enact a Global Compact of shared values and principles in the areas of human rights, labor, the environment and anti-corruption. From an operational point of view, the initiative was launched on 26 July, 2000 during a meeting, at the UN headquarters in New York, of leaders from business, labor organizations and civil groups.

The Global Compact is a voluntary initiative, open to the participation of companies and to the involvement of labor, human rights, environmental and development organizations. It encompasses ten principles, drawn from the Universal Declaration of Human Rights, the ILO Declaration on Fundamental Principles and Rights at Work, the Rio Declaration on Environment and Development, and the United Nations Convention Against Corruption. If companies decide to participate in this initiative, the Global Compact asks them to act on these principles in their own corporate domains. The Compact thus promotes good practices by corporations; it does not, however, endorse companies. The Global Compact asks business to support and respect the ten universal principles in the fields of human rights, labor standards, the environment, and anti-corruption. Some of the most important firms in the world are among the participating companies, all of which have sent a letter of intent from the company CEO to the UN Secretary-General and submit yearly evidence of their efforts to advance the Compact's ten principles.

Another relevant contribution to the international debate on CSR came from the G8 Evian Summit 2003. For the first time, a G8 Summit Document focused on CSR. According to the G8 Declaration 'Fostering Growth and Promoting a Responsible Market Economy':

> Corporate integrity, strengthened market discipline, increased transparency through improved disclosure, effective regulation and corporate social responsibility are common principles that are the foundations for sound macro-economic growth.

In the second paragraph, headed 'Corporate Social Responsibility', the G8 representatives stated:

> Consistent with the outcomes of the World Summit on Sustainable Development, we support voluntary efforts to enhance corporate social and environmental responsibility. We will work with all interested countries on initiatives that support sustainable economic growth, including the creation of an environment in which business can act responsibly. We also welcome voluntary initiatives by companies that promote corporate social and environmental responsibility, such as the OECD Guidelines for Multinational Enterprises and the UN Global Compact principles consistent with their economic interest. We encourage companies to work with other parties to complement and foster the implementation of existing instruments, such as the OECD Guidelines and the ILO 1998 Declaration on Fundamental Principles and Rights at Work.

The variety of perspectives and the increasing number of institutional actors shaping the CSR panorama demonstrate that the CSR issues are much more than a temporary fad. The systematic exchange of views and knowledge at different political and institutional levels has revealed both the common ground and the differences, above all the absence of a common and shared language concerning the right way to interpret CSR at the company level. However, apart from the natural differences that derive from the necessity to draw CSR boundaries around the social and local contexts of reference, there is a common and clear understanding as to which social and ecological sustainability problems can be influenced positively by companies and their operations.

2.3 CSR AND SUSTAINABLE DEVELOPMENT

Along with the debate on the role and responsibilities of companies in society, the European CSR process has led to an intensive debate concerning the potential contribution of business to sustainable development. Although CSR and sustainable development have different roots – that is, the perspective of business primarily focuses on social matters for CSR, while the environmental protection debate is concerned with sustainable development – the two concepts are becoming increasingly integrated: in fact, *sustainability* means the capability of an organization to continue its activities over time while taking into account the impact of these activities on natural, social and human capitals (AccountAbility, 1999, p. 94). In other words, through the integration of social and environmental concerns into business operations, that is, through the adoption of CSR philosophy and practices, companies address their strategies and operations towards sustainable development.

Through this lens, a sustainable company is fully aware of its responsibilities toward its social context and adopts all the methods and tools functional to the improvement of its social and ecological performance.

In general, across time the paradigm of sustainable development has shifted from a focus on the environment to a broader and more complex meaning. According to the definition by Pearce, Markandya and Barbier (1989), development is considered as a vector of socially desirable objectives such as an increase in real income per capita; more equitable income distribution; broader access to resources; maintaining and increasing environmental quality; improving public health and nutritional status; improving education, and ensuring the basic freedoms. Given this premise, sustainable development is a condition in which the vector of development increases steadily over time. Therefore, unless development is sustainable, there is no development.

The sustainable development paradigm was established at the political level as a guiding principle since the Declaration of the United Nations Conference on the Human Environment, held at Stockholm from 5 to 16 June 1972. Although the concept was not yet defined in specific terms, the Declaration represents the raising awareness of the necessity to adjust the direction of economic development. In the preamble (paragraph 6) we read:

> A point has been reached in history when we must shape our actions throughout the world with a more prudent care for their environmental consequences. [...] To defend and improve the human environment for present and future generations has become an imperative goal for mankind – a goal to be pursued together with, and in harmony with, the established and fundamental goals of peace and of worldwide economic and social development.

And according to principle 13:

> In order to achieve a more rational management of resources and thus to improve the environment, States should adopt an integrated and co-ordinated approach to their development planning so as to ensure that development is compatible with the need to protect and improve environment for the benefit of their population

Maintenance of essential ecological processes and life support systems, the preservation of genetic diversity and the sustainable utilization of species and ecosystems represent the three principles ratified by the World Conservation Strategy in 1980. However, the official definition of sustainable development was promoted by the World Commission on Environment and Development (WCED), in the report titled 'Our Common Future' (1987).

> Sustainable development – a development that meets the needs of the present without compromising the ability of future generations to meet their own needs.

The report also underlined the link between sustainability and CSR, the latter with an instrumental role in fostering the pursuit of sustainable development objectives.

States and people shall cooperate in good faith and in a spirit of partnership in the fulfillment of the principles embodied in this Declaration and in the further development of international law in the field of sustainable development

On this note the Rio Declaration on Environment and Development of the United Nations Conference on Environment and Development (UNCED, Earth Summit, 3 to 14 June 1992) ends. Together with the Convention on Biological Diversity, undersigned during the Earth Summit, and Agenda 21, the Conference clearly set the necessity to find common and universal ways of tackling social and environmental threats. As we can see from principle 5:

All States and all people shall cooperate in the essential task of eradicating poverty as an indispensable requirement for sustainable development, in order to decrease the disparities in standards of living and better meet the needs of the majority of the people of the world.

With specific reference to Europe, the Fifth European Community Environmental Action Programme 'Towards Sustainability' (1993-2000) was launched by the European Commission in 1992 and approved by the Council on February 1, 1993. In the program, the main features of sustainability are identified:

- maintaining the overall quality of life;
- maintaining continuous access to natural resources;
- avoiding lasting environmental damage;
- considering as sustainable a development that meets the needs of the present without compromising the ability of future generations to meet their own needs.

On January 24, 2001, the European Commission presented the Sixth European Community Environmental Action Programme 'Environment 2010: Our Future, Our Choice (2001-2010)'. Sustainable development is considered as critical to the overall long-term welfare and is recognized as a global objective.

[...] Sustainable development is more than a clean environment. The social and economic implications of environmental action must be taken into account when pursuing sustainable development. So, whilst this Action Programme targets the environmental dimension of sustainable development, it also aims to improve the [...] quality of life of citizens in the European Union more generally.

In 2001, the European Commission also adopted the communication 'A Sustainable Europe for a Better World: A European Union Strategy for Sustainable Development' (Commission's proposal to the Gothenburg European Council). In the communication, sustainable development is considered as:

a fundamental objective that requires dealing with economic, social and environmental policies in a mutually reinforcing way.

In the Strategy for Sustainable Development adopted by the Gothenburg European Council on June 16, 2001, and based on the Commission's communication, the relationship with the Lisbon Strategy is made evident.

The European Council agrees a strategy for sustainable development which completes the Union's political commitment to economic and social renewal, adds a third, environmental dimension to the Lisbon strategy and establishes a new approach to policy making. The arrangements for implementing this strategy will be developed by the Council.

The international path of sustainable development continued in 2002 with the World Summit on Sustainable Development (WSSD; Johannesburg, South Africa, 26 August to 4 September). Here the commitment to sustainable development is reaffirmed and a collective responsibility to advance and strengthen the interdependent and mutually reinforcing pillars of sustainable development at the local, national, regional and global levels is assumed.

One of the most recent institutional interventions, dated 2005, coincides with the Communication 'Draft Declaration on Guiding Principles for Sustainable Development', adopted by the European Commission on May 25. The definition and role of sustainable development that emerge from the Communication are the following:

Sustainable Development is a key objective for all European Community policies, set out in the Treaty. It aims at the continuous improvement of the quality of life on earth of both current and future generations. It is about safeguarding the earth's capacity to support life in all its diversity. It is based on the principles of democracy and the rule of law and respect for fundamental rights including freedom and equal opportunities for all. It brings about solidarity within and between generations. It seeks to promote a dynamic economy with a high level of employment and education, of health protection, of social and territorial cohesion and of environmental protection in a peaceful and secure world, respecting cultural diversity.

A set of objectives and principles are then listed, as necessary to concretely enact the sustainable development pillars. In particular they are:

- key objectives: environmental protection, social equity and cohesion, economic prosperity, meeting our international responsibilities;
- policy guiding principles: promotion and protection of fundamental rights, intra- and intergenerational equity, open and democratic society, involvement of citizens, involvement of businesses and social partners, policy coherence and governance, policy integration, use of best available knowledge, precautionary principles, make polluters pay.

During the Brussels European Council (June 16-17, 2005) the Heads of State and Government adopted the 'Declaration on Guiding Principles for Sustainable Development' to guide all the policies and actions.

Finally, on December 13, 2005, the Commission adopted its review of the Sustainable Development Strategy and transmitted it to the European Council, the European Parliament, the Economic and Social Committee and the Committee of the Regions. The 'European Sustainable Development Strategy 2005-2010. A platform for action' (CEC, 2005) has been adopted by the European Council in June 2006.

Reliance on the multiple perspectives on sustainable development is important because, as argued above, today the concepts of CSR and sustainable development overlap in many areas, sharing the credit for the successful integration of economic, social and environmental objectives. From this perspective, CSR could be considered as a micro-level (that is, business-level) interpretation of the sustainable development issues. CSR constitutes an element of sustainable management. Achieving a new model of development and pursuing sustainability concern not only socio-economic systems but also the individual actors involved in the dynamics of change.

2.4 DEVELOPING A DEFINITION OF CSR

A sustainable company develops by taking into consideration the economic, social and environmental dimensions of its activities. In this sense, economic and competitive success, as well as social legitimacy and an efficient use of natural resources are integrated into a broader company final objective. A sustainable company is therefore a responsible company, where *responsible* refers to the ability of firms to interact with and integrate the needs and requests of its social context.

Despite the variety of formal definitions and ways to name such changed perspectives, CSR, corporate sustainability (CS), corporate citizenship (CC), triple bottom line (TBL), socially responsible behavior (SRB) and many other terms (see figure 2.1 for some other examples) all became more or less synonyms for the emerging effort to determine the meaning of *business in society*.

More in depth, CSR encompasses the economic, legal, ethical, and philanthropic expectations placed on organizations by society at a given point in time (Carroll and Buchholtz, 2002). Therefore, by pursuing economic, social and environmental objectives (Elkington, 1994), the CSR-oriented company increases its intangible assets of knowledge and trust, which support the processes of value creation (Wood, 1991; Joyner and Payne,

2002). The stakeholder value (Figge and Schaltegger, 2000) created makes it possible to reward, in specific and appropriate ways, the different social stakeholders who contribute resources (see Figure 2.2). Therefore sustainability becomes the strategic objective of socio-economic systems and responsible companies (Tencati, 2002b; Perrini and Tencati, 2003), which aim to pursue long-term economic development, consistent with promoting social needs and protecting the environment (Margolis and Walsh, 2003; Walsh, Weber and Margolis, 2003).

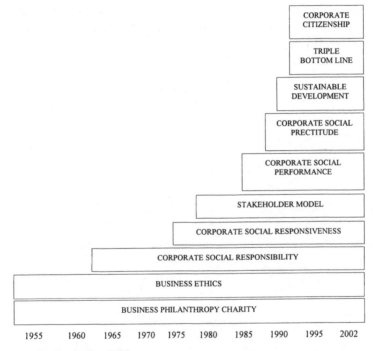

Source: De Bettignies, 2002

Figure 2.1. Concepts of CSR

Concretely, current emerging CSR issues include product responsibility, responsible downsizing, SMEs' role and corporate influence on public policy. Civil society, consumer campaigns and media attention have focused on major national and international brands; however, international standards are increasingly being developed to provide a global framework for CSR and corporate sustainability management.

To sum up, the CSR concept is focused on a stakeholder model, and can be considered as equidistant from the stakeholder theory (Donaldson and Preston, 1995), the triple bottom line approach (Elkington, 1997) and the integrative social contracts theory (Hasnas, 1998; Van Buren III, 2001). In other words, socially responsible behavior depends on the context in which companies operate, and is dynamically linked to the different categories of stakeholders (Dunfee, 1991; Hasnas, 1998). Therefore, CSR combines economic prosperity, social cohesion and environmental protection; it is functional in reaching the company's overall objective of long-term value creation.

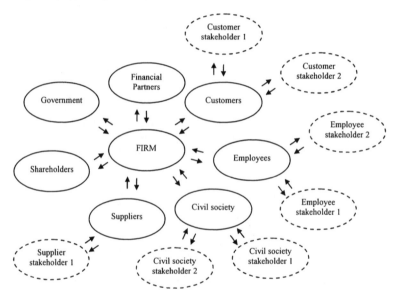

Source: based on Matten and Crane, 2004

Figure 2.2. Stakeholder map

CSR is defined in terms of the responsiveness of businesses to stakeholders' legal, ethical, social, environmental and economic expectations; it is also adopted by companies aiming to pursue long-term economic development, consistent with promoting social needs and protecting the environment. And the main categories of stakeholders considered are: human resources; shareholders/members and financial community; customers; suppliers; financial partners; state, local authorities and public administration; community, and the environment.

On the basis of this preliminary review, the CSR definition and approach proposed by the EU appear to be the most comprehensive and up-to-date. Furthermore, they will continue to be a reference point for future decisions in the field of European public and private policies promoting corporate socially responsible behavior.

3. CSR across Europe: public policies and ongoing initiatives

3.1 INTRODUCTION

The European Commission's Green Paper on CSR and its subsequent Communication in 2002 officially sanctioned the existence of a direct link between a company's decision to adopt socially responsible strategies and conduct and the ability to pursue the objectives of competitiveness, employment, social cohesion and environmental protection that are the foundation of the strategic decisions made in Lisbon.

The role of companies in this process of change has been discussed on many occasions, but what is expected of the public sector? How have the EU Member States interpreted their contribution to making social responsibility a national priority?

A clear reference to the role of government in CSR can be found in the text of the 2002 Communication, which speaks of the commitment of the Member States in three parallel areas of action: the promotion of CSR, of dialogue between the various actors, and of the exchange of experience and good practices at all levels; transparency regarding responsible practices and specific management tools; and the integration of CSR into national strategy and the consequent development of specific supporting policy.

Based on these general indications, the Member States have implemented CSR initiatives using a variety of solutions and approaches; for example, embracing the liberal tradition and minimizing public intervention, with the public sector playing the role solely of a promoter of change and facilitator of dialogue, as is being done in the UK; taking a more regulatory approach, such as in France; fostering a partnership-oriented strategy, which is typical of the Nordic nations; or focusing on a multi-stakeholder model, as has happened in the Mediterranean countries, Italy included (for a detailed analysis of the Italian experience see chapter 8).

3.2 THE UK LIBERAL APPROACH

The idea that CSR is first and foremost the responsibility of the private sector can be clearly seen in the UK's definition of corporate social responsibility (www.csr.gov.uk):

> The Government sees CSR as the business contribution to our sustainable development goals. Essentially it is about how business takes account of its economic, social and environmental impacts in the way it operates – maximizing the benefits and minimizing the downsides.

In other words, CSR is the responsibility of the private sector, but also includes voluntary social action that goes beyond mere philanthropic commitment and is closely related to a company's financial performance and competitiveness; as the definition continues:

> Specifically, we see CSR as the voluntary actions that business can take, over and above compliance with minimum legal requirements, to address both its own competitive interests and the interests of wider society.

In March 2000, in order to provide ongoing support for this strategy, Kim Howells was appointed Minister for Corporate Social Responsibility within the Department of Trade and Industry (DTI), although all of the various departments are involved in one way or another. This was the first initiative of its kind anywhere in the world. The responsibilities assigned to this post included the dissemination of CSR knowledge, the promotion of consensus regarding British and international codes and practices, and the definition and dissemination of a framework for social and environmental reporting and labeling. The current Minister for CSR is Malcolm Wicks.

Regarding public policy in the promotion of CSR, the British government places particular emphasis on periodically assessing the state of the art and best responsible practice throughout the UK. Each year since 2001, the UK has issued a government report on CSR in order to coordinate national policy and promote the paradigm of social responsibility, especially among small and medium-sized enterprises (SMEs).

Similar objectives are being pursued through government support of the Business in the Community (BITC) movement, the purpose of which is 'to inspire, engage, and support and challenge companies, to continually improve the impact they have on society' (www.bitc.org.uk). Government has entrusted this independent organization with a fundamental role in the process of disseminating and promoting responsible management, that of preparing the Corporate Responsibility Index, which involves self-evaluations of socially responsible companies and, based on this index, identifying those companies that could best attract socially responsible investing (SRI).

Another important initiative, which is based on public-private partnerships, is the National Strategy for Neighbourhood Renewal, launched by the DTI in January 2001 to involve the private sector on a large scale in the social and economic renewal of depressed areas that are at risk of being left behind.

The British government has also developed policy to improve CSR conduct and transparency. The many initiatives being promoted include the Voluntary Principles on Security and Human Rights in the Extractive Sector in December 2000 and the Extractive Industries Transparency Initiative (EITI) in September 2002, both concerning one of the industries most at risk both socially and environmentally and both attempting to establish common principles that can, in the first case, increase respect for worker rights and, in the second case, increase the level of transparency in financial relations between the public and private sectors. In the same way, the Ethical Trading Initiative (ETI) was strongly supported by the Department for International Development in 1998 in order to orchestrate the efforts of companies, NGOs and trade unions to improve working conditions throughout the entire value chain. More specifically, the companies involved in the initiative are required to implement a specific code of conduct and to provide annual progress reports. The results are monitored and verified by a multi-stakeholder commission.

There are also two recent initiatives in the area of social and environmental reporting: the General Guidelines on Environmental Reporting (October 2001) and the White Paper on Modernizing UK Company Law (July 2002).

The guidelines are an attempt to define a framework for companies, and larger organizations in particular, interested in the issue of environmental reporting. In January 2006 the Department for Environment, Food and Rural Affairs (DEFRA) produced a set of Environmental Reporting Guidelines – Key Performance Indicators (KPIs), which supersede previous Guidelines.

The White Paper has innovated corporate reporting, in that it recommends that economically significant companies include in their annual report's information, the quality of relations with stakeholders and the impact the company has had on the community in which it operates. Specifically, this involves adding an Operating and Financial Review (OFR). According to the proposal of the British government, as presented in the Draft Regulations on the Operating and Financial Review and Directors' Report, a consultative document published in May 2004 and subject to evaluation by the publics concerned until 6 August 2004, the OFR is an annual report (mandatory for publicly listed companies) intended primarily for shareholders that identifies the main drivers of corporate performance, both past and future. The report must cover certain traditional topics, such as business units, objectives, strategies, results and the main risks to which the company is exposed, but must also deal with the outlook for the future and, as necessary to properly evaluate the company, provide information concerning the environment, its employees and customers, and relations with the community and other stakeholders. Regulations to implement the OFR came into force on 22 March 2005, but in November 2005 the OFR was repealed by Gordon Brown, Chancellor of the Exchequer, to reduce the bureaucratic and administrative burdens on companies.

In the area of training initiatives, in 1990, the National Training Task Force, with the support of the Employment Department and in collaboration with certain influential organizations in the private sector, such as the Confederation of British Industry (CBI), the Trades Union Congress (TUC), and the Institute of Personnel and Development (IPD), issued a national standard – Investors in People – defining the optimal level of training and development practices with a view to improving corporate performance.

With regard to SRI, an amendment to the Pensions Act of 1995 has been in effect since July 2000. The Pensions Disclosure Regulation states that all pension funds must disclose whether they take account of ethical, social and environmental issues when making investment decisions.

The final area of intervention is that of government incentives designed to support CSR. The UK stands out from the rest of the EU Member States as the only nation with comprehensive tax legislation in the area of CSR. Included within this category of public initiatives are the Community Investment Tax Relief, which went into effect in January 2003, and Payroll Giving, which was strengthened in April 2000. The former provides tax relief aimed at encouraging private investment, through the Community Development Finance Institutions (CDFIs), in private organizations, both for-profit and non-profit, that operate in disadvantaged communities. This program is based on an implied assumption, that poorer communities need entrepreneurs capable of generating earnings and creating, jobs and that these businesses should be financially supported, not directly, but through the CDFIs that are fully aware of the specific needs of the area, given that they are physically close, and that are specialized in managing financing in areas in which investment levels are extremely low.

Payroll Giving, on the other hand, allows workers to make donations to registered volunteer organizations (charities), deducting the amount directly from their paycheck. This form of tax-exempt donation was introduced in the UK with the Finance Act of 1986, but it was only in 2000 that the donation limit was eliminated. This was accompanied by an intensive marketing campaign, in which the government undertook to add a 10% supplement to all donations for a period of three years.

Finally, the government is an active promoter of the OECD Guidelines for Multinational Enterprises, having introduced the National Contact Point within the DTI, as well as the ILO Conventions, and actively favors green procurement policies.

3.3 THE FRENCH REGULATORY MODEL

Although recognizing the importance of independent private initiative to stimulate innovation and good practice, the traditional

French view of the state as a major actor, the guarantor of the public interest and, as such, characterized by a higher level of social responsibility, adds a strong regulatory component to the role of the public sector.

In fact, France is the European nation in which the state is most involved in CSR, having adopted a regulatory approach and thereby centralizing social responsibility management. This is done by the Ministère des Affaires Sociales, du Travail et de la Solidarité, which plays a leading role in stimulating social dialogue in France in the areas of employment, vocational training, the fight against exclusion, and health and pensions.

In other words, CSR acts as a catalyst in involving both the public and private sectors in these areas, while at the same time being an objective in itself. More specifically, French CSR strategy is structured on three levels:

- the creation of a clear, nationwide reference system;
- constant monitoring of the state of the art in implementation practice;
- the development of socially responsible investing.

This action plan is embodied in French Law 240 of 2001 concerning 'new economic regulations' and in the subsequent implementing regulation (No. 221, February 2002), which supplement existing commercial law to oblige publicly listed companies to prepare an annual report that takes account of the social and environmental consequences of doing business. The institutionalization of the triple bottom line has the primary purpose of granting an additional right to shareholders: to receive information not only on the more traditional aspects of financial performance, but also on social and environmental issues, seen as an indispensable part of properly assessing a company's soundness.

The law does not encroach upon a company's freedom to interpret the CSR paradigm based on specific company needs, its strengths and its weaknesses. In fact, the law is neither a framework nor does it seek to provide reporting guidelines; rather, it responds to the need to induce substantial change in the way in which companies disclose information regarding their own performance. This is achieved by requiring companies to include information in their annual reports regarding the quality and quantity of certain social and environmental issues, but it leaves it up to the companies themselves to determine the most appropriate methods of achieving this in terms of their own operations. However, as regards improving the quality of the information provided by publicly listed companies, the results obtained following these legislative reforms are far from satisfactory.

Although legislation is the distinguishing characteristic in its approach to CSR, France has not stopped there. As in the other European nations, it has taken action in the areas of promotion, transparency and the development of specific supporting policy.

With regard to promotion, during the French presidency of the G8 in 2003, the government actively supported (including providing funding) the ILO Declaration on Fundamental Principles and Rights at Work, the OECD Guidelines and the UN Global Compact.

Among the activities aimed at ensuring transparency, in addition to the law discussed above, further legislation was adopted in 2001 that called for the elucidation of the social and ethical principles adopted in the investment policies of the Fonds de Réserve pour les Retraites.

Among the policies developed in direct support of CSR, of particular note was the formal adoption in June 2003 of a National Strategy for Sustainable Development, with a decisive contribution from the Conseil National du Développement Durable (CNDD), established in January 2003 by the French government and composed of 90 members from various economic and social groups.

Finally, since March 2001, French law governing public tenders authorizes the inclusion of social and environmental clauses in contracts.

3.4 THE DANISH PARTNERSHIP-BASED MODEL

Denmark has long been known in Europe for its highly developed welfare system, which is primarily aimed at ensuring constant social welfare over time through generous transfer schemes, high-quality services and a comprehensive educational system, all with a decidedly public makeup.

This approach has been experiencing a period of crisis since the 1980s, attracting its first critics and prompting initial attempts at reform in a highly dynamic international landscape characterized by heightened competition.

In the spotlight are policies to fight unemployment in particular. The traditional strategies to reintegrate the unemployed and marginalized, which are based on transfers that can ensure a level of subsistence, financed by general taxation rather than by worker and employer contributions, are deemed to be economically unsustainable and harmful to national competitiveness. At the same time, they are considered politically misguided, in that they make recipients a 'passive customer' of the public system, and socially damaging, a direct cause of skill obsolescence and the diminished ability to work of those who have been unemployed for long periods of time, as well as of other related difficulties that such people have in rejoining the labor force.

This led in the early 1990s to extensive reforms in employment policy, setting the threefold objective of preventing exclusion from the workforce, creating the conditions for maintaining one's job, and expanding/improving the possibilities of reintegration of those who have been unemployed for long periods of time, individuals with limited job skills and so on.

This landscape of profound change and redesign of social policy comprises the Danish government's initiatives regarding CSR.

A decisive stance in the debate on the importance for companies to move beyond mere observance of the law in corporate management was taken in 1994 with the campaign 'Our Common Concern – The Social Responsibility of Companies', promoted by the Ministry for Social Affairs. This initiative defined the government's official role in promoting the dissemination of CSR, which is to encourage social partnerships and research in order to reduce social exclusion and achieve an inclusive labor market.

The emphasis on the importance of adopting actions based on partnership, which is the core of Danish public policy, is based on the belief that social challenges must be faced by focusing on cooperation between the players influenced by these challenges and those who can influence them.

More specifically, public initiatives to promote corporate social responsibility are designed around three lines of actions:

- the dissemination of knowledge: During its Presidency of the European Union (July-December 2002), Denmark included CSR among its priorities, which comprised the organization of the second European conference on the issue (in November 2002);
- research: The Danish government finances the Danish Institute of Social Research to monitor large-scale progress in the area of social responsibility and the degree of inclusion of the labor market, and supports the Human Rights Impact Assessment (HRIA), which was developed by the Danish Centre for Human Rights in order to assist companies in evaluating business practices and detecting any violations of human rights;
- information campaigns, research, and other initiatives aimed at creating public-private partnerships: The Danish government's strategy requires that the promotion of CSR takes place through partnerships between the various social actors. This has led to decisions such as the establishment of the Coordinating Committee for Preventive Labor Market Measures and the Employment Council, both of which are made up of representatives from labor unions, employee associations, and associations of municipal governments and civil society and are aimed at monitoring the labor market, playing an advisory role for the Ministry for Social Affairs. Perhaps the most significant initiative in the area of partnerships for the promotion of responsibility was the establishment, in June 1998, of The Copenhagen Centre (TCC), an independent body created after the World Summit on Social Development held in Copenhagen in 1995 and the Danish CSR campaign. TCC acts as an intermediary among public authorities, businesses, trade unions and social organizations and is primarily responsible for stimulating public debate, cooperation between the social partners, and the sharing of experiences by conducting studies, organizing and facilitating networks, and publishing reports, all in order to 'make CSR real' (www.copenhagencentre.org).

At the same time, government action has not been limited merely to promoting CSR, but has also included initiatives in the area of transparency.

First of all, with regard to non-financial reporting, in 1995 the Ministry for Energy and the Environment issued Statutory Order No. 975 of 13 December regarding the obligation for certain special types of activity (e.g., in the chemicals and natural gas industries, as well as in steel, metals, wood, plastics and other materials) to prepare a 'statement of green accounts'. Then in 2001, the Annual Accounts Act was amended to meet the information needs of all stakeholders. It is now possible to include in the traditional annual report a supplement regarding CSR initiatives. Also in 2001, the Ministry for Social Affairs drafted a set of guidelines for social and ethical reporting (Socialetiske Regnskaber – Virksomhederog Organisationer), while the Labor Ministry, together with business organizations and trade unions, participated in the preparation of a guide to social reporting for SMEs.

Activities to improve transparency promoted by the Ministry for Social Affairs also include the launch in 2000 of the Social Index, an instrument for self-evaluation and disclosure of the level of social responsibility of Danish companies, particularly regarding employment policies and social inclusion. Participating companies that achieve a score of 60/100 or higher can use a social label in their reports, on their products, and so on.

The Ministry of Trade and Industry's Consumer Information Centre has a vast database on business ethics in which companies register the ways in which they handle and internalize recognized national and international business standards.

Public support policies also form part of government social responsibility initiatives. Since 2001, public authorities can require companies that provide services to them or receive benefits and subsidies from them to fulfill social obligations. Finally, Denmark promotes the dissemination of OECD Guidelines through a Tripartite National Contact Point composed of representatives of government, labor and the private sector.

More recently, the Danish Ministry of Economic and Business Affairs, the Confederation of Danish Industries and the Human Rights and Business Project of the Danish Institute for Human Rights launched the CSR Compass on 15 June 2005. The CSR Compass is an interactive tool aimed at supporting small- and medium-sized Danish enterprises in documenting compliance with environmental and social requirements from foreign buyers. In addition, the tool provides guidance to Danish companies on how to define social and environmental standards with which their suppliers are obliged to comply (www.humanrightsbusiness.org).

3.5 THE GERMAN MODEL: A SOCIAL MARKET ECONOMY

The interest of the German government in issues related to CSR has in certain respects developed in a context similar to that in Denmark: a traditionally strong, high-level welfare system meeting basic social needs that has been faced, since the early 1990s, with rising unemployment and pressing national imbalances resulting from the reunification process.

The traditional division of responsibilities in the area of social policy fell into crisis, accompanied by a rising, increasingly unsustainable level of public spending and a widespread skills gap in the highly specialized segments of the private sector.

These trends prompted the German parliament to establish a research commission on the Future of Civic Activities in December 1999 to survey the state of the art in civic activities, the relationship between these activities and the levels of social cohesion desired, and the methods by which to strengthen them. This event officially marks the start of the government's commitment to CSR. The commission's final report, presented in the summer of 2002, clearly shows that the role of companies in contributing to social welfare is closely related to the voluntary assumption of responsibility beyond purely financial aspects, not so much for philanthropic reasons, but as a driver of competitive success and national reconstruction:

> Companies too are facing new challenges to help fashion civil society and promote civic activities. The goal is to develop a corporate culture in which the profit motive is linked with an orientation towards the common good and the assumption of social responsibility in the community. [...] Enterprises depend on intact communities and well-trained employees, and by engaging in civic activity they can

contribute to this. (Campaign Report on European CSR Excellence 2002-2003, pp. 60-61)

Currently, CSR policy is the responsibility of the Ministry of Economics and Labor (Bundesministerium für Wirtschaft und Arbeit, or BMWA), which is responsible for promoting CSR (Soziale Verantwortung der Unternehmen), increasing transparency, and defining public support initiatives, all of which start from an understanding that responsible action is an essential element of renewed development.

Direct funding for the UN Global Compact and the co-funding of the second Global Compact Learning Forum (December 2002), as well as the 2003 Training Campaign to increase business awareness of the importance of investing in employee development, have had the objective of disseminating awareness of the intrinsic value and potential of socially responsible initiatives.

Most of these promotional initiatives have centered on the launch of public-private partnerships.

The adoption of such a collaborative strategy largely involves projects intended for the labor market, on the theory that a properly functioning labor market is the first indicator of the level of a nation's social cohesion and its qualification as socially responsible. Take, for example, the TeamArbeit initiative launched in June 2003, a partnership between companies and representatives from various civil society groups to fight unemployment, or the action program 'Life-accompanying Learning for All', aimed at promoting networks designed to provide long-term education for disadvantaged people.

Two other initiatives are also extremely interesting: one, the New Quality of Work Initiative (Initiative Neue Qualität der Arbeit, or INQA), on the importance of the quality of the workplace to employee performance; and another that, through a federal law that went into effect on 1 May 2002, seeks to achieve equal treatment for the disabled. Although focusing on different aspects of employment, the various projects share a quest for synergies among the various social actors.

The use of incentives for businesses, however, remains the distinguishing characteristic of the German experience in the area of promoting social responsibility. In that regard, the government is supporting the dissemination of the Eco-Management and Audit

Scheme (EMAS) by providing benefits/incentives for companies that decide to adopt the European system. At the same time, financial support is provided for small and medium-sized businesses that implement environmentally friendly policies, such as those that use environmental consulting services or choose to introduce management systems.

As regards action concerning the transparency of conduct and socially responsible activities, the federal government has promoted a roundtable on company codes of conduct which, by involving a variety of representatives of civil society, has the objective of designing a framework for improving social and working conditions in developing countries. Since 1 August 2001, pension funds have also been required to disclose whether their investment policies take ethical, environmental and social factors into account.

Finally, with regard to public policy in support of the dissemination of socially responsible practices, alongside the adoption of a Strategy for Sustainable Development in April 2002, the federal government is committed not only to supporting, through subsidies, the reintegration/rehiring of employees of companies undergoing reorganization, but also to fully funding the Training Place Developer Programme for companies in eastern Germany in order to strengthen their ability to provide training programs for their employees. The government is also sponsoring a program to promote social and environmental standards in developing countries in the areas of sustainable agriculture, fair trade and forest certification.

And as in the UK, France and Denmark, Germany is also engaged in promoting and disseminating OECD Guidelines and has established the National Contact Point within the Ministry of Economics and Labor.

3.6 BELGIUM AND THE ROLE OF THE SOCIAL LABEL

The interest of the Belgian government in the potential of promoting and disseminating the CSR paradigm is fairly recent. In fact, the first initiatives of note were taken in 2001 with the organization of the first European conference on CSR during its EU Presidency (July-December 2001).

Another initiative launched in 2001 by the Ministry for Employment and Tourism was the Trivisi Pioneering Enterprise for People, the Environment and Society, a multi-stakeholder initiative to analyze the characteristics that distinguish a sustainable business, as well as to exchange ideas and experience and define specific management tools.

However, it was in 2002 that the importance of integrating social aspects in management was legally sanctioned, preceding the other European nations. More specifically, the Social Label Law came into effect on 1 September 2002. It is intended to stimulate socially responsible production, offering companies the possibility of obtaining a label that certifies the products – not the organization – of companies that comply with the eight fundamental ILO conventions.

Labels are awarded for a period of up to three years by the Ministry of Economic Affairs acting on the binding opinion of a multi-stakeholder committee (the Comité pour une Production Socialement Responsable) composed of sixteen members.

Although the Belgian government's activities regarding social responsibility are commonly associated with the establishment of the Social Label, they are not limited to this. In fact, in the area of transparency, the new Loi Pensions Complémentaires (LPC) of 15 May 2003 requires pension fund managers to disclose, in their annual reports, the adoption of any ethical, social and environmental principles when making investment decisions.

With regard to public policies in support of CSR, the federal government has established a Federal Council for sustainable development and has introduced social clauses for certain types of federal tenders, which favor the inclusion of disadvantaged groups and respect for the environment.

Finally, Belgium also actively promotes the OECD Guidelines and supports the work of the ILO.

3.7 THE SPANISH MODEL: ACROSS CSR AND BUSINESS ETHICS

Although more slowly than the countries of Anglo-Saxon orientation, Spain, too, has been keenly interested in issues related to corporate social responsibility for about a decade. This interest is no longer just a generic request for companies to respect social needs, but is now seen as a driver for innovation and an opportunity to stimulate competitiveness at all levels.

Unlike in other countries, CSR has come about in Spain primarily in the form of business ethics. Originating in the mid-1980s in academia, this line of research, based on a renewed focus on the respect of individual rights and a widespread sense of solidarity typical of Mediterranean countries, has been a driving force in accelerating the process of internalizing the stimuli generated by the international debate.

Through this mutual integration of cultural factors and specific initiatives, CSR is now seen as a vital component of a company's core business and a decisive factor for the future competitiveness of the country as a whole.

As a direct expression of national trends, the Spanish government's first initiative focused primarily on business ethics. In 1997, a team of experts was commissioned to prepare a report on codes of ethics for the board of directors of publicly listed companies. The result of this study – the so-called Olivencia Report – proposed a Code of Good Governance with 23 recommendations regarding best practices in the area of governance for Spanish organizations. Adoption of the code is voluntary, but companies that choose to follow its recommendations can publicize this decision in order to provide investors and other stakeholders with an initial signal of their adoption of principles of responsible conduct.

However, it was not until 2002 that the government made more concerted efforts in the CSR field.

Focusing first on activities to promote dialogue and disseminate knowledge, in the summer of 2003, following a resolution passed by the Spanish parliament in December 2002, a committee of CSR experts was established within the Ministry of Labor and Social Affairs (Ministerio de Trabajo y Asuntos Sociales, or MTAS). The committee's objectives include the possibility of creating a certifying body for social quality and implementing a social label.

The ministry also included a module centered on issues of environmental responsibility in the training and national inclusion plan. Training courses are also being promoted on occupational health and safety, and a manual has been written on 'good environmental practice' in agriculture, construction and manufacturing.

The government has also established numerous responsible conduct awards, including the Flexible Company Award to stimulate research into innovative methods of work-life balance, the Infanta Cristina Award for Corporate Social Action for projects of social inclusion, and the Prince Phillip Award for Corporate Excellence to recognize companies that have excelled in their direct commitment to quality and the quest for competitiveness.

The Ministry of Labor and Social Affairs has also promoted the Optima Program for equal opportunities. Companies that choose to enter the program are required to develop an action plan that, following evaluation, could lead to certification as a Collaborating Organization for Equal Opportunities between Men and Women.

In October 2002, the autonomous government of Aragon issued an *Orden* to provide public funds as an incentive for small and medium-sized enterprises engaged in the implementation of socially responsible management tools, such as codes of conduct in line with the recommendations for the Global Compact or the OECD Guidelines, sustainability reporting systems, and certifications.

With regard to public activities in support of transparency as an essential component of social responsibility, at the beginning of 2003, Parliament initiated a debate on changing the law regarding institutional investors and pension funds, proposing – in line with developments in the UK, France, Germany and Belgium – to take action involving fund management methods, making it mandatory to disclose any ethical, social and environmental principles followed in making investment decisions.

Similarly, the Comisión Nacional del Mercado de Valores (CNMV) adopted a document regarding the characteristics that investment funds must have in order to be defined as ethical, social or green. All of these initiatives are aimed at increasing transparency and preventing fund managers from making purely 'cosmetic' transactions. The only law on the issue of transparency is Law No. 26/2003 of 17 July, which is centered on the responsibility of company directors and thereby intended to increase the level of protection for private investors.

Generally speaking, the Spanish government's level of intervention in the area of CSR is thus far low, leaving ample room for private initiative. Although the pressure from NGOs in demanding more active government involvement is increasing,

Spanish organizations continue to defend voluntary social action as an aspect essential to its effectiveness. What companies seek, on the other hand, is a general European framework for CSR that would provide common minimum standards and a certain level of comparability between nations and individual initiatives.

3.8 THE PORTUGUESE APPROACH TO CSR

In Portugal the interest in CSR issues and behaviors is growing fast and it combines a deep social knowledge and interest in human resources conditions, gender equality at work, and help for people with disabilities. Most of the tools defined by private organizations are based on business incentives and awards whose scope is promoting CSR principles in terms of improving human conditions and rights at work in their family life.

The Ministry of Labour has been one of the first institutions to act, in requiring all companies with more than 100 employees to issue a report on the social balance and send it to the Ministry.

In Portugal since the 1990s the issue that has ahd the most attention is human resources. A lot of work has been done in this direction with the objective of ensuring:

- male and female equality of treatment at work;
- equal opportunity in recruiting processes, career advancement, vocational training;
- balance of employees' work activities with their home lives;
- balanced participation of male and female workers in decision making processes;
- non-discriminatory language in internal and external communications.

The Commission for Equality in Work and Employment grants its 'Equality is Quality' award organized for those firms who can demonstrate good practices in ensuring equal opportunities in their processes and business behaviors.

The Institute for Development and Inspection of Working Conditions grants the 'Prevenir Mais, Viver Melhor No Trabalho' prize to communicate good practices of employees and firms in matters of health and safety conditions at work.

The National Institute for Employment and Professional Training and the Secretariat for the Rehabilitation and Integration of Disabled People have granted, since 1991, the 'Prémio de mérito' award to employees and firms who testify good practices in professional rehabilitation and integration of people with disabilities.

Moreover the Ministry of Labour through the law 141/85 and Decree-Law 9/92 requires all companies with more than 100 employees to issue every year a report on the social balance and send it to the Ministry. Information about organizations' human resources management, social investments and actions to improve employees' quality of work are essential in this reporting tool.

3.9 THE GREEK MODEL FOR BUSINESS IN SOCIETY

Studies about Corporate Social Responsibility, stakeholder perceptions, triple bottom line and corporate citizenship have not been so common in Greece.

The European Business Campaign Marathon held in Athens on the 29th and 30th of November 2001 can be seen as a starting point in which academic communities, business, and public sector and media initiated their process of CSR enlightening. At this event, the Hellenic Network for Corporate Social Responsibility started to develop a common understanding to answer the question: what is the Greek model for business in society? A discussion has begun about human resources management, socially responsible behaviors, corporate governance, socially responsible investments, sustainable development and related issues.

The conference has definitely had a significant impact in terms of giving a good push to opening up dialogue and debate on CSR issues.

With regard to the private sector, at the moment there is only one initiative, but it is developing by networking and acquiring new affiliates. The Hellenic network for CSR has its main interests in labor conditions and refugees, and is participating in two Equal projects:

- Employment of people with mobility problems;
- Employment of economic refugees and immigrants.

The Hellenic Network for CSR is based in Athens, and was formed in June 2000 by 13 companies and 3 business organizations as a non-profit organisation. Its mission is to promote the meaning of CSR to both Greek businesses and Greek society with the ultimate target of a balanced achievement of profitability and sustainable development.

We can add to this basically Greek initiative the various campaigns carried on by large companies already interested in CSR issues which have subsidiaries in Greece, and the dissemination campaigns of institutional parties such as the European Union, CSR Europe, MORI and so on.

The Ministry of Labour and Social Affairs is in charge of managing and coordinating public and private efforts to develop CSR practices in the Greek economy.

The Greek government is not only interested in disseminating European studies about management of human resources, health and safety at workplaces, and adaptation to change, but promotes initiatives of social partnership, mainly at the level of enterprises.

The Institutions strongly involved in this process are:

- The Greek Economic and Social Commission
- Ministry of Development (The Greek Institute of Hygiene and Security at Work)

The voluntary approach to corporate social responsibility is the basis on which Greek partners started developing their own CSR model. In order to preserve national diversity and innovative approaches in building CSR into a competitive advantage, it is left to stakeholders to determine the different strategy each company uses to achieve CSR issues.

The Minister for Labour, Dimitris Reppas, sees this new focus on corporate responsibility as a unique opportunity to raise the stakes: 'Businesses, by voluntarily undertaking commitments and by surpassing the boundaries of their common regulatory and contractual obligations, on the one hand actually highlight their social responsibility and on the other create and develop higher standards for social development, culture, environmental protection and the respect of fundamental rights.'

3.10 FINAL CONSIDERATIONS

Thanks in part to the driving force provided by the European Commission, CSR is now becoming an integral part of the national strategies of EU Member States.

The cases presented above, together with the great dynamism in Italy regarding these issues, associated in particular with the CSR-SC Project promoted by the Ministry of Labor and Social Affairs (see chapter 8), provide a number of significant examples of a broad process of change aimed at creating a model of sustainable development.

They demonstrate how, in the actual definition of policy to promote CSR and more appropriate management models, it is essential to take account of a nation's specific needs, such as its social, cultural and political traditions and the particular features of its economy, in order to define and build solutions that best meet the real needs of the region for which they are intended.

The search for a common European framework is also important to foster dialogue and the involvement of the various social partners, but the breadth and variety of CSR actions are a true asset for all of Europe. We need to define a model of social responsibility according to guidelines that can capitalize on local successes and close certain structural gaps in order to enhance the quality of national systems and their ability to create and disseminate lasting economic, social and environmental value.

4. The evolutionary path of the concept of CSR

by Clodia Vurro

4.1 INTRODUCTION

The evolution of the concept of CSR and the related issues of social and environmental accountability can be seen as the result of two parallel paths: one encompasses the efforts of policy makers and organizations to spread the idea of socially responsible behavior and CSR practices through initiatives, formal definitions and so on. The other path includes academic research, which has progressed from an initial, vague awareness of the relationship between companies and social/environmental issues to the identification of a more defined set of management tools and rules of conduct.

In the political arena, the European Union (EU) has been actively dealing with the issues related to CSR since 2001, when it presented the Green Paper 'Promoting a European framework for CSR'. This paper was the EU's response to the strategic goal adopted in March 2000 by the European Council in Lisbon: 'to become the most competitive and dynamic knowledge-based economy in the world, capable of sustainable economic growth with more and better jobs and greater social cohesion' (CEC, 2001d, p. 3). The Green Paper was followed in 2002 by an official communication entitled 'CSR: A business contribution to Sustainable Development' (CEC, 2002b), which, together with the earlier document, represents the latest outcome of many years of discussion in Europe, at both the theoretical and institutional level, about the social implications of business activities and the role of companies in supporting local and national community development.

More specifically, the EU has contributed to the global debate on CSR by providing an enabling environment for CSR through the development of dynamic frameworks based on a European definition of CSR. In the Green Paper, CSR was defined as a principle whereby companies: 'decide voluntarily to contribute to a better society and a cleaner environment' and 'integrate social and environmental concerns in their business operations and in their interaction with their stakeholders' (CEC, 2001d, p. 4-6). This framework aims, in short, to provide guidance and 'reference points' on key issues of the CSR agenda, thus enhancing the transparency and credibility of CSR practices and tools. In this sense, the EU interpretation of CSR, which calls for the steadfast involvement of appropriate stakeholders, is consistent with one of the most recent trends in the academic literature regarding CSR: the 'stakeholder management model'.

On the academic end, the number of theoretical and empirical contributions is growing at an increasing rate, stimulating a proliferation of theories, approaches and terminology.

A first impression of business-in-society research and CSR-related issues is well described by Carroll, one of the most prestigious scholars in the discipline (1994, p.14):

An eclectic field with loose boundaries, multiple memberships, and differing training/perspectives; broadly rather than focused, multidisciplinary; wide breadth; brings in a wider range of literature; and interdisciplinary.

Rapid growth of the field is unfortunately engendering confusion as to what constitutes CSR: It is critical to analyze and clarify the multidimensional concept of social responsibility. This is the first, mandatory step towards the definition of both joint and shared CSR patterns (Willis, 2003), able, in turn, to help everyone – from the simple stakeholder who wants to choose among worthwhile companies to the researcher who labors intensely– to distinguish faddishness from stability and attain a wide consensus on the scope and content of CSR benchmarks.

An examination of how the CSR concept and its related issues have been exploited across time and theoretical perspectives clarifies what the *fil rouge* in the CSR literature is and how it has influenced the various ways of integrating business into society and in turn social demand into business. Whether explicit or not, the emphasis has been on the concept of value and on the shift from shareholder supremacy, focused on the ability of the firm to maximize the value for shareholders, to the idea that long-term value creation can be significantly influenced by the needs and requests of numerous and different categories of stakeholders.

In general terms, this extended perspective entails a more comprehensive way of integrating the firms' context of reference into different levels of its operations. It represents the main result of a complex set of changes: from globalization to the gradual affirmation of the concept of sustainable development.

The globalization process undoubtedly continues to offer substantial opportunities to companies that want to extend their business boundaries. At the same time, crossing geographical boundaries through more or less radical productive delocalization is a risk that may cause conflicts with a firm's stakeholders.

In fact, acting globally allows firms to manage an enormous pool of resources. But their responsibilities simultaneously become global; local mistakes can wield an unprecedented ripple effect.

Moreover, in a global setting there is far more competition to attract capital, clients and productive settlements. In such a venue, the incentive to reduce costs, cutting 'unnecessary expenses' such as social and environmental ones, is high. One immediate effect of this cost-cutting approach is more intense competition from those countries with few, if any, limits on cutting, for example, occupational health and safety or environmental expenses.

It follows that the proactive adoption of social and environmental behaviors and standards and an openness to dialogue and cooperation with stakeholders, provide the way to consensus and legitimacy, and foster the creation of long-term value.

In addition to globalization, technological development and the evolution of market sectors and industries also lead to a renewed view of the relationship between business and society. In fact, the role of technological devices in supporting the free circulation of ideas, culture, ways of life and capital and fostering globalization should not be underestimated.

At the same time, this overlap between industries and sectors has to a large extent contributed to the current plethora of competition, causing manufacturing processes to migrate to low-cost productive regions.

Finally, the principle of sustainable development represents the last main stimulus to the evolutionary path of the CSR concept, a solution to the loss of faith in an unlimited growth capacity that does not consider the environmental limitations of the eco-systems. On this basis, as well as the lengthy global debate ongoing since the United Nations Conference on Human Environment in 1972, the principle of sustainable development is applied to three main areas of intervention: the need to identify limits to preserve the natural environment; the need to integrate the responsibility toward future generations into current concerns; and the need to extend measurement practices, focusing not only on quantitative measures but also on the quality of growth, keeping in mind the limits of the planet.

The CSR path is therefore consistent with the concept of sustainable development, supported by the strong link among social, environmental and economic systems. In addition, a sustainable company is one able to carry on its activity indefinitely, as long as it remains mindful of the effects of its actions on social, environmental and economic assets.

The remainder of this chapter offers a history of perspectives on the responsibilities of business in society and the evolution of the related concept of CSR across boundaries and attitudes.

4.2 AN OVERVIEW OF THE INTERNATIONAL LITERATURE ON CSR

During the last fifty years, the concept of CSR has changed its focus many times. The dearth of consensus on the relationship between business and society proceeds from the subjectivity that characterizes responsible behaviors. In other words, if being socially responsible implies developing the ability to interact with society, then the heterogeneity of both the managerial and academic literature and the actual CSR behaviors must refer to the endless possibilities of interpreting social phenomena and the consequent links between companies and their stakeholders.

Notwithstanding this panorama, the evolutionary path of the CSR paradigm can be divided into five main phases. Because a detailed review of the literature on CSR is beyond the scope of this study, the focus instead will be on the main characterizing themes and contributions.

4.2.1 Early Developments

The first step in the history of CSR occurred in the nineteen twenties, when both academic and managerial literature began to assign social duties to companies (Clark, 1939; Kreps, 1940). But the earliest modern contribution to the subject came in the nineteen fifties, when Bowen (1953, p. 6), stressing the social responsibilities of business, wrote about CSR in terms of:

> The obligations of businessmen to pursue those policies, to make those decisions, or to follow those lines of action which are desirable in terms of the objectives and values of our society.

During these years, however, the attention remained focused on large companies characterized by a progressively wide range of action. The public began to fear that corporate power was expanding too rapidly.

In other words, the focus of the academic literature was limited to corporations. Research attempted to describe and evaluate how responsive managers were to public expectations.

4.2.2 Formalizing CSR and First Criticisms

The second evolutionary step, in the nineteen sixties, introduced the idea of corporate power as central in the debate over CSR and the business-society relationship (Davis, 1960). In his 'Iron Law of Responsibility', Davis wrote that:

> Whoever does not use his social power responsibly will lose it. In the long run those who do not use power in a manner which society considers responsible will tend to lose it because other groups eventually will step in to assume those responsibilities (p. 63).

In other words, the social responsibilities of business are consistent with the extent of their social power.

Within this context two concepts assimilate into the general thinking, essential to the modern definition of CSR: to be socially responsible, it is necessary that a company consider the expectations of the surrounding community (Frederick, 1960) and confront them voluntarily, beyond the legal prescriptions. In this sense, McGuire (1963, p. 144) argued that:

The idea of social responsibility supposes that the corporation has not only economic and legal obligations, but also certain responsibilities to society which extend beyond these obligations.

But the nineteen sixties also brought the first criticisms of the effectiveness of the CSR paradigm (Friedman, 1962). In particular, critics stress the vagueness of CSR definitions and the lack of reference points, along with the difficulties of foreseeing the economic effects of responsible behavior. The nineteen sixties ended with Friedman's 'well-known pronouncement': the business of business is business. Nothing more than maximizing profits, nothing less. Acting in a way that does not destroy value for shareholders, companies should satisfy their own expectations and needs.

4.2.3 The 1970s: Classifications and Models

The persistence of some skepticism about the necessity to introduce CSR within corporate operations (Friedman, 1970) also characterized the third phase of the CSR path.

The theories advanced during the nineteen seventies, in response to critics, try to lend clear, rigorous formalization to the CSR concept. Throughout this period, most studies attempted to define the distinctive features and rules of CSR (Manne and Wallich, 1972). Even if the contributions were extremely heterogeneous, all of them agreed that socially responsible companies have to act voluntarily to conform to CSR paradigms, beyond legal prescriptions (Davis, 1973).

An important attempt to formalize the main dimensions of the CSR concept and describe socially responsible behavior was offered by Carroll (1979), who proposed this definition of CSR (p. 500):

> The social responsibility of business encompasses the economic, legal, ethical and discretionary expectations that society has of organizations at a given point in time.

In other words, besides essential and required economic and legal responsibilities (that is, to be profitable and obey the law), Carroll identified expected and desired responsibilities, the former dealing with conformity to social norms, the latter including totally voluntary philanthropic contributions to the community of reference. In other words, while the ethical responsibility responds to social expectations, discretionary responsibilities are contributions to communities regardless of what they expect.

Some theories of this period (Preston and Post, 1975; Ackerman, 1975) centered on the idiosyncratic relationship between companies and their social context: society interacts with business at large, giving it a certain legitimacy and prestige. As a result, it becomes necessary for enterprises that 'detection and scanning of, and response to, the social demands that achieve social legitimacy, greater social acceptance and prestige' (Garriga and Melé, 2004) emerge, while they continue to support their own long-term economic operations and to create value.

Delving deeper, Preston and Post (1975) asserted the existence of public responsibility rather than social responsibility, stressing the fact that (p. 95):

> The scope of managerial responsibility is not unlimited, as the popular concept of social responsibility might suggest, but specifically defined in terms of primary and secondary involvement areas.

In this sense, an active company involvement is legitimized when strictly linked to the essential economic task of the firm – the primary involvement areas (that is, procuring suppliers, engaging employees and so on) – and to all those activities that result (that is, career opportunities, workforce development and so on).

Also, during the nineteen seventies, the need to analyze the relationship between CSR and corporate social performance became evident, and this in turn became the intense focus of the next phase.

4.2.4 Stakeholder Theory and Corporate Social Performance

The fourth CSR step, in the nineteen eighties, consisted of three main research venues: stakeholder management, ethical theories and in-depth studies on corporate social performance.

The location and classification of 'those groups who can affect or are affected by the achievement of an organization's purpose' (Freeman, 1984, p. 49) are the fulcrum of the stakeholder theory. It represents a concrete consciousness rising above awareness of others who tout links to the company, in order to truly become a 'responsible player'. The Stakeholder Approach has many different interpretations, ranging on a continuum. In fact, at one extreme, stakeholder approach is interpreted more as a managerial issue focused on how to integrate social demands.

Those drivers that are commonly identified as the forces behind the affirmation of the CSR concept are synonymous with the foundation of the stakeholder approach. Liberalization, globalization and the information technologies have all contributed to the complexity and intensity of stakeholder relationships. As a result, stakeholder management emerged as an innovative and comprehensive framework responding to changes in the business environment. Stakeholder power and orientation became strategic drivers to foster long-term sustainability.

However, the stakeholder approach can also be considered an ethically based theory (Garriga and Melé, 2004) when it affirms that stakeholder thinking is introduced 'both to explain and to guide the structure and operation of the established corporation' (Donaldson and Preston, 1995, p. 70). It is in this sense that stakeholder approach cannot be limited to descriptive, managerial and integrative dimensions but must be extended to a normative content.

Donaldson and Preston (1995, p. 67) argued that the fundamental basis of stakeholder theory is normative, involving the acceptance of two basic ideas:

> Stakeholders are persons or groups with legitimate interests in procedural and/or substantive aspects of corporate activity. Stakeholders are identified by **their** interests in the corporation, whether the corporation has any corresponding functional interest in **them**. The interest of all stakeholders is of **intrinsic value**. That is, each group of stakeholders merits consideration for its own sake and not merely because of its ability to further the interests of some other groups, such as the shareowners.*

Recognizing the presence of different and complementary perspectives on stakeholder approach, the statement that best summarizes stakeholder theory is: 'Business can be understood as a set of relationships among groups which have a stake in the

---

*Emphasis in the original

activities that make up the business' (Freeman, Wicks et al., 2004, p. 9).

In other words, it is no longer a matter of value distribution among stakeholders, but rather a radical change in the basic way of thinking about modern corporations. In support of this view, the capacity of a firm to generate sustainable wealth over time is claimed to be determined by the relationship with critical stakeholders (Post, Preston and Sachs, 2002b).

Although not explicitly in this phase of the CSR evolutionary path, stakeholder approach was increasingly associated with a concept that can be considered complementary to CSR: the concept of corporate social performance (CSP). In fact, the stakeholder management approach has shown, also by means of empirical evidence (e.g., Post et al., 2002b; Cummings and Doh, 2000), that managing exclusively with a traditional profit-maximization motive is insufficient, essentially because of the changed environment in which companies operate. This is why the CSP concept deals mainly with a search for social legitimacy, justifying CSP as an unavoidable consequence of the critical interdependencies that exist among the firm, its employees, customers, investors, communities and constituencies in general. Companies are more and more becoming conscious of their assimilation into an open, dynamic organism that interacts with a wider system – the environment of reference – on a continuous basis. As a result, adopting socially responsible behavior and pursuing corporate social performance become crucial, in order to manage relations with both environment and stakeholders.

In other words, since corporate social performance emerges as (Wood, 1991, p. 693):

> A business configuration of principles of social responsibility, processes of social responsiveness, and policies, programs, and observable outcomes as they relate to the firm's societal relationships,

it is clearly set in the context in which a company operates and represents a strategy (Ullmann, 1985) for dealing with the players or stakeholders that compose each context. In other words, social performance is a strategy for dealing with stakeholder demands.

Moreover, the numerous definitions of CSP share three analytical perspectives (e.g., Carroll, 1979; 1991; Schwartz and Carroll, 2003; Wartick and Cochran, 1985; Wood, 1991). The first one relates to the definition of CSR or the principle of social responsibility. Linked to this are the detailed issues in which social responsibility consists and finally, the processes of responsiveness that comprise a sort of philosophy of rising to social expectations.

By now, however, correlation studies specifically focused on the relationship between stakeholder power and orientation are lacking in the literature on CSR. Roberts (1992) conducted a study on the relationship between power and social responsibility disclosure, but focused on a limited number of stakeholders (i.e., community, stockholders and government) and did not consider the impact on social performance. In addition, the effectiveness of stakeholder management has been tested through case-based studies and not yet been conceptualized in terms of stakeholder orientation.

But is it enough for companies to claim socially responsible behavior to avoid growing stakeholder pressures rather than to respond to an actual interest in achieving a better or 'good' society? The ethical theories graft themselves onto this question and, on this subject, Frederick (1986) speaks about corporate social rectitude as the need to introduce moral values and ethical codes to support socially responsible behavior. At the same time, the need for responsible action to be measured in order to have some effect clearly becomes essential. These studies base themselves on an assumption: the CSR paradigm is not only the last result of a process, but also a process itself, to be included in decision making, whose results have to be evaluated and measured (Jones, 1980).

4.2.5 New Directions and Expectations

During the fifth and last phase – from the nineteen nineties to today – the term *CSR* has continued to change and enrich itself with new themes: stakeholder theory and 'social contract', and then the 'integrative social contracts theory' (Donaldson, 1982 and 1989; Donaldson and Dunfee, 1994, 1995, 1999a, 1999b). In *Ties That Bind*, Donaldson and Dunfee write (1999a, p. 246):

All organizations, wherever situated, and whatever their characteristics, must recognize the interests of stakeholders whenever failing to do so may violate a hypernorm [...] it then becomes the obligation of all organizations to recognize this principle with regard to stakeholders. [...] Thus [...] an organization that sells carcinogen-contaminated pajamas in the Third World must take heed! Knowing that they are prohibited for sale in the United States and Europe and are unacceptably dangerous to their intended users, fails to recognize a mandatory stakeholder duty.

Given the existence of a sort of implicit social contract between business and society, companies surely have some indirect obligations towards society. While hyper-norms provide rules for any social contracting, the microsocial contracts show explicit or implicit agreements that are binding within an identified community.

But the nineteen nineties are also the years of the concept of corporate citizenship (Andriof and McIntosh, 2001; Matten and Crane 2004). Although presenting different definitions and frameworks on these themes, research contributions on corporate citizenship and business citizenship share one feature: they tend to be focused on rights, responsibilities and possible partnerships of business in society, assuming a strong sense of responsibility of business towards communities of reference.

The broadening of communities and the progressive affirmation of global responsibilities within the global markets, have led to an alternative model of corporate citizenship: global citizenship. In fact, while through the nineteen eighties corporate responsibility was disproportionately an American phenomenon, this is no longer the case. The geographical boundaries of CSR research are now extending along with the boundaries of global firms, giving rise to the concept of global business ethics (Donaldson and Dunfee, 1999a).

Moreover, the stream of research on corporate citizenship has been recognized as the source of another recent debate concerning the roles and responsibilities of business in society: the debate over social entrepreneurship. In this context, the link between the crisis of the welfare state, the globalization phenomenon, and the deregulation process on the one side, and an increasing economic and social power of some large multinational companies on the other, has convinced both business and academics that corporate actors undoubtedly belong to a community and must take its needs into account. According to this view, social entrepreneurship (hereafter, SE) represents a further development of the theory and practice of corporate citizenship, in that it arises directly from the needs of society (i.e., social problems) and aims explicitly to enhance societal well-being by initiating social change (Perrini and Vurro, 2006). In other words, SE can be viewed as the main outcome of the overlap between different but complementary theoretical perspectives. It focuses on those organizations explicitly devoted to delving into social problems through innovation within the entrepreneurial setting. For this reason, the concept is increasingly considered at the nexus of business entrepreneurship, strategic innovation and social issues in management.

The amount of theoretical and empirical research on the CSP and business case for CSR also increased during this phase. By now, this category of research, specifically on the relationship between CSR activities and behaviors and corporate economic and financial performance, remains the most controversial one. Most of the existing theories rely on the assumption that the stronger the firm's involvement in CSR programs and activities is, the greater the economic and financial results become.

Notwithstanding the increasing number of studies on this subject, it is surprising to discover a substantial inconsistency in the results obtained, in term of both existence and direction of the correlation between the constructs. Margolis and Walsh (2003) counted 127 studies devoted to exploring the CSP-corporate financial performance (hereafter, CFP) relationship in the period 1972-2002. Their results are puzzling: in spite of the fact that the majority of inquiries found a significant positive relationship, conflicting results were reported even in cases based on the same sample of firms. As a consequence, the relationship continues to be recognized as ambiguous and complex, not allowing for much theoretical generalization on the implications of responsible business conduct.

It is useful to divide the studies on the business case for social responsibility into two main groups: the one side includes theoretical frameworks focused on the concept of CSP as defined by Wood (1991), and aimed at clarifying the nature of the relationship between CSP and financial performance. In general, these studies claim a non-linear relationship (i.e., an inverted U relationship) between the two constructs, justifying the inconsistencies in the empirical studies by the fact that companies surveyed were in different positions on the curve. With regard to the construct definition, Carroll (1979) is considered to have introduced a model of corporate performance that also includes the social dimension. A recent evolution of Carroll's approach (Schwartz and Carroll, 2003) is based on a three-domain model of CSR, composed of three areas of responsibility: economic, legal and ethical. Schwartz and Carroll's contribution (2003) focuses on a shift from the traditional pyramid framework (Carroll, 1991), in which CSR domains were characterized by a sort of hierarchical organization in favor of the economic responsibilities, to a Venn model framework with overlapping categories, supporting the idea that 'none of the three CSR domains (i.e., economic, legal, or ethical) is prima facie more important or significant relative to others' (2003, p.508).

The other side of the debates on the link between social responsibilities and business results includes all the empirical studies aimed at exploiting the CSP-CFP relationship in quantitative terms or following a more descriptive methodology. Although the whole body of research on this issue is extensive and, as said above, the majority of them support the business case for CSR, results suggest that the relationship is complex and contingent on situational, company- and plant-specific factors that are difficult to detect and control for. In addition, the issue of the causal sequence between financial performance and corporate social performance remains unresolved.

This evidence is increasingly compelling a different approach to the exploitation of the effect of CSR on corporate performance, suggesting the inadequacy of those frameworks focused only on traditional measures of economic and financial performance. By now, in fact, the majority of CSP-CFP relationship studies have not been concerned with the strategic importance of business's contribution to society; rather, they have found justification in an attempt to demonstrate the superiority of the CSP theory to the claim of the neo-classical theory that *the business of business is business* (Friedman, 1970).

Such a theoretical superiority is demonstrated by the proof that CSP is significantly and positively correlated with CFP: only in this case business contributions to social and environmental concerns are consistent with profit-maximization strategies.

Increasingly the perspective has been rejected that legitimizes CSP as an unavoidable consequence of the critical interdependencies that exist among the firm, its employees, customers, investors, communities and constituencies in general.

Since companies are open organisms continuously interacting with their specific context of reference, CSR and socially responsible behavior represent the strategy for dealing with the context and managing relations with the different categories of stakeholders.

Therefore, more than in the past, current studies attempt to shed light on the strategic posture (Vogel, 2005) that justifies the business case for CSR, shifting the current debate to perspectives and research inquires that are not focused exclusively on economic performance.

As Frederick (1998) wrote, the fulcrum of this phase lies on a conceptual shift from the 'mere' CSR construct (that is, CSR from an ethical-philosophical point of view), to a more action oriented concept of social responsiveness, a sort of operationalization of the main concept.

This process of operationalization is well represented by the large number of studies on the multiple ways of enacting CSR, which recognize the existence of a sort of parallelism between corporate socially responsible behavior and the aptitude of companies to systematically provide better responses to the social, economic and environmental requests of their stakeholders.

For these reasons, in addition to the initial trend to adhere to the CSR paradigm, more and more companies have paid growing attention to the importance of demonstrating CSR commitment through clear and verifiable data and information, similar to more traditional financial documents. Consistent with that trend, which considers the relational dimension of corporate behavior and the necessity of suitable management tools and evaluations of companies' relational performance, a new *zeitgeist* has emerged: the unavoidable link between the measurement of social and environmental performance and the ability to manage these dimensions of corporate behavior.

In other words, more than in the past, companies are aware of the unquestionable necessity of a good reputation and their interlocutors' trust to be able to create value – all this by embedding sustainability and social responsibility into the day-to-day business operations. In this sense, being socially responsible, which encompasses increased engagement and transparency about what companies stand for, how they create long-term value for their shareholders, clients and employees and how they contribute to society, necessitates being trustworthy and able to deliver profitable growth.

Social, environmental and sustainability reports are placed in the context described above: on the one hand, they substantially contribute to both formalizing firms' positions on CSR and providing a viable opportunity to assert commitment to good business practices; on the other hand, reporting practices, that is, pulling and collecting information from business units with different priorities, represents not only a step towards evaluating and measuring the overall corporate responsibility performance, but also, and most important, a concrete opportunity to identify strengths and weaknesses across the whole spectrum of corporate responsibility.

The theoretical roots of such actual corporate behavior can be found in the emergence of the so-called *triple bottom line* (TBL) approach, developed since the nineteen nineties with specific reference to the measurement of CSR (Elkington, 1997; Norman and MacDonald, 2004). TBL refers to the contemporary evaluation of the economic, social and environmental corporate dimensions, and can be considered in line with the EU definition of CSR and sustainable development. It supports the belief that the aptitude for profit is only one of the outcomes of an organization's activities, not its sole interest.

From a different perspective and sustained by the assumption that reporting represents the external and systematic result of companies' thought about what CSR is and how it can be shared with stakeholders, a number of studies have focused on social and environmental disclosure and on analysis of the content and role of company non-financial reporting. This alternative approach to CSR emphasizes social and environmental reporting as representative of the role of information in firm-society dialogue (Gray et al., 1995). In this sense, many studies have been conducted that attempt to determine the amount and type of social and environmental disclosures that companies are publishing (see for example, Guthrie and Parker, 1990; Gray et al., 1995; Deegan and Gordon, 1996).

Other studies have focused more on reporting itself, exploiting the determinants of disclosure on the one hand (Adams, 2002; Roberts, 1992; Patten, 2002), and the effect of disclosure and reporting practices on performance on the other (see for example: Blacconiere and Patten, 1994).

Finally, part of the recent research on disclosure and reporting practices has focused on the role of standards of reporting in encouraging corporations to disclose critical social and environmental data and information. At the moment, along with the increasing number of companies reporting, there is a greater diversity in the types of reports issued (Willis, 2003), making it necessary to look for a common standard both to support the measurement and evaluation process and to facilitate the consequent assurance process.

In this setting, standardization is much more than necessary, and this can be easily demonstrated by the role that the Global Reporting Initiative (GRI) has played in increasing the amount of sustainability reporting in recent years. The number of companies known to use or reference the GRI's sustainability reporting guidelines currently stands at 817 (March 2006), while only 140 used the tool two years ago (SustainAbility, 2004).

This evidence has stimulated a fruitful debate on the role of reporting standards in reducing the comparability gap among companies and across time. All this led by the advantages of the standardization itself (Willis, 2003; Tencati et al., 2004): reduction of selective disclosure, comparability among different reports, reduction of the risk of releasing misleading information, creation of a common, shared knowledge base and so on.

The diffusion of standards is considered to be a concrete opportunity to enhance the companies' willingness to social and environmental disclosure, by both reducing the ability of firms to selectively disclose and strengthening the stakeholder knowledge about what information a corporation should disclose.

4.3 A ROAD MAP FOR CSR

The previous sections have shown the heterogeneity of the approaches toward the relationship between business and society: from business ethics to the corporate citizenship theme; from the analysis of the determinants of socially responsible behavior to the actual way of demonstrating corporate involvement; from stakeholder management to the identification of corporate social and environmental performance indicators.

Although the main strength of the CSR concept and related issues is undoubtedly the variety of approaches and theoretical frameworks, this last section aims to summarize those features that with more or less emphasis have emerged along the complex CSR path.

Across time, each one of the themes concerning the role and responsibilities of business in society has had its apex, with a convergence of academic interests and research inquiries. As a farsighted eye has no difficulty viewing distant objects, but is unable to focus on nearby objects, it is difficult to clearly understand what CSR means today. Areas are overlapping, with an increasing emphasis on integration both at the theoretical and practical levels. What is certain at the present time is a matter of fact: whether the perspective is skeptical or not, CSR has 'won the battle of ideas', as emphasized by a recent cover story in the *Economist* (January, 2005).

First of all, CSR is less and less often a separate aspect of the corporate scene, opposed to an ideal and hierarchically superior economic responsibility. The classical approach to economic and financial performance maximization is no longer supportable, because it is incomplete. An alternative paradigm has emerged, with the integration of socially, economically and environmentally complementary responsibilities. The superiority of such an approach is not in the straightforward link between CSR activities and behaviors and reinforced business performance, but rather in the necessity to take into account those changes that have occurred in a firm's frame of reference, in terms of expectations and requests. According to this view, CSR is not a tool in service of economic responsibility, but a composite and multidimensional strategic response to a changed situation. The corporate objectives have not changed, but evolved to a renewed managerial vision, embedded in the supremacy of stakeholder-based relationship sets.

The second consideration in tackling CSR themes concerns the boundary between what behaviors are and are not consistent with CSR. By now, companies are interpreting their relationship with their social context in myriad ways, emphasizing specific relationships (for example, with employees or customers) or corporate proficiency in environmental protection. But this still does not answer the question. The *red line* that distinguishes, among behaviors and practices, what is consistent with a CSR paradigm is the voluntary action. CSR represents that 'bundle of policies and programs that private firms undertake on a voluntary basis as a response to societal pressure and expectations' (Vogel, 2005, p. 7) or a 'concept whereby companies integrate social and environmental concerns into their business operations and interactions with their stakeholders on a voluntary basis' (CEC, 2001d). Social responsibilities are different from legal ones. Even though there can be different approaches to CSR, from reactive to collaborative, a responsible firm is more and more seen as a proactive force within its community and in its relationships with stakeholders. In other words, bribery or the violation of human rights in a developing region exposes a company to legal liabilities. Limiting themselves to legal obligations, or avoiding CSR practices or stakeholders' requests leaves a company open to a bad outcome. For instance, consumers might prefer a competitor's product, employees might evaluate other employment opportunities, or investors might prefer companies with better social rating and so on.

A third point concerns the link between CSR and firms' stakeholders. It is not possible to deal with social responsibility without answering the question: 'Responsible to whom?' As a consequence, the necessary prerequisite to CSR behavior is a deep understanding of the context of reference and the categories of stakeholders that comprise it. This does not require the satisfaction of all requests from stakeholders, but rather the development of scanning and prioritization skills. It is necessary to progressively integrate CSR into strategies and business operations, permanently modifying the corporation. CSR is increasingly considered a way of life shared within the company and with stakeholders.

Finally, the role of representing what companies have done in the areas of CSR has to be considered in the study of the relationship between business and society. If we accept the idea that CSR rests at the nexus of the relationships between companies and their stakeholders, the importance of accountability and reporting should not be underestimated.

5. CSR as a source of competitive advantage

A happy convergence between what your shareholders want
and what is best for millions of people
(Kofi Annan, 2001)

5.1 INTRODUCTION

The debate over the ethical conduct of business, fostered by academics and international institutions, as well as public and private actors, has been constantly sustained by an underlying dilemma: the existence of a sort of contradiction in associating morality with market and ethics with business activities.

At the same time, few would disagree that there is some relationship between CSR practices and the ability of firms to achieve their objectives. In fact, the number of reported cases of companies convinced of the advantages of integrating CSR philosophy into their day-by-day operations provides sufficient evidence that CSR is a source of competitive advantage.

Beyond multinationals, pioneers in this field with remarkable commitment, increasingly small- and medium-sized companies are developing or simply adopting tools and approaches to manage social and environmental issues within the scope of their strategic and competitive activities. In general, literature and managerial practice provide evidence that CSR contributes to the creation of value, and thus to a competitive advantage for the company.

From this perspective, CSR is not to be considered as an expense, but rather an element that, if integrated into the company's governance, contributes to the company's performance and competitiveness, by enhancing the development perspective and reducing the 'risk profile'.

Here follows a list of the broad areas in which CSR can accomplish positive results:

- with reference to human resources and the company climate, CSR practices foster a better, safer and more motivating working environment, in line with the corporate goals of effectiveness and efficiency. As a consequence, the corporate ability to attract and keep qualified and motivated human resources is increased;
- in relation to the final market, the CSR commitment increases brand value, through the development of a steady and long-lasting relationship with consumers, on the basis of trust in and loyalty to the brand;
- in the area of social and environmental responsibility, the company reputation is strengthened, thus reducing the risk of boycotting by third organizations;
- at the international competitive level, which is more and more complex and dynamic, where social and environmental dumping cases trigger competitive imbalances, CSR can become a qualifying and distinctive element by transforming threats into opportunities, with full respect for the rules of the market and consumer sensibility;
- in terms of easier access to financing, due to more favorable risk profiles, socially responsible behavior also improves relations with financial institutions.

The importance of such benefits, as well as the strategic importance of intangible assets, increases.

Proceeding from this premise, the remainder of the chapter is structured as follows: first, the main effects of CSR on performance are summarized. They are grouped into four areas: (i) related-to-internal organization effects; (ii) related-to-consumer market performance effects; (iii) related-to-financial market performance effects; (iv) related-to-general stakeholder network effects. Second, according to the stakeholder view, the contribution of CSR to value creation and company sustainability is described. Finally, criticisms of the hypothesis that CSR contributes to firms' competitiveness are provided.

5.2 THE EFFECTS OF CSR

Analyzing the effects of CSR practices is undoubtedly one of the trickiest subjects in dealing with CSR and the impacts of socially responsible behavior on corporate overall performance. More than one hundred empirical tests have been carried out over the last twenty years but the results are inconclusive. In other words, this complex relationship depends on situation, company- and plant-specific factors that are difficult to detect.

As highlighted in chapter 4, academic research on the business case for CSR can be divided into three main areas of research: theoretical frameworks, empirical testing and descriptive studies (Salzmann, Ionescu-Somers and Steger, 2004). In this chapter we do not focus on the results of that research; rather, the aim is to clarify the many ways in which CSR can influence firm's management and performance.

We identify one main assumption that justifies the business case for CSR. From the perspective of sustainability, as explained above, companies are not just tools for organizing economic activity in terms of the production of goods and services, but pervasive economic and social organisms interacting with a stakeholder network and accountable to it. As explained by Paine (2003, pp. 91-92):

> Even when we aren't working, we spend much of the time interacting with corporations in the person of individuals who represent them or act on their behalf. Corporations also supply us with the most basic goods and services we need to run our households, but we also depend on them for transportation, communications, energy, and other essential utilities to maintain the fabric of our daily lives. [...] The visible hand of the corporation touches nearly every aspect of our lives. [...] Through their employment policies, corporate decision makers determine when we must work, when we may meet with our children's teachers, when we may visit the doctor.

Given these premises, the next step is the attempt to clarify the relationship between CSR and value, through the lens of their components.

The literature uniformly recognizes, in a broad sense, four main sets of possible effects of CSR on corporate performance. They are: (i) related-to-internal organization effects; (ii) related-to-consumer market performance effects; (iii) related-to-financial market performance effects; (iv) related-to-general stakeholder network effects. The following sections summarize the main findings in each of the identified areas.

5.2.1 CSR and Internal Organization

Along with the increasing importance of intangibles for company success, in terms of the ability of firms to create, to manage and to transfer knowledge (Cohen, 1998; Glazer, 1998; Miles, Snow, Mathews, Miles and Coleman, 1997; Ruggles, 1998), and according to the decreasing importance of the other sources of competitive advantage (Pfeffer, 1994; Snell, Youndt and Wright, 1996), the quality of the workforce has become the critical source of competitiveness for companies.

As argued by Greening and Turban (2000, p. 256):

A firm will be successful in this endeavor if it has a quality-workforce to take advantage of and manage such knowledge. It should be pointed out that although a quality workforce may be a necessary condition for success in the new knowledge economy, it is not a sufficient one. The successful firm must be able to take advantage of such talent and develop it into skills that are valuable, rare, nonsubstitutable, and unable to be easily imitated by competitors.

The authors find support for the hypothesis that CSR, in terms of corporate responsiveness to social pressure, that is, corporate social performance, can have a positive impact on a firm's attractiveness as an employer. In particular they investigate the corporate image resulting from corporate social performance through the quality of product and services, the nondiscriminatory behavior and diversity management and the treatment of the environment.

In other words, an overall positive corporate social and environmental performance, not limited to employment issues, can generate competitive advantage, through attracting a quality workforce and fostering the accumulation of intangibles.

Similar results (Kotler and Lee, 2005) corroborate this, indicating that a company's participation in social initiatives can have a positive impact with prospective and current employees, as well as citizens and executives. According to their March 2001 survey, employees working in companies reported to have cause-related programs were 38 percent more likely to say they were proud of their company than employees in companies not reported to have these programs. Even before 11 September, 48 percent of respondents indicated that a company's commitment to causes is important in the decision to work for the company. After 11 September, that percentage rose to 76. And in their 2002 Citizenship Study with a national cross-section of 1,040 adults, 80 percent of respondents said they would be likely to refuse to work at a company if they were to find that it was guilty of poor treatment of and attitudes toward personnel.

On a different note, CSR can increase efficiency in the way internal organization is managed. For example, CSR intervention to improve the corporate climate could reduce opportunism and shirking while at the same time instilling greater confidence in the firm. This could lead to improvements in employee relations – for example, a decrease in absenteeism and carelessness or internal theft. In Paine's words (2003, pp. 39-40):

> Thus, we would expect a high regard for truth and honesty to contribute to better planning, better decision making, and more efficient problem solving. Why? Because the underlying information is more apt to be accurate, the analysis more objective, and the decision makers free to acknowledge problems and risks. We would also expect to see fewer resources wasted on unrealistic projects undertaken for reasons of ego gratification or political accommodation.

In more general terms, firms that adopt socially and environmentally productive practices can reduce the waste of resources in redundant activities (think, for example, of fact checking) and devote time and resources to highly valuable activities such as training or research and development.

5.2.2 CSR and the Consumer Market

Along with the growth of the consumerism movement, and the increasing consumer demand for corporate transparency, CSR practices and information about companies have become quality indicators, strengthening company and brand positioning. In this context, CSR practices represent a useful and 'intuitively appealing heuristic on which individuals can focus when evaluating a firm' (Jones and Murrell, 2001, p. 63).

The accent here is on the more general impact of CSR on corporate reputation (Greening and Turban, 2000), which in turn affects the accumulation of intangibles in terms of trust and market reciprocity.

Trust is a fundamental asset in every business and non-business relationship. Indeed, the high level of abstraction of the construct makes it useful for understanding many types of relationships (inter-personal, intra- and inter-organizational, social, business and so on) that are studied using different approaches (Ring and Van de Ven, 1992, 1994; Zaheer and Venkatraman, 1995; Zaheer, McEvily and Perrone, 1998; Das and Teng, 1998, 2001).

Trust literature offers a huge variety of definitions for trust. It has been generally defined as 'an expectation referred to the trustee's willingness to keep promises and to fulfill obligations' (Rotter, 1971; Barber, 1983; Dwyer, Schurr and Oh, 1987; Hagen and Choe, 1998). Expectation is sometimes associated with the antecedents of trust, such as the level of competencies, honesty and goodwill of the trustee (Barber, 1983; Blomqvist, 1997), and also altruistic motivations.

According to the two analytical levels based on the distinction originally proposed by Lewicki and Bunker (1996), trust can manifest itself as knowledge-based. In this sense, it is based on the knowledge of CSR actions or initiatives of the firm in question, of its abilities and its technical competencies. The second level of trust is value-based, that is, trust based upon the company's perceived integrity as well as on its elevated value system. In this case, the customers fully identify themselves with the brand. For this reason, the impact of CSR programs is stronger in terms of value-based rather than knowledge-based trust.

Moreover, each of the trust types discussed above can be associated with one or more customers' behavioral intentions. For this purpose, we agree with those who consider the behavioral dimension of trust as a fundamental pre-requisite of this very construct. Without an intention to act, trust is indeed meaningless. If a customer states his/her trust in a brand, yet his/her trust is not turned into actual willingness to purchase, no trust-based relationship exists (Moorman, Zaltman and, Deshpandé, 1992).

Therefore, we can assume that trust should be translated into an intention to purchase the brand. This intention determines brand loyalty as a direct consumer response. It is defined as the tendency to be loyal to a focal brand, which is demonstrated by the intention to buy the brand as a primary choice (Oliver, 1999; Yoo and Donthu, 2001). Trust in the firm's ability to differentiate the product/service through CSR orientation should turn into an intention to re-purchase as well as the willingness to pay a premium price.

The direct effect of the single dimension of CSR on customers' behavioral intentions is very low. In particular, the hypothesis is that the only CSR dimension able to influence the intention to pay a premium price and the brand loyalty level is the consumer dimension. In fact, the belief that the firm produces high-quality products to satisfy its customer's needs, that it is very focused in controlling all the activities along the whole supply chain and protects voluntarily rights and interests of its customers, is part of the firm's brand equity and, for this, could have a direct effect on customers' behavioral intentions. The other dimensions of CSR should have only an indirect effect, mediated by trust, on premium price and brand loyalty.

Moreover, companies that demonstrate that they are engaging in practices that satisfy and go beyond regulatory compliance requirements are given less scrutiny and more free rein, reducing the risk of boycotting by third organizations. In addition, the consumer-related market performance effects require that consumers be sensitive to CSR issues. In other words, a set of consumer-related factors may influence the intensity and type of CSR initiatives.

5.2.3 CSR and the Financial Market

A further benefit of socially responsible behavior concerns the relationship with the financial market in terms of easier access to funds via the already-mentioned 'more free rein' profile. Companies can, in fact, adhere to CSR practices, to manage and ideally eliminate risks associated with misconduct, carelessness or insensitivity. CSR can reduce risks at different levels: from the easily identifiable (for example, the environmental risk, the risk of customer dissatisfaction, insurance or legal expenses, and so on) to the hidden risks such as decreases in productivity, damages to corporate image, deterioration of the relationships with the company stakeholders, and so on.

In this sense, potential investors and lenders would perceive firms engaged in CSR as less risky than the others. However, the prerequisite of such an argument is the visibility of CSR commitment.

As in the other cases, the effect of CSR on the different areas of corporate performance is strictly related to the ability of firms to disclose social and environmental information. In other words, the existence of a positive correlation between the quantity and quality of disclosed information about the net financial position and the cost to access credit should be taken into account. Investments in CSR activities and the ability to manage stakeholders have a direct impact on lenders' and potential investors' perceptions of company risk. This can increase a firm's access to market capital. In this way, disclosure can play a fundamental role in the process. The ability of the company to manage multiple stakeholder relationships decreases risk; with the visibility gained through disclosure, shareholders and financial partners at large can interpret CSR activities as a 'signal of a firm's successful attempts at satisfying stakeholder groups' (Orlitzky and Benjamin, 2001).

The relationship between CSR and the financial market can be considered according to a firm's easy access to financing, but also in terms of a wider range of possible financial sources. In this context, socially responsible investing (henceforth SRI) represents a new opportunity for those companies able to adhere to and practice the CSR way of life.

SRI consists of managing financial assets according to ethical, social and environmental criteria. It includes green investment funds, social and ethical investment funds, traditional investment funds, pension funds and open-ended investment companies (which adopt social criteria to optimize their portfolio choices), ethical private banking, separate management for institutional clients such as foundations, religious bodies, non-profit bodies (which carefully select their capital allocation) and closed funds (which invest according to ethical criteria). If we expand our analytical framework, the concept of ethical financing can be extended to include funds that transfer one part of the commissions to bodies and associations for social purposes and subjects that develop forms of alternative financing to support third-sector and microcredit activities.

SRI dates back to the nineteenth century, when some religious groups first introduced the concept in the United States. However,

Developing Corporate Social Responsibility

it was only in the nineteen sixties, when the public became increasingly sensitive to social and environmental issues, that an overt demand for SRI emerged. In the late nineteen seventies, this concept began to attract a larger number of investors who were especially concerned about the system of apartheid in South Africa. Investment choices were designed to exclude companies that did business with that country, combined with other forms of pressure adopted by the international community to force the South African government to change its discrimination policies. Subsequently, the number of ethical SRI products began to notably increase, first in the United States, followed by the UK and the other European countries. From the mid-nineteen nineties this trend increased even more.

The total SRI assets under management amount to around 2,000 billion Euros (Table 5.1).

Table 5.1 Worldwide socially responsible investments (million Euros)

Country	Retail Funds		Institutional Funds		Total	
	SRI Assets under Management	%	SRI Assets under Management	%	SRI Assets under Management	%
North America	103,165.42	80 99%	1,621,515.34	85.51%	1,724,680.76	85.23%
USA	100,544.24	78 94%	1.596,041.17	84.17%	1,696,595 41	83.84%
Canada	2,611 19	2.05%	25,474.17	1 34%	28,085.36	1 39%
Australia	1,402.20	1.10%	7,096.28	0.37%	8,498.48	0.42%
Europe	22,816 53	17.91%	267,630 15	14 11%	290,446.68	14.35%
Total	127,384.15	100%	1,896,241.78	100%	2,023,625.93	100%
%	6.29		93.71		100	

Source: USA - Social Investment Forum (2004). Canada - Social Investment Organization (2003). Australia - Ethical Investment Association (2004). Europe - E. Capital Partners (2004); Eurosif (2003)

The growing interest of investors in the social and environmental dimension of portfolio choices is due not only to ethical considerations but also to the profit motive. In this connection, in the last eleven years ethical stock indexes have been set up and are used as benchmarks for financial products and to measure the performance of fund managers (Box 5.1).

BOX 5.1 Ethical indexes

- The *Domini 400 Social Index* (DSI). Kinder, Lydenberg, Domini & Co., Inc. (KLD), an American social rating company began preparing this index at the end of 1989. The DSI was officially launched on 1 May 1990. KLD Research & Analytics introduced two new indexes in January 2001: the KLD Broad Market Social Index (KLD BMSI) and the KLD Large Cap Social Index (KLD LCSI). In 2002, the KLD Nasdaq Social Index (KLD-NS Index) was launched;
- the *Citizens Index*, set up in the US in 1994, is managed by Citizens Advisers;
- the **Dow Jones Sustainability World Indexes** (DJSI World) were first published on 8 September 1999 and the Dow Jones STOXX Sustainability Indexes were launched in October 2001. The Dow Jones Sustainability Indexes were the result of a joint effort by the Dow Jones Indexes, STOXX Ltd. and the SAM Group, a Zurich-based company that deals with sustainable asset management;
- the *Jantzi Social Index* (JSI), launched on the Canadian market in January 2000 and managed by Michael Jantzi Research Associates;
- the *Triodos Sustainable Investment Index*, managed by Triodos Research, a division of Triodos Bank, and calculated by Nyfer, an independent institute for economic research of the Nijenrode University in the Netherlands;
- the *Ethical Index Euro*. E. Capital Partners, an independent, Italian financial advisor, began to define the index in May 2000 and officially presented it in October 2000. The process of ethical rating adopted by E. Capital Partners is based on the method developed by Finetica, a think tank of Bocconi University set up in conjunction with the Pontificia Università Lateranense (the University of Vatican

City). The index is part of the larger Ethical Index Management System;

- **Ethibel Sustainability Index** (ESI). Developed by Ethibel, a Belgian intermediary advisor for the financial the corporate world founded in 1992, ESI provides a comprehensive perspective on the financial performance of the world's leading companies in terms of sustainability for institutional investors, asset managers, banks and retail investors. ESI groups four regional indexes: ESI Global, ESI Americas, ESI Europe and ESI Asia Pacific;

- The **ASPI Eurozone®** (Advanced Sustainable Performance Indices). A family of indexes that track the financial performance of 120 leading Eurozone sustainability performers. ASPI uses Vigeo's rating system, which centers on a positive approach to sustainability and SRI. The indexes were established in July 2001 and have since been considered as an important new standard or benchmark for corporate sustainability and SRI fund managers or mainstream fund managers wishing to engage in CSR. On 15 June 2005, the merger between Ethibel and Vigeo was approved and the Vigeo Group was born: it is one of the leading European companies in the SRI and social rating fields;

- **FTSE4 Good Index Series** comprises four sets of stock indexes introduced on 31 July 2001 (FTSE4Good Global indices, US indices, Europe indices, UK Indices) and were developed by FTSE together with EIRIS, the Ethical Investment Research Service. FTSE is the index company owned by the *Financial Times* and the London Stock Exchange. All the licensing fees are donated to UNICEF.

In order to set up ethical indexes and to select adequate portfolios for SRI, processes of ethical and social rating have been developing during the last few years (Calcaterra and Perrini, 2002;

Calcaterra, Giorgieri and Perrini, 2002). These processes are used to select companies and stocks that meet ethical financing requirements. Ethical and social rating activities are based on specific screening methodologies. Generally, the corporate analysis is founded on an integrated approach, which combines the classical financial criteria found in traditional financial analysis methods with a scientific method, which entails the monitoring of a firm's approach and behavior towards society. In fact, the connection among financial objectives that guarantee the economic stability of an enterprise, the ability to create and increase value in invested capital, the production of cash flow, the ethical and social objectives that determine the enterprise's social sustainability, and the environmental management, results in a full analysis of the firm's relationships both with the marketplace and with all the other stakeholders.

The analysis of the sustainability of an enterprise takes into consideration the viewpoints of and the relationships with all interested parties associated with the company; that is, customers, suppliers, competitors, collaborators, public authorities, civil society, as well as investment lenders and other providers of funds. Particular attention is paid to the objectives of the enterprise over the long term. The company evaluation takes into account the enterprise's sensitivity towards economic, social and environmental issues as well as the clarity and coherence of the company's business mission and goals in relation to the objective of sustainability. The company's business strategy is also analyzed for transparency, and strategic management objectives and competencies.

The ethical screening process, based on negative and positive criteria, is used to evaluate and define investment portfolio management. The object of this analysis is to determine a company's contribution to sustainable development. A positive ethical evaluation is inviting to investors; whereas titles receiving a negative evaluation are placed back into the basket of titles which, at the moment of evaluation, do not conform to the criteria of ethical analysis defined for the SRI.

The enterprise-screening methodology applied at the international level focuses on many types of investment risk; that is, the investor's capacity to financially sustain a company share that reveals, during the evaluation, non-ethical characteristics and therefore affects the level of share risk as it pertains to the rest of the portfolio. The evaluation of ethical sustainability is therefore the key point of the ethical rating process and is based on the in-depth examination of the company, its strengths and weaknesses in relation to the society in which it operates, the environment, stakeholder relations, market relations and strategies, as well as on external impact analyses, such as market sector trends and country factors that influence the company's ability to respect the evaluation conditions applied. Particular importance is assigned to management's ability to communicate and respect official company strategies in the case of adverse market conditions, and to the analysis of management actions in relation to criteria of ethics and social sustainability (Box 5.2).

BOX 5.2 Ethical screening

The analysis of ethical sustainability of the enterprise is primarily focused on the following areas (Perrini, 2002):

- market sector(s) analysis;
- company general evaluation that assesses both market and internal management issues, identifying the corporate structure and principal operating characteristics, market positioning and competitor analysis, as well as the political and regulatory/legal aspects of the country of affiliation.
- company social evaluation, which assesses the quality of the enterprise's relationships with its stakeholders: customers, competitors, employees, management, public authorities, civil society, shareholders, fund lenders and providers;
- assessment of the corporate environmental impact.

5.2.4 CSR and the Community Relationships

Along with the affirmation of corporate citizenship as a further consideration in the debate over the role of business in society, a last main focus on CSR behavior has to do with the role of companies in the local and global community of reference, in terms of civic positioning (Paine, 2003). The focus is again on reputation, this time referred to the entire community, not just in the marketplace. For instance, companies might seek to establish themselves as a progressive force of social betterment. Others might want to build good relationships with civic stakeholders, such as governments, NGOs and local communities.

In this context, the possible areas of intervention can be widely differentiated: on one hand, a company could support the *corporate giving* or philanthropic activity that consists of donations, gifts, gratuities, benefactions and other exclusively monetary corporate contributions to socially/environmentally useful organizations and related projects.

On the other hand, there are all the direct interventions carried out by companies, in terms of initiatives and plans promoted in and in favor of the community. In this area, companies explicitly finance programs and hence contribute their human resources, knowledge, reputation and so on. In this specific case, direct interventions can occur in different fields: starting from training and education to culture, sports, research and innovation concerning productive processes or even social solidarity, drug rehabilitation communities, community orchestras and so on. All this is eventually accompanied by some forms of voluntary charity or, in general, social and ethical activities that witness the company's will to proactively contribute to the community at large and its development.

The company's voluntary and above all proactive involvement in the community well being represents the key point of CSR practices (Stroup and Neubert, 1987), this together with all the other forms of communication and engagement of the community in company activity. As stakeholders composing the network of relationships to which each company belongs, become more active and able to make a greater contribution to the development and evaluation of company policy, their action-plans are a direct result of holding regular discussions on what can and needs to be given priority.

5.3 HOW CSR CONTRIBUTES TO THE PROCESSES OF VALUE CREATION

International scandals started in 2001 with Enron (Stiglitz, 2003), and national downfalls (e.g., Bipop-Carire, one of the most important banking groups, in 2001, Cirio and Parmalat, two of the most important food corporations, in 2002 and 2003), and demonstrated that 'shareholder value' is not a sufficient principle to manage a company. In some ways, the pursuit of this goal is self-defeating (Clarkson, 1995, 112; Kay, 2004a and 2004b, 182-184; Freeman, Wicks et al., 2004, 9-11), in that this short term approach destroys the basis for the long-term success and survival of a firm.

Therefore, new perspectives on governance are emerging, focused on sustainability as a more comprehensive concept capable of integrating companies with critical stakeholder groups. More specifically, the sustainable development of a firm depends on the sustainability of the relationships with its stakeholder network. In this sense, sustainability should be the leading principle that informs business/stakeholder management and therefore also the corporate performance evaluation and reporting systems, which in turn should be built according to a comprehensive stakeholder framework.

In other words, each firm seeks to create wealth, that is, value. But in order to achieve this, the firm cannot ignore the context in which it operates. In fact, a network of relationships connects the company to a great number of interrelated individuals and constituencies, that is, stakeholders (Ulrich and Krieg, 1973; Freeman, 1984; Donaldson and Preston, 1995; Clarkson, 1995). These relationships influence the way a company is governed and, in turn, are influenced by the company's behavior (for a review of the stakeholder theory see chapter 4).

This means that if the entire set of stakeholder relationships becomes strategic for the long-term success and survival of a company, shareholder value cannot be considered a sufficient objective and measurement of the quality of a company's management. More specifically, a firm can develop over time only if it is able to build and maintain sustainable and lasting relationships with all the members of its stakeholder network. Therefore, we believe that a company creates value when it adopts a managerial approach that focuses on sustainability.

A sustainability-oriented company develops over time by considering the economic, social and environmental dimensions of its processes and performance as these relate to the quality of stakeholder relationships. In this kind of firm economic and competitive success, social legitimacy and efficient use of natural resources are interconnected according to a synergetic and circular view of the company's aims. In this context, broad and shared processes of value creation ensure that a company will develop and survive in the long run by fulfilling, in different ways, the requirements of its stakeholders, who provide the resources the firm needs to manage its operations.

This is not only a normative approach. Many examples, also in Italy, show that it is possible to achieve positive financial and competitive performance through a careful attention to social relationships and an effective management of the environment. For example, social capital is at the basis of the long-term success of many Italian districts (e.g., in the ceramic tile industry: Porter, 1990, 210-225; Jarboe, 2001, 8-9) and organizations, such as many local public utilities companies, which play a meaningful role in the development of local communities through wealth creation and distribution.

With specific reference to the Italian experience, Coop represents a case worth of consideration. It is the largest Italian retail chain, with a 17.7% market share in the grocery market, and in 2004 it was owned by 6,030,000 members, grouped in 175 territorial consumers' cooperative societies. The retail network comprised 1,290 points of sale, encompassing 1,370,000 square meters and 55,700 employees. The turnover was 11,335 million Euros. This dominance on the market is supported and strengthened by Coop efforts towards sustainability along its entire stakeholder network.

For example, since 1991, Coop has released an annual social report on its relationships with the most important stakeholder groups (members, consumers, employees, civil society, cooperative movement). This Social Balance is focused on the programs carried out and the wealth distributed. This report is considered a fundamental tool to support the social/societal strategy of the group.

Moreover, since December 1998 Coop Italy, the national consortium that carries out purchasing, marketing and quality-control activities for territorial cooperatives, has been certified according to Social Accountability 8000, the ethical sourcing standard. Coop Italy was the first European company to obtain SA 8000 certification. It first adopted SA 8000 internally and subsequently involved all the suppliers of Coop-labeled products (about 300 all over the world) in this project focused on the protection of workers' rights. Also thanks to the Coop's intervention, Italy has the greatest number of SA 8000-certified facilities in the world (see chapter 8).

Coop has also diversified, distributing Fair Trade products, organic foods, Eco-labeled products and Forest Stewardship Council (FSC) labeled goods. With regard to the relationship with local communities, since the late nineteen nineties, Coop has developed a broad campaign, called Advantages for the Community, aimed at fulfilling specific social needs in the fields of education, training and welfare policies. This community program is based on partnerships among territorial cooperatives, public institutions and NGOs.

Therefore, if we adopt a sustainability approach to the governance of the firm, critical managerial implications derive from that. In fact, sustainability especially means: (i) strategic importance of intangible assets; (ii) implementation of stakeholder engagement and cooperation processes; (iii) adoption of stakeholder-based performance evaluation and reporting systems.

5.3.1 Fostering Value Creation through Intangible Assets

In the world of the twenty-first century, civil society plays an increasing role, and consumer models in the most advanced economies evolve towards goods and services that have a strong intangible and symbolic component. Public concern and awareness of critical issues, such as environmental emergencies (air pollution, energy consumption, water supply, climate changes, and so on), the protection of employees' rights throughout the supply chain, the role of companies in the communities to which they belong, rules of corporate governance and so on, are widespread and increasing.

As a result, the capability of a firm to continue its activities and operations over time depends on its stakeholder relationships. Therefore, the main value-drivers for a company are the intangible assets, directly affecting the quality of these relationships. Intangibles refer to intellectual and social capitals and include know-how, brands, trust, reputation, and so on (Ghoshal and Bartlett, 1999; Lev, 2001; Castaldo, 2002; Lipparini, 2002). The intangibles can be divided into two categories. The first one includes knowledge resources, that is, knowledge, capabilities and skills available in the organization or in its stakeholder network. Knowledge could have a large impact on the 'development and maintenance of favorable and productive stakeholder relations' (Post, Preston and Sachs, 2002b, 25). A broad set of knowledge resources could enable a company to better understand different stakeholder needs, define innovative solutions in order to meet stakeholder expectations and create sustainable value. The second one concerns trust resources, which include trust, reputation, image, brand-equity and the overall license to operate, that is, the social consensus necessary for corporate survival.

Through its activities and choices a company creates and enhances (or destroys and reduces) its intangibles. CSR activities can contribute to the increase of companies' intangible assets of knowledge and trust, which in turn support the processes of value creation. In fact, a sustainability-oriented company is committed to following an innovative path, which involves all aspects of the firm and its stakeholder network. This allows, on the one hand, improved management operations (through, for example, cooperative sourcing policies or eco-efficient investments) and, on the other, enhancement of the company's value proposition and involvement of the entire stakeholder network (through, for example, social- or eco-labeled products or direct interventions in the local community).

In this context, CSR contributes to the sustainability of business in society by strengthening the ties to stakeholders through superior corporate social and environmental performance (determined by innovative solutions supported by knowledge resources), which increases the level of trust that different individuals and constituencies have in a company and its products. The stronger is the social commitment demonstrated by the company, the broader is its 'license to operate' (that is, the increase of resources that accrue from an increased trust). Thus, the sustainability-oriented company is also a responsive one (see Figure 5.1).

The stakeholder value created by a sustainability-oriented and responsive company makes it possible to reward, in specific and appropriate ways, the different stakeholders who contribute resources. Sustainability, therefore, becomes the strategic objective not only of socio-economic systems but also of firms, which aim to pursue long-term economic development, consistent with promoting social cohesion and protecting the environment (CEC, 2004, p.5).

5.3.2 Fostering Value Creation through Stakeholder Engagement and Cooperation

As stakeholders become more active and able to make a greater contribution to the development and evaluation of company policies, their needs and requirements must be taken into account. In the relational view of the firm (Post, Preston and Sachs, 2002a), stakeholders become an essential part of the extended organization and their role is crucial for a successful strategic management. So, stakeholder engagement processes are the determinants of collaborative and cooperative approaches aimed at supporting sustainability-oriented efforts.

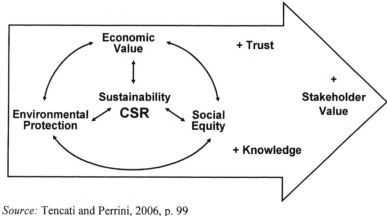

Source: Tencati and Perrini, 2006, p. 99

Figure 5.1 Corporate goals, intangibles and value creation in a sustainability-oriented and responsive company

A relevant case history regards mining companies in Latin America, where they are changing their traditional behavior and starting to strongly involve communities, NGOs and public authorities in defining a shared vision of the local development and overcoming the previous conflicts that characterized the relationships between international enterprises and local players (Pélouas, 2004).

The current processes of many local implementations of Agenda 21 provide other excellent examples of this new view based on the participation of stakeholders in decision making. In fact, local authorities, public institutions, enterprises, NGOs and citizens support a shared framework in order to define, plan and carry out new patterns of development affecting a specific territorial area (Sancassiani, 2004). This means that the concepts of sustainability and stakeholder engagement should be applied not only within a firm's environment but call for an extended implementation to identify new broad governance solutions more suitable to the current complex social needs.

If, as argued by the Commission on the Private Sector and Development (2003, p. 30), 'one of the most compelling ways to help firms succeed is by increasing the power of the linkages and networks they are part of', cooperation with stakeholder groups becomes crucial under this perspective.

Shared responsibility among public authorities, enterprises and citizens has been fundamental to the European strategies for protecting the environment since the early nineties (European Community, 1993): voluntary programs, such as EMAS (Eco-Management and Audit Scheme) and Eco-Label, aimed at promoting environmental innovation at process and product level, were launched by the European Community in that period and are based on this collaborative approach (CEC, 2001a).

In some industrial areas and districts (consider, for example, the ceramic tile district of Modena/Reggio Emilia in northern Italy), new relationships among local players have been developed during the last decades in order to reduce the overall impact on the environment through material and energy recovery policies and shared managerial improvements according to principles of industrial ecology (Frosch and Gallopoulos, 1989, p. 94):

In an industrial ecosystem [...] the consumption of energy and materials is optimized, waste generation is minimized, and the effluents of one process [...] serve as the raw material for another process. The industrial ecosystem would function as an analogue of a biological ecosystem.

Facing social problems cooperatively is also of fundamental importance. Public-private sector agreements and partnerships should be promoted to support social cohesion and the development of local communities, and fight unemployment/underemployment and social exclusion (Copenhagen Centre, 1998).

In general, creating effective partnerships among public institutions, enterprises and civil society is recognized as the most important instrument to foster economic growth, poverty eradication and sustainable development, the implementation of Agenda 21, and the achievement of the internationally agreed development goals (World Summit on Sustainable Development, 2002a, Principle 18; World Summit on Sustainable Development, 2002b, 42-54).

5.3.3 Supporting Value Creation through Evaluation and Reporting Systems

Another implication of the adoption of a sustainability approach is the need for *ad hoc* performance evaluation and reporting systems. Over the last fifteen years, more than one hundred standards and management solutions were developed to evaluate and report the economic, social, environmental and sustainability performance of companies (ISO Advisory Group on Corporate Social Responsibility, 2003). They range from stakeholder-based frameworks to models based more on the integrated evaluation of different dimensions of corporate performance.

However, these new proposals have the purpose of broadening, integrating and improving the traditional financial/economic approaches to the corporate performance measurement, taking stakeholder needs and requirements into due account. With regard to this issue, Lynn Sharp Paine (2003, p. 120) points out that some non-financial variables are important on their own terms and not only as a means to financial ends; indeed, they may be critical success determinants:

> Therefore, managers must care about them for the same reason they care about financial performance – because they are intrinsically im-portant and part of what is expected of leading companies today [...]. This expanded conception of corporate performance is implicit in the

calls for corporate accountability that have become commonplace in recent decades.

It is out of the scope of the chapter to provide a list of the existing CSR evaluation and reporting systems (see chapters 6 and 7). At this stage, what is important is the relevance of grounding the evaluation processes on managerial tools capable of monitoring and tracking from a qualitative and quantitative viewpoint the overall corporate performance according to a stakeholder framework.

Furthermore, both internal and external corporate performance should be measured. This means that the degree of trust and stakeholder satisfaction generated by the corporate behavior should be carefully evaluated (Zadek, Pruzan and Evans, 1997).

5.4 IS CSR ALWAYS A COMPETITIVE ADVANTAGE?

On the basis of the previous discussion, CSR may involve a remarkable competitive advantage and have an impact on firms' performance. The reason is that socially responsible behavior may generate commitment to stakeholders, and, thus, consensus, cooperation, and satisfaction of their expectations. CSR is even more crucial in globalizing network society, by creating new rules and a new organizational culture, by fostering innovative learning processes and by increasing productivity of work, that is, by improving corporate performance in a broad sense and broadening the stakeholders' approval.

However, the relationship between CSR and company performance is anything but straightforward. This is demonstrated, as explained in chapter 4, by the low consistency of results of the studies that focus on the correlation between corporate social and financial performance. It is not only the impact that is unclear, but also the direction of the effect. This means that it is not clear whether social performance should precede or be followed by economic and financial performance (Margolis and Walsh, 2003).

In his recent book (2005), Vogel proposes a critical view of the business case for social responsibility, arguing that (p. 16):

To be sure, improving the bottom line is not the only possible reason for CSR. Many executives genuinely care about conducting their businesses in ways that are more environmentally sustainable, that respect human rights, and that foster economic development. Self-regulation can also reduce the likelihood of more government regulation or place a firm in a better competitive position if and when new regulations emerge.

In other words, the superiority of the CSR paradigm cannot be limited to profitability motives, but supported by the possibility that CSR fosters competitiveness, providing sources of differentiation.

Moreover, there is a problem related to the flexibility of conforming CSR policies to the contexts in which companies operate. CSR *per se* crosses geographical boundaries, in the sense that all companies have responsibility with respect to their stakeholder networks. At the same time, it would be impossible for global humanity to agree upon a particular set of rules that would spell out in detail the boundaries of responsible behavior in economic relationships (Donaldson and Dunfee, 1999a). In that there are no universalistic rules to suggest the best way of organizing or the best way of interacting with the firms' interlocutors, rationales vary and uncertainty permeates actions; CSR activities should be different as firms recognize differences abroad.

Once we have agreed upon a process or broad common frameworks by which moral rules can hold, contingent on the specific circumstances, painting partial portraits of the role of business in society becomes worthy of consideration. Such a global versus local tension represents the current European situation better than any other ones do: while the economic trends push towards the internationalization of business operations, the weight of local social contexts and the community-firm collaborative relationship appear to be the unavoidable key to comprehending the European economic structure.

On that basis, we are likely to hear continuing calls for companies to become more efficient and more profitable, and at the same time responsive to their constituencies, accountable for the impact of activities and respectful of law and accepted ethical standards. In this context, it is possible to expect many more enterprises to recognize the benefits of honoring human values and presenting a moral face to the world as they carry out their business.

However, the moralization of the corporations represents a radical departure from the mechanistic conception that has dominated corporate thinking. In fact, the attribution of moral personality to companies necessitates fundamental changes in internal structure and management. This shift has implications for corporate leadership. Management has to bring a dual perspective to their decisions, which must pass the test of both ethical and economic rationality. Guidance systems will be aligned with the accountabilities that flow from these imperatives. Leaders will recognize that corporate performance has moral as well as financial implications and that the pursuit of excellence requires attention to both. And they have to innovate, restructure the workforce and the supply chain, manage safety and battle corruption to meet both companies' and stakeholders' expectations and build a competitive advantage.

6. European and international standards, tools and methodologies on CSR

6.1 INTRODUCTION

From the notion of CSR it is possible to derive the complementary concept of *accountability* (AccountAbility, 1999), which means that the company is held accountable for its actions. If companies want to manage CSR and sustainability issues and obtain the trust of their social stakeholders they must not only communicate, but also give concrete evidence that they are committed to continual, long-term improvement.

Therefore, a sustainability and responsibility-oriented company must define appropriate systems to measure, control and evaluate corporate performance. Over the years, many social and environmental standards and management solutions have been developed to evaluate and report the economic, social, environmental and sustainability performance of companies. These tools provide information of a qualitative, quantitative and economic nature and influence the interactions between a firm and its stakeholders (see Table 6.1).

In the economic field a turning point was reached in 1986 with the definition of the shareholder value paradigm (Rappaport, 1986).

The first social auditing systems were developed, between the late nineteen sixties and early nineteen seventies, in the United States and then in Europe and especially in Germany and France (Rusconi, 1988). The social reporting processes enter a new phase at the beginning of nineteen nineties through the initiatives developed mainly by the cooperative movement in Europe.

Table 6.1 Corporate performance management tools

economic dimension	social dimension	environmental dimension	sustainability dimension
Operating budget and annual report Return On Investment (ROI) Return On Equity (ROE) Leverage Current ratio Periodic performance measurement (Economic Value Added, EVA) (Stewart, 1991) Specific performance indicators (Marketing, Production, Logistics, R&D, Quality) Value of economic capital (Guatri, 1991) Shareholder Value (Rappaport, 1986)	Social audit (Abt, 1977) and social report (Gruppo per il Bilancio Sociale, 2001) Social accounting (Zadek et al., 1997; Gonella et al., 1998) Socio-efficency Indicators (Schaltegger et al., 2002: p. 9) AccountAbility 1000 (AA1000) (AccountAbility, 1999) BS 8800 and Occupational Health and Safety Assessment Series Specification (OHSAS 18001). http://www.bsi-global.com Social Accountability 8000 (SA8000). http://www.sa-intl.org Ethical indexes (Domini 400 Social Index, Citizens Index, Dow Jones Sustainability Indexes, Ethical Index Euro, FTSE4Good Index Series) (Tencati, 2002b, pp. 196-197) Ethical and Social Rating (Perrini and Tencati, 2003, pp. 14-16)	Environmental report and LCA (Hallay, 1990; Hallay and Pfriem, 1992) Environmental accounting (Bundesumweltminis terium and Umweltbundesamt, 1995; Burritt et al., 2002) Ecolabels. http://www.eco-label.com Eco-efficiency Indicators (World Business Council, 2000) Performance Indicators (ISO 14031). http://www.iso.org/iso/en/iso9000-14000/index.html Environmental management regulations and standards (EMAS and ISO 14001). http://europa.eu.int/comm/environment/emas/index_en.htm; http://www.iso.org/iso/en/iso9000-14000/index.html	GRI. http://www.globalrep orting.org Balanced Scorecard (Kaplan and Norton, 1992; Figge et al., 2002; Zingales and Hockerts, 2003) SIGMA Project. http://www.projectsi gma.com Q-RES Project (2002; 2004) ISO 26000. http://www.iso.org/sr http://www.uni.com Integrated Framework for Sustainability Performance Measurement, Management and Reporting (Schaltegger and Wagner, 2006) Sustainability Evaluation and Reporting System (SERS): the SPACE framework (Tencati, 2002a; Perrini and Tencati, 2003)

The first environmental reports were drawn up by research centers and companies in Germany, the Scandinavian and Anglo-Saxon countries in the late nineteen eightees and coincided with the public's growing awareness of the importance of environmental issues (Hallay, 1990; Brophy and Starkey, 1996). Subsequently, this tool began to be commonly used even in the less aware countries from the ecological point of view (Bennet and James, 1999).

The triple bottom line approach and the first attempts in the field of sustainability accounting were born in 1994 (Elkington, 1994), but a fundamental driver of their growth trend was the Global Reporting Initiative established in 1997.

In the next paragraphs we will examine the principal methods of environmental, social and sustainability performance management which a company can adopt.

6.2 CORPORATE SOCIAL PERFORMANCE MANAGEMENT

6.2.1 Social Audit

The success of the CSR concept modifies opportunities and limits within which a company operates. The mere pursuit of profits is no longer sufficient since the company has also to consider the needs of different stakeholders capable of influencing its own success.

Therefore, it becomes crucial to measure the company's capacity to meet stakeholder needs, and to strike some sort of balance between what the company offers and what it receives from the social system. In order to address these issues, the first social auditing systems were developed, between the late nineteen sixties and early nineteen seventies, in the United States and then in Europe.

The many different approaches and the fact that it is generally a voluntary tool which measures the social results of companies – and is thus subject to the influence of specific variables of a cultural, political and economic nature – has made it impossible to develop a generally accepted model of social reporting.

The methods adopted diverge in content and final objective. However, despite these divergences it is possible to formulate a definition of social auditing by combining the different experiences which have been developed up to now.

To sum up, social audit can be considered as the control, at a given time, of the impact which the activities of an organized system (in particular, a company) have on the well-being of the individuals that in some way interact with the company. It might be useful to see how the different approaches to social accountability are classified (Table 6.2).

Table 6.2 Approaches to social accountability

Stated or 'named' approach	Examples of organizations using these approaches	Description
Capital valuation	Skandia	Regularly disclosed process to understand, measure, report on and manage various forms of capital (which could include intellectual, human, social, environmental, organizational, structural and financial capital)
Corporate community involvement reporting	BP, Diageo (Grand Metropolitan), NatWest Group	Description, illustration and measurement of community involvement policies and activities through occasional reports. This approach may also include benchmarking against other company performances
Ethical accounting statement	Sbn Bank, Scandinavian public sector	Regularly disclosed process, based on shared values that stakeholders develop through ongoing dialogue, aimed at designing future actions
Ethical auditing	The Body Shop International	Regular, externally verified process to understand, measure, report on and improve on an organization's social, environmental and animal testing performance through stakeholder dialogue
Social auditing	Ben & Jerry's Homemade, VanCity Credit Union, Black Country Housing Association, Co-op Bank	Regular, externally verified process to understand, measure, report on and improve on an organization's social performance through stakeholder dialogue
Social Balance	Coop Italia, Unipol	A regular reconstruction and aggregation of financial data across stakeholder groups which specifies financial costs associated with 'social activities'
Value-added statement	Credito Valtellinese, Telecom Italia, MPS, Acea, South African Breweries	Process to quantify the value-added generated by an organization and its distribution to stakeholder groups
Statement of principles and values	Shell International	Statement that develops and describes an organization's principles in meeting its financial, social and environmental responsibilities
Sustainability reporting	Shell, Baxter International, Procter & Gamble	Evolving reporting process that identifies ways forward and reports on progress against sustainability principles and targets

Source: based on Gonella, Pilling, Zadek (1998),in Bennett, James (1990, pp.55-56)

They include different ways of measuring social impact and different ways of carrying out activities regarding Social and Ethical Accounting, Auditing and Reporting (SEAAR) (AccountAbility, 1999).

6.2.2 AccountAbility 1000 (AA1000) Framework and Series

In order to overcome the above-mentioned problems and make the approaches to social accountability more uniform so that information coming from different sources can be compared, in November 1999 AccountAbility (ISEA, Institute of Social and Ethical AccountAbility) published AccountAbility 1000 (AA1000).

AA1000 is an accountability standard designed to ensure the quality of the social and ethical accounting, auditing and reporting process. It is a foundation standard, which can be used in two ways: as a tool to underpin the quality of specialized accountability standards (like the Sustainability Reporting Guidelines of the Global Reporting Initiative, Social Accountability 8000 on ethical sourcing, the ISO standards on the development and certification of environmental and quality management systems); and as a stand-alone system and process for processing and communicating social and ethical accountability and performance.

The principles of the AA1000 standard are organized according to a hierarchical order. The fundamental concept, found at the top of the pyramid, which regulates the SEAAR process is accountability defined as the capacity 'to explain or justify the acts, omissions, risks and dependencies for which an organization is responsible to people with a legitimate interest'. The principle of accountability means that a company is transparent, and responsible, complies with agreed standards. Accountability generates the principle of inclusivity. Inclusivity is based on the remaining principles: completeness, materiality, regularity and timeliness regard the scope and nature of the process; quality assurance (independent audit of the process), accessibility and information quality (implying that the information can be compared, is reliable, relevant and understandable) concern the meaningfulness of the information; embeddedness (systems integration) and continuous improvement affect the management of the process on an ongoing basis. Together with a set of user guidelines, AA1000 therefore provides a framework, which allows the company to effectively implement SEAAR processes and satisfy stakeholder needs. In fact, the main objective of the standard is to involve the interested parties. Only by building solid relationships with stakeholders is it possible to define shared social and ethical objectives, improve the organization's capacity to respond by enhancing its corporate performance and thus contribute to sustainability. In 2002 AccountAbility, launched the new AA1000 Series, consisting of the AA1000 Framework and a set of specialized modules. The first module is the AA1000 Assurance Standard, issued on 25 March 2003 (AccountAbility, 2003).[1]

6.2.3 SA8000, the New Standard for Ethical Sourcing

The Council on Economic Priorities Accreditation Agency (CEPAA)[2] has promoted the development of Social Accountability 8000 (SA8000), a system which protects workers' rights by defining a set of auditable standards for a third party verification.

The CEPAA is an organization set up at the beginning of 1997 by the Council on Economic Priorities (CEP), one of the first institutions to deal with the issue of CSR. The CEPAA immediately set up an Advisory Board, which helped the agency draw up SA8000.

This Board was originally made up of representatives from NGOs such as Amnesty International and the Abrinq Foundation for Children's Rights (Brazil), consulting companies, auditing and certification bodies such as KPMG and SGS-International Certification Services, companies such as Avon, The Body Shop, Toys 'R' Us, Otto-Versand and Reebok, distribution companies, trade unions and universities, and so on. The SA8000 standard was officially launched on 15 October 1997.

A revised version was issued at the end of 2001. Based on the International Labour Organization Conventions and other documents such as the Universal Declaration of Human Rights and the UN Convention on the Rights of the Child, SA8000 is a standard for companies that aims to guarantee fundamental workers' rights.

It is specific enough to be used to audit companies and suppliers in the same way in different sectors and countries. SA8000 represents a significant innovation since it is the first social standard whose application can be controlled by independent third parties. SA 8000 basically provides a reference framework to control the ethical production of all the goods manufactured by companies of all sizes throughout the world.

This standard represents an important opportunity for companies to demonstrate their commitment to carrying out processes and products in a really ethical way. As of 30 September, 2005, the number of SA 8000 certified organizations throughout the world totaled 763, with 260 facilities certified (34.1% of total) in Italy. The certified companies which meet the required standards are entitled to display the SA 8000 Certification Mark. The certification is valid for three years with audits carried out every six months.

6.2.4 GBS Proposal

The Gruppo di studio per il Bilancio Sociale (the Study Group for Social Reporting),[3] also called GBS, held its first meeting on 15 October 1998 in Milan. Many Italian universities, research institutes and consulting firms participate in GBS activities. In April 2001 GBS published the Social Reporting Standards.

According to the GBS proposal the Social Report has the following objectives:

- to provide all stakeholders with a comprehensive picture of the company's performance, establishing an interactive social communication process;
- to provide relevant information on the company's operations in order to broaden and improve stakeholders' awareness and ability to evaluate and make choices, also from an ethical-social standpoint (Gruppo di Studio per il Bilancio Sociale, 2001, p.13).

Furthermore, the social reporting process must comply with the following principles in order to ensure its quality: responsibility, identification, transparency, inclusivity, consistency, neutrality, accrual basis, conservatism, comparability, meaningfulness, clarity and intelligibility, regularity and timeliness, uniformity, relevance, materiality and significance, verifiability of the information, reliability and true and fair presentation, third party independence.

Finally, the social report is composed of the following three elements:

- the corporate identity, which comprises corporate structure, ethical values, mission, strategies and policies;
- the creation and allocation of value-added;
- the social account, which provides a broad picture of the outcomes achieved by the company through the implemented strategies and policies, and of the impacts generated by its behavior on the different stakeholder groups in relation to the adopted commitments.

In Italy, the GBS model is a point of reference for social reporting and it has been applied by private and public organizations.

6.3 CORPORATE ENVIRONMENTAL PERFORMANCE MANAGEMENT

6.3.1 Corporate Environmental Reporting

In general, the corporate environmental report is a tool a company uses to manage and control corporate activities and support communication with the stakeholders, especially those interested in environmental issues (Azzone et al., 1997).

These groups include the following: employees and collaborators; clients/consumers; suppliers; local and/or national communities; state, local authorities and public administration; mass media; special interested parties (consumer associations, environmental groups and so on); banks; insurance companies; investors (individual shareholders, institutional investors and so on).

The perceived environmental risk of a company's activities can, in fact, influence the stakeholder attitude (either positively or negatively) towards the company.

A careful communication strategy must, therefore, make the stakeholders aware of the degree of eco-compatibility of production processes and products and provide reliable and understandable information related to the company's current and future plans with regard to environmental protection. In this sense, the environmental report, meaning the information system, which controls the company's ecological performance, has come to play a crucial and necessary role.

BOX 6.1 The Eni Enrico Mattei Foundation framework

The Eni Enrico Mattei Foundation (FEEM), a research institute which studies issues related to environment, energy and economic development, has defined a model environmental report that can be a useful management and information tool. The aim is to provide companies with a reference framework which improves on the partial approaches adopted up to now and furnishes concrete information to help companies communicate better and make the right decisions regarding environmental management. The model suggested is based on building a complete accounting system which includes physical indicators and monetary measurements of the costs incurred to reduce or prevent pollution. The FEEM corporate environmental report is divided into three separate accounts: the resources account (input); the pollutants account (output); and the environmental expenditure account. The model therefore consists of an input-output analysis together with the environmental expenditure. In this way, the environmental report becomes an intelligent container of environmental information since it adopts precise methods to gather and organize the basic data which are fundamental for each subsequent elaboration. Since 1994, the Eni group has used this model to draw up its environmental reports.

Source: Bartolomeo, Malaman, Pavan and Sammarco (1995)

BOX 6.2 The IÖW framework

Between the autumn of 1987 and 1988 the Nordrhein-Westfalen region commissioned the Institut für Ökologische Wirtschaftsforschung (IÖW), in conjunction with Umwelt-future (a German association of entrepreneurs), to develop and implement a new model of corporate environmental report. For this purpose, the Tecklenburg plant of the Bischof & Klein Company, which produces flexible packaging, was chosen. In 1987 the company employed over 2000 workers and had a turnover in Germany of 400 million Marks. The Tecklenberg plant employed 80 workers and manufactured bags and containers. The environmental reporting system developed by the IÖW (called ecobalancing) is made up of four elements: (1) corporate ecobalance or input-output analysis; (2) process ecobalances; (3) product ecobalances; (4) site assessment. The first element of the German model is the typical input-output analysis also found in the FEEM scheme, which considers the company or plant analyzed as a kind of black box. The process ecobalances aim to audit the environmental impact related to the internal functioning of the black box not examined in the preceding phase. The production processes are subsequently subdivided according to criteria of space and time and inherent to the product. Each process thus identified is then analyzed by using a specific input-output matrix of the materials and energy flows. The product ecobalances coincide with the LCA (Life Cycle Assessment) of the company's main products and the site assessment represents a register of all the ecologically relevant aspects not included in the previous phases (the need to reclaim some sites, use of land, modifications in the landscape). In the German-speaking countries, the IÖW framework is considered a reference scheme used to draw up ecobalances.

Source: Hallay (1990); Hallay and Pfriem (1992)

Drawn up mainly on a voluntary basis, the environmental report reflects the specific corporate, economic, legal and social context in which it developed. Due to the wide variety of methods and content and the complexity of the issue, a definitive and generally acceptable model of corporate environmental report is still not available.

Therefore, there is no homogeneity among the data obtained by different companies and comparisons are very difficult. Because of this, many organizations[4] have drawn up guidelines for environmental reporting in order to help companies implement environmental accountability schemes. There are, however, at least two environmental reporting schemes worth analyzing in greater detail since they present important and interesting features: the framework of the Eni Enrico Mattei Foundation (Box 6.1), and the IÖW framework (Box 6.2).

6.3.2 Environmental Management Systems

In the nineteen nineties public opinion and companies became aware of the importance of environmental issues. As environmental awareness increased and companies began to include this variable in their corporate policies, standards to regulate environmental management systems were developed.

In March 1992 the British Standards Institution (BSI) published the first environmental management systems' standard, which shares the same management principles as BS 5750 (subsequently replaced by the BS EN ISO 9001 standard) on quality assurance systems and represents a direct outgrowth in the area of environmental protection.

The BS 7750 was tested over a two-year period and involved at least 500 participants including 230 companies. On the basis of the results obtained during this phase and the content of the new EMAS regulation, the modified and definitive version of BS 7750 was issued in January 1994.

On 29 June 1993, the Council of the European Communities adopted the EEC Regulation No. 1836/93 allowing voluntary participation by companies in the industrial sector in a Community eco-management and audit scheme (EMAS). It was published on 10 July 1993 in the Official Journal of the European Communities and came into force in April 1995.

As the first article of the regulation clearly underlines, EMAS is established for the evaluation and improvement of the environmental performance of industrial activities and the provision of relevant information to the public.

EMAS aims to promote continuous improvements in the environmental performance of industrial activities by: the establishment and implementation of environmental policies, programs and management systems by companies, in relation to their sites; the systematic, objective and periodic evaluation of the performance of such elements; the provision of information of environmental performance to the public.

Many parts of the EMAS regulation coincide with BS 7750 and this demonstrates the influence the 1992 version of the British standard had on the new European regulation. In fact, at that time, the BS 7750 specification was the only tool which regulated environmental management systems.

In September 1996 the standard ISO 14001:1996 Environmental Management Systems – Specification with guidance for use was published. It was largely based on the BS 7750 approach. In November 2004 the revised edition of ISO 14001 was issued.

Following a revision based on the experience acquired during the first five years it was applied, on 19 March 2001 the European Parliament and the Council of the European Union adopted the EC Regulation No.761/2001 allowing voluntary participation by organizations in a Community eco-management and audit scheme (EMAS II). The regulation came into force on April 27 2001 and replaced EEC Regulation No. 1836/93. The main elements of the revised EMAS regulation are: it applies to organizations; the adoption of ISO 14001 as the specification for the Environmental Management Systems Requirements; the promotion of organizations' participation, in particular of small and medium-sized enterprises; the strengthening of the role of the environmental statement to improve the transparency of communication of environmental performance between registered organizations and their relevant interested parties and the public.

EMAS, therefore, is no longer exclusively applied to industrial sites but to all types of organizations according to the ISO 14001 standard. Moreover, the greater integration between EMAS and ISO 14001 makes it possible to better coordinate the European regulation and the international standard.

The advantages a company can obtain by introducing a management system, especially one which integrates quality, health, safety and environment (the Integrated Management System, IMS), are of an organizational, managerial and economic nature.

The advantages include the following: clear and coherent definition of responsibilities and operating procedures; elimination of inefficient duplications and overlapping from the organizational point of view; one single file of records; full value given to in-company competence; improved evaluation of corporate risk profile and performance; better analysis, control and evaluation methods; better management of the relationships with the different stakeholders; reinforcement of corporate image; greater compliance with regulatory standards; easier access to financial and insurance markets; reduction in management costs including auditing costs; more efficient use of raw materials and resources; fewer serious occupational injuries; fewer criminal lawsuits; keeping hidden losses and liabilities to a minimum.

In short, management systems (and relative standards) are performance indicators since they point out companies which are active from the managerial viewpoint and pay close attention to developing and maintaining correct relationships with stakeholders. Moreover, they are tools for corporate performance measurement and evaluation since setting objectives and targets, which companies have to reach, is part of them. Corporate performance is subsequently controlled through auditing procedures.

6.4 CORPORATE SUSTAINABILITY PERFORMANCE MANAGEMENT

6.4.1 Global Reporting Initiative

The Global Reporting Initiative (GRI) is an international, long-term, multi-stakeholder project designed to develop, promote and disseminate a common framework for voluntary reporting of the economic, environmental and social performance of an organization (its activities, products and services). The Sustainability Reporting Guidelines provide this framework.

GRI is the result of a process begun in the autumn of 1997, which aimed to develop an international framework for environmental reporting. During the first meetings held at the beginning of 1998, GRI expanded its scope and decided to focus on defining guidelines for sustainability reporting, including not just environmental factors but also economic and social ones. In partnership with the United Nations Environment Programme (UNEP), which plays a key role, the GRI network includes the active participation of companies, entrepreneurs' associations, workers' associations, research institutes, universities, government representatives, NGOs, consulting firms, rating agencies, auditing firms, and associations of chartered accountants.

A provisional version of the Sustainability Reporting Guidelines was published in 1999. After being tested in some companies, the revised, final version was published in June 2000. For each dimension of sustainability (environmental, economic, social) the Guidelines include categories, aspects and indicators.

After the guidelines were applied in an increasing number of companies,[5] in April 2002 a draft document containing the 2002 Sustainability Reporting Guidelines was released.

The process of stakeholder consulting ended on 26 May and during the Johannesburg Summit the new guidelines were issued (Global Reporting Initiative, 2002). In the 2002 version, the performance indicators were revised, reorganized and integrated especially as regards the economic category and social ones (labor practices and decent work, human rights and society).

In January 2006 the draft version of the G3 Sustainability Reporting Guidelines was issued for public comment (Global Reporting Initiative, 2006).

The guidelines represent an excellent tool to initiate a process which will integrate economic, social and environmental reporting. In fact, they provide indicators to measure the performance of the organization in the three areas of sustainability and help enterprises draw up specific integrated indicators (ratio indicators). The GRI guidelines therefore provide an interesting sustainability report framework. Following the social report and the environmental report it represents the third phase in the development of control and reporting systems, which measure a company's corporate social and environmental performance.

6.4.2 Balanced Scorecard

Proposed by Kaplan and Norton in 1992, the balanced scorecard is a measurement and management system which evaluates corporate performance through a set of measures built around four perspectives: financial; customer; internal business processes; learning and growth (Kaplan and Norton, 1992, 1996).

The balanced scorecard is a multi-dimensional model to monitor corporate performance. It aims to overcome the limitations of the traditional economic and financial measurements and integrate them with indicators of a quantitative and technical nature. This tool thus makes it possible to describe and explain what has to be measured in order to assess the effectiveness of strategies (Parker, 2000).

These indicators furnish a balanced picture of the corporate dynamics since they also check the development of corporate competence and intangible assets (like the relationships with consumers based on the trust) essential for the company's continual success.

The balanced scorecard is a very important performance measurement methodology, which has been widely used by companies. However, the fact that it is not always applied properly has raised doubts as to whether the managerial tool is really effective. Moreover, Kaplan and Norton themselves proceeded to revise the system and drew up a balanced scorecard strategy map (Kaplan and Norton, 2000).

In any case, due to its multidimensional features and flexibility, this evaluation system can also be oriented to control the sustainability performance of an organization through the introduction of elements of sustainability according to the triple bottom line approach. The balanced scorecard is therefore important for sustainability since it can be constructed to include economic-financial, social and environmental indicators in an organic way so that the real performance of an organization can be more closely evaluated.

6.4.3 SIGMA Project

If companies have to contribute to achieving overall sustainability by modifying their policies and behaviors, management tools must be developed to help companies reach this objective.

The UK Sustainable Development Strategy called for a government commitment to sponsor the creation of a sustainability management system. Thanks to the support and involvement of the Department of Trade and Industry, the Department of the Environment, Transport and the Regions, the SIGMA Project[6] (Sustainability: Integrated Guidelines for Management) was launched in July 1999. It aims to create a strategic management framework for sustainability, namely a set of instruments and requirements for sustainable management, which might serve as an international reference standard. On 31 May 2001, the pilot version of the SIGMA Guidelines was presented and was available on the Internet until 31 May 2002 so that interested parties could evaluate it. The new SIGMA Guidelines were launched on 23 September 2003. The Sigma Guidelines include (SIGMA Project, 2003): (i) a set of Guiding Principles to help organizations understand and deal with the elements linked to sustainability. These Principles consist of two core elements: 1. The holistic management of five kinds of capital (Natural Capital, Social Capital, Human Capital, Manufactured Capital and Financial Capital) that reflect an organization's overall impact and wealth. 2. The exercise of accountability, by being transparent and responsive to stakeholders and complying with relevant rules and standards; (ii) a management framework which integrates sustainability into core processes and mainstream decision-making. It is basically a management system for sustainability which follows the traditional Plan, Do, Check, Act pattern; (iii) a series of instruments and approaches the organization can use to implement effective strategies, initiate a cultural change, promote learning and reach its objectives. The SIGMA Toolkit includes well-known instruments like benchmarking, the balanced scorecard applied to sustainability (sustainability scorecard), environmental accounting, stakeholder engagement and the GRI guidelines.

The SIGMA Guidelines therefore represent an effort (still underway) to organize and synthesize all the best management proposals. The aim is to obtain a framework which is really integrated and goes beyond the partial approaches of the individual standards regarding quality (economic performance), safety (social performance) and the environment, and develops a new management paradigm.

6.4.4 Q-RES Project

The Q-RES Project was conceived in September 1999 and launched in 2000 by CELE, the Centre for Ethics, Law and Economics of the LIUC University in Italy. It aims to develop a management framework for the social and ethical responsibility (RES) of corporations, based on the idea of the social contract between the firm and its stakeholders, by developing a new type of quality standard, externally certifiable.

The Q-RES model consists of an integrated and complete set of tools to introduce ethics into companies. It also defines excellence criteria in the management of social and ethical responsibility, taking into consideration emerging international standards and current best practices. The Q-RES management model includes six tools for managing the social and ethical quality of corporations (Q-RES, 2002; Q-RES, 2004; CEC, 2004):

1. Corporate ethical vision: It defines and makes explicit the concept of justice of the company, from which the criterion to balance stakeholders' claims derives. The responsible behavior that the company has to comply with in the relations with stakeholders is based on that concept of justice. The ethical vision expresses the concept of a social contract between the company and its stakeholders.
2. Codes of ethics: They are the main tools to implement social and ethical responsibility within a business organization. Their function goes beyond the legal regulation.
3. Ethical training and communication: Ethical training in the company is directed to the company employees and aims at enabling each organization member to apply moral reasoning tools to address ethical questions connected with corporate activities.
4. Organizational systems of implementation and internal control: They are the ethical infrastructure which is needed to support an effective implementation of corporate social and ethical responsibility.
5. Social and ethical accountability: The process of social and ethical accountability aims at broadening the perspective of corporate social communications from relations between the firm and shareholders to relations among the company and all its stakeholders, in the social contract perspective.

6. External verification: It is the activity whereby a third party checks the consistency between the social and ethical responsibility tools adopted by the company and the excellence criteria defined by the Q-RES Guidelines. Therefore, external verification/certification provides trustworthiness to the company's declarations concerning its commitments on social and ethical responsibility.

Some Italian companies, professional associations, consulting firms and business organizations participate in the project through the Q-RES Working Table. In Europe, a constructive dialogue has been established with similar initiatives (such as SIGMA Project in the UK and the Values Management System initiative in Germany) (Q-RES, 2005).

NOTES

1. For further information see the website of AccountAbility, http://www.accountability.org.uk.
2. Social Accountability International (SAI) is the new name adopted by the CEPAA in the summer of 2000.
3. For further information, see http://www.bilanciosociale/gbs.html and the website of GBS, http://www.gruppobilanciosociale.org.
4. Some of these are: CEFIC-European Chemical Industry Council; CERES-Coalition for Environmentally Responsible Economies; GEMI-Global Environmental Management Initiative; PERI-Public Environmental Reporting Initiative; UNEP-United Nations Environment Program; WBCSD-World Business Council for Sustainable Development.
5. As of 25 January 2006, 781 organizations from more than 50 countries adhered to the Guidelines including: Acea S.p.A., Aéroports de Paris, AstraZeneca, AT&T, BASF, Baxter International, BC Hydro, Body Shop International, Bristol-Myers Squibb, British Airways, BT, Cable and Wireless, Canon, Chiquita Brands, Co-operative Bank, Cosmo Oil, Daikin, Danone, Electrolux, Ford Motor Company, Fuji Xerox, General Motors, Henkel, ING, Johnson&Johnson, J. Sainsbury, KLM, Matsushita Electric Group, McDonald's, Motorola, NEC, Nike, Nissan, Nokia, Novo Group, NTT, Pioneer Group, Polaroid, Procter & Gamble, Saint-Gobain, Shell International, South African Breweries, Telecom Italia, Thames Water, Van City Savings Credit Union, Unipol Assicurazioni, Volkswagen, Volvo Car Corporation, Waste Recycling Group. For further information see the website of GRI, http://www.globalreporting.org.
6. The project resulted from a partnership between organizations with different expertise: BSI; AccountAbility; Forum for the Future.

7. SERS, the Space-Bocconi framework

7.1 INTRODUCTION

In the previous chapter the main initiatives with regard to corporate performance management have been presented but in over fifteen years more than a hundred proposals were defined (ISO Advisory Group on Corporate Social Responsibility, 2003). This multiplicity, complexity and the absence of a clear reference framework generate undesired effects among companies and their own stakeholders:

- confusion for companies and lack of management and organizational innovation. The existence of several standards and acronyms, the development of different and at the same time similar proposals especially focused on big firms' expectations can complicate companies' attitude towards sustainability and CSR. This can lead to a slowing down of the adoption and implementation of more advanced and aware managerial models, especially in small and medium-sized enterprises, rather than supporting and promoting them;
- confusion and lack of clarity for the companies' stakeholders. If firms do not use an effective and clear approach in order to manage, assess and report their own performance, the different constituencies (employees, citizens/consumers, investors, public actors and so on) have difficulties in analyzing and appreciating the sustainability efforts of enterprises.

Furthermore, this absence of shared, sound and recognized processes and methods might reward free riders that adopt fraudulent behavior and communicate unfair and untrue results.

Moreover, even if we consider the most advanced methodologies in the sustainability field (Figge et al., 2002), the balanced scorecard in its different versions and the GRI Sustainability Reporting Guidelines are not designed to take into account in an explicit, clear and complete way the different relationships which companies develop with their stakeholders.

With regard to the balanced scorecard, Lynn Sharp Paine (2003, p. 120) suggests that:

> some nonfinancial variables are important on their own terms and may be critical success factors even if they are not causal drivers of financial results. [...] Matters such as honest accounting, treating employees with dignity, disclosing product risks, or being a good corporate citizen are not merely means to outstanding performance – they are increasingly part of its very definition. This expanded conception of corporate performance is implicit in the calls for corporate accountability that have become commonplace in recent decades. [...] These calls for accountability have taken various forms – media investigations, legal challenges, boycotts and direct action by consumer, labor, civic, religious and other nongovernmental organizations.

And Freeman, Wicks et al. (2004, p. 11) add:

> There are few secrets in today's world. Executives live in the fishbowl, on full display. They need a way of thinking that easily integrates the many changes that they face. Focusing simply on 'stockholders' and 'shareholder value' is not helpful.

Also the triple bottom line approach has evident limits. According to John Elkington himself (2004, p. 16): 'The TBL agenda as most people would currently understand it is only the beginning. A much more comprehensive approach will be needed that involves a wide range of stakeholder'. And GRI (2002, p. 9) adds that:

> like any simplification of a complex challenge, this definition has its limitations. [...] Defining sustainability in terms of three separate elements (economic, environmental, and social) can sometimes lead to thinking about each element in isolation rather than in an integrated manner.

The concept of extended enterprise, based on a relational view of the firm focused on stakeholder linkages (Post et al., 2002a), goes beyond previous work on the triple bottom line and balanced scorecard: 'The key to solving the core strategic problem is to understand the firm's entire set of stakeholder relationships' (Post et al., 2002a, p. 8).

Furthermore, the traditional environmental, social and sustainability reports are defined more as public relations products than as effective methodologies to control and manage the corporate performance. For example, after his analysis of corporate environmental reports, Pontus Cerin (2002a, p. 62) emphasizes that 'the environmental reporting of today therefore functions more as a marketing tool than an accounting innovation'. Moreover, 'the large and the dirty firms are the ones that produce most environmental reports' (Cerin, 2004, p. 315; Cerin, 2002b): so, through this kind of information companies create their own reputation, influencing the selection processes in the sustainability indexes.

Finally, the balanced scorecard, the GRI Sustainability Reporting Guidelines, and the SIGMA Project, are instruments not suitable for SMEs because of their complexity, limited flexibility, and the need for formal procedures. Until now, only some hundred companies all over the world adopted the Sustainability Reporting Guidelines, and this result is very far from a widespread involvement of firms. For this reason, GRI launched in November 2004 a handbook for SMEs, still too focused on procedures and not on the monitoring of outcomes according to a stakeholder framework (Global Reporting Initiative, 2004).

In conclusion, in order to face the strategic challenge related to the management of stakeholder relationships and meet the managerial needs coming especially from SMEs, we believe that there is a strong need for a clear and modular methodology for a sustainability performance management system. In the following section, we present and describe our framework, defined to monitor and track from a qualitative and quantitative viewpoint the overall corporate performance according to a stakeholder view (see chapter 4) and based on a flexible structure that makes it suitable for companies of different industries, sizes and countries.

7.2 SUSTAINABILITY EVALUATION AND REPORTING SYSTEM (SERS)

The proposal – developed by SPACE (the Research Centre of Bocconi University on Risk, Security, Occupational Health and Safety, Environment and Crisis Management) and called the Sustainability Evaluation and Reporting System (SERS) – aims to aggregate different management tools (e.g. social reporting, environmental reporting, and key performance indicators) into a comprehensive model.

This integrated approach derives from theoretical analyses and empirical experiences carried on in almost fifteen years of research activities in the fields of management of sustainability and social, environmental and sustainability performance evaluation and reporting; it depended on the collaboration with companies and institutions (SPACE, 1993; Pogutz and Tencati, 1997; De Silvio and Tencati, 2002; Tencati, 2002a; Perrini and Tencati, 2003).

The goal is to build an efficient and effective methodology for an overall assessment of corporate sustainability in order to foster and support new accounting and reporting efforts in companies (with a particular focus on SMEs), contribute to the integration between financial and non-financial performance measures, improve the quality of decision-making processes and of the overall business management, and strengthen the corporate accountability and responsiveness towards the different stakeholder groups.

SERS is composed of three modules (see Figure 7.1):

- the Overall Reporting System (or the Sustainability Reporting System) which comprises:
  - o the Annual Report;
  - o the Social Report;
  - o the Environmental Report;
  - o a Set of Integrated Performance Indicators;
- the Integrated Information System;
- the Key Performance Indicators for Corporate Sustainability.

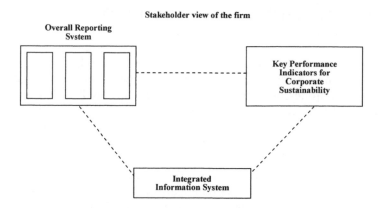

Figure 7.1 Sustainability Evaluation and Reporting System (SERS)

7.2.1 The Overall Reporting System

The annual report

The annual report includes the profit and loss account, the balance sheet and the statement of cash flows. Ratios and indicators should be included in order to check the corporate competitiveness in the finance, marketing, operations, technology, and quality fields.
Furthermore, significant information from a social and environmental point of view are already presented in annual reports with regard to issues related to risk management, potential liabilities, research and development policies and so on. In any case, every country has a specific regulation on this topic.

The last financial scandals brought policy-makers to strengthen the rules regarding financial accounting in order to ensure higher levels of transparency and fairness in financial accounting and reporting activities. However, if we adopt a stakeholder view of the firm, this tool is not sufficient to cover all aspects of corporate performance, including social and environmental ones.

The social report

The social report measures the impact of the company and its activities on the different stakeholder groups. Therefore, it is a methodology capable of supporting the management decision-making process and the corporate communication/engagement policies. According to the SERS approach, it is composed of the ethical policy, the value-added statement and the analysis of stakeholder relationships (see Table 7.1).

More specifically, the value-added statement is a traditional tool in social reporting: for example, it was adopted in the nineteen seventies by the group of German companies called Sozialbilanz-Praxis (Rusconi, 1988, pp. 84-88) and it is the link between the traditional financial accounting and the social reporting. It measures the (financial) value added generated and distributed by the company to the different stakeholder groups (employees, financial partners, state and local authorities, community, shareholders) or invested into the firm. It is a first picture of the (stakeholder) value created and distributed.

Table 7.1 The social report according to the SERS scheme

Corporate Identity
- Brief Description of the Company
- Ethical Policy
➔ Charter of Values and Principles (Ethical Code)
➔ Mission
➔ Charter of Commitments towards Stakeholders
➢ Employees
➢ Members/Shareholders, Financial Community
➢ Clients/Customers
➢ Suppliers
➢ Financial Partners (Banks, Insurance Companies and Financial Services)
➢ State, Local Authorities and Public Administration
➢ Community
Economic Wealth created and distributed by the Company:The Value Added
Relationships with Stakeholders

The analysis of stakeholder relationships aims to describe through qualitative and quantitative information the state of the interactions between a company and its stakeholders. This analysis also comprises forms of social accounting in order to understand the economic costs and benefits related to social activities and policies (e.g. internal costs and benefits related to the occupational health and safety management).

An interesting example of social report used as a fundamental tool to improve the stakeholder management is provided by the Banca Lombarda experience (see Box 7.1).

BOX   7.1   Banca Lombarda: Social report and improvement of the stakeholder management strategy

The Banca Lombarda Group is the result of a merger and some acquisitions realized between 1998 and 2000. From 31 December 1997 to 31 December 2003 it increased its total assets from 8.8 billion Euros to 31.5 billion Euros, and changed from a local banking group into one of the leading Italian banking groups mainly operating in the regions of Lombardy and Piedmont.

As at 31 December 2003, the Banca Lombarda Group had about 1.3 million customers, primarily comprised of individuals and small and medium-sized companies, and it carried on its operations through 783 branches and a network of about 600 financial consultants. Banca Lombarda is listed at the Milan Stock Exchange (Banca Lombarda, 2005).

Between 2002 and 2003 the Group decided to develop a social report as an internal information system in order to assess and improve its stakeholder management strategy. As the long-term success of Banca Lombarda, also in financial terms, depends on the quality of the relationships with the stakeholder network and, in particular, with the local communities in which the Group operates, the development and adoption of an instrument capable of mapping the critical stakeholder groups and assessing the related corporate social performance became crucial. The scheme proposed by SPACE according to the SERS framework was adopted by the company to design and elaborate the social report. First of all, the corporate identity was defined through the explicit identification of the ethical policy, i.e. the

---

principles and values at the basis of the corporate behavior, and the commitments towards the stakeholders. At that time, the most critical stakeholder groups were employees, stockholders, clients and the community(ies). The commitments, which represent the ultimate goals of a real social/societal strategy, were used to assess the value creation and distribution processes and the quality of stakeholder relationships. With regard to this last point initiatives devoted to stakeholder engagement (e.g. questionnaires, satisfaction surveys) were carried out. The outcomes of this long and demanding process, which involved representatives of the controlled banks operating at the local level, coordinated by top managers of the holding company, were used to build a clear and shared organic strategy for an effective stakeholder relationship management.

Therefore, the implementation of the social report allowed the Group to achieve the following advantages:

- clear definition of the role of the firm in the community through a map of the different stakeholder groups and the development of an explicit social and societal strategy;
- control and assessment of the value added and distributed;
- support of planning and decision-making processes;
- improvement of the quality of the company's relationships with stakeholders and enhancement of the related corporate reputation;
- increase and strengthening of the social consensus and license to operate.

The Environmental Report

Although a single, definitive model of environmental report does not yet exist because of the special features of the tool (still prevailing voluntary approach, focus on the national, industrial, corporate specificities and so on), we can attempt to define the boundaries that should characterize a comprehensive environmental information system. According to the nature of the environmental information (physical data or financial items) and the object which these measurements refer to (processes or products), it is possible to classify the principal methodologies developed up to now to monitor the relationships between corporate activities and the natural capital as follows (see Table 7.2).

Table 7.2 Environmental accounting: main methodologies

Types of environmental information / Object of analysis	Energy and material flows	Financial Items
Processes	Ecobalance or Input-output analysis	Cost/benefit accounting related to environmental management of processes
Products	Product ecobalance or Life-Cycle Assessment (LCA)	Cost/benefit accounting related to environmental management of products

The environmental reporting framework within SERS aims to include all the methodologies identified and combine an accounting system collecting physical data with the measurement of (internal) costs and benefits related to the environmental management choices made as regards processes and products (Emblemsvåg and Bras, 2001; Burritt et al., 2002). According to this approach, the environmental report comprises input-output analysis, LCA and cost/benefit account related to environmental management of products/processes. Therefore, the SERS model is designed to define the boundaries an environmental information system should have by identifying a general and complete environmental reporting scheme, which can be applied to any size of organization or business across all industries. Two important kinds of information flows are the object of the environmental reporting system: flows related to physical data – energy and materials accounting; and flows related to financial items – monetary environmental accounting (see Figure 7.2).

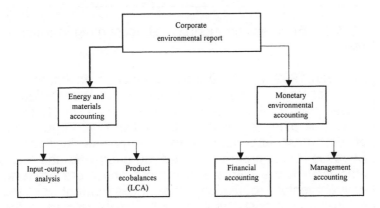

Figure 7.2 Environmental report: the SERS model

Energy and materials accounting (Hallay, 1990; Beck, 1993) collects information regarding the environmental impact of company activities. In particular, we can distinguish two methods: the input-output analyses and the product ecobalances (LCA). The first ones collect and organize the information on energy and material consumptions and the related emissions caused by the operations. The second ones measure the environmental impact of the main products of the firm in terms of resources consumption and pollution along their entire life-cycle (the cradle-to-cradle approach).

Monetary environmental accounting (Bundesumweltm inisterium and Umweltbundesamt, 1995; United States Environmental Protection Agency, 1995) is a method designed to determine the financial costs/benefits borne by the company and associated with the environmental management activities carried out by the firm itself and represents the second important dimension in developing a corporate environmental report. It is a matter of building a tool to measure economic quantities related to environmental management to improve decision-making. This monetary environmental accounting has to be well integrated with the existing financial and management accounting systems (Burritt, 1997). Therefore, defining this kind of environmental accounting is very complex and few companies in the world have introduced an advanced system of measuring environmental costs and benefits (see Box 7.2).

BOX 7.2 Enel: environmental cost accounting in a power plant

Between 1999 and 2000 a pilot project on environmental cost accounting was carried out in the thermoelectric power plant of La Casella, near Piacenza, in Northern Italy. This plant is owned by the Italian Enel Group, one of the most important power companies in Europe. Because of a program aimed at improving the eco-efficiency of the plants and a more and more pressing environmental regulation, the measurement of the environmental costs, that is, of the costs related to the environmental management, became strategic. Therefore, this project was implemented in order to develop an innovative environmental cost accounting system, which could be applied also in other plants of the Group. According to the achieved results, the environmental costs represent about 18% of the overall operating costs, i.e. purchasing costs plus salaries, wages and employee benefits. This information supported the introduction of an Environmental Management System, developed according to the requirements of the Eco-Management and Audit Scheme (EMAS) Regulation, with the purpose of improving the environmental performance of the plant and the local relationships.

Source: De Silvio and Tencati, 2002

A Set of Integrated Performance Indicators

The Sustainability Reporting System allows a company to check and report the annual overall corporate performance. Its goal is to build a true and fair view of the business situation in order to strengthen, improve and manage stakeholder relationships in a sustainable way.

It is a fundamental tool in meeting the information needs coming from different stakeholder groups and affecting the concept of corporate social accountability. Thus, in order to achieve a more complete view of the business behavior, a company should also define and present a set of integrated performance indicators, that is, cross-cutting indicators (Global Reporting Initiative, 2002, p. 4 and pp. 82-84). In general, cross-cutting indicators relate physical and technical quantities to financial ones (for example, an indicator could relate the total amount of waste generated during the year to the value added).

In this way, a firm goes beyond a simple triple bottom line approach in order to adopt a more comprehensive and integrated perspective, capable of defining a really more reliable and material picture of the corporate activities and related implications.

7.2.2 The Integrated Information System

This is the core of performance evaluation and reporting processes. Based on the new ICT – Information and Communication Technologies – solutions such as the Enterprise Resource Planning (ERP) systems, this element enables an organization to collect, process and share physical/technical and financial data. Programs to introduce environmental and social accounting systems for the purpose of integrating and improving the existing financial and cost accounting methodologies have to start from this level.

The goal is to build a satellite accounting system (United Nations, 1993; United Nations, European Commission et al., 2003) focused on social and environmental performance, capable of collecting and organizing all the relevant data (including financial ones) and connected with the other specific accounting/information systems. Through the integration of the different databases it is possible to extract and provide to operators and decision-makers the necessary information to assess the overall performance of the company and its sustainability.

7.2.3 The Key Performance Indicators for Corporate Sustainability

These are specific indicators developed in relationship with the corporate information requirements. The aim is to provide a tool to continually monitor an organization's performance trends. Number and types of measures should be defined on the basis of real corporate needs. In this way the Key Performance Indicators (KPIs) represent a Dashboard of Sustainability (International Institute for Sustainable Development, 2001) supporting management decision-making processes.

Sets of indicators proposed by many organizations, such as Global Reporting Initiative (2002), World Business Council for Sustainable Development (2000, 2003), Eurostat (2001a, 2001b, 2005) and European Environment Agency (2002, 2003), can be used in drawing up an organization's specific measurements, but they cannot limit the corporate choice. Indicators can focus on the financial, operating, marketing, environmental, social, cross-cutting (e.g. with regard to the eco-efficiency and the socio-efficiency of the organization: Schaltegger, Herzig et al., 2002, p. 9; Schaltegger and Burritt, 2005, pp. 188-192) aspects of business management. Key Performance Indicators are also used in the Overall Reporting System and in order to define them the company should carry on stakeholder engagement activities (Stakeholder Research Associates Canada et al., 2005; AccountAbility, 2005).

These Key Performance Indicators are the crucial element of the SERS methodology. A small or medium company could not have sufficient time and resources to define a long and complicated Sustainability Reporting System. But this kind of firm certainly needs a map for an ongoing assessment of its performance and of the related quality (i.e. degree of sustainability) of the relationships with its stakeholders. This map is really provided by a set of KPIs. And this consistent and clear dashboard of sustainability could also be used as a fundamental tool to communicate the information required by the different stakeholder groups.

Therefore this set of indicators must be the result of a process of stakeholder engagement, involving the different constituencies in the KPIs' definition. Moreover, in line with the adopted stakeholder view of the firm (Donaldson and Preston, 1995; Clarkson, 1995; Figge and Schaltegger, 2000; Post et al., 2002a;

O'Higgins, 2002), and the sustainability concept (Tencati, 2002a, pp. 3-36; AccountAbility, 1999, p. 94), the key performance indicators should be organized according to a framework based on stakeholder categories (see Box 7.3).

BOX 7.3 Coop Adriatica: KPIs and sustainability report

Coop Adriatica is one of the most important territorial cooperative societies of Coop (see chapter 5). The 2003 turnover was 1,700 million Euros. Coop Adriatica has 760,000 members and 8,130 employees. In 2004 it issued its second sustainability report. As a fundamental part of the document a set of key performance indicators is presented. Besides the financial/economic measures, the indicators related to social and environmental issues are organized according to a framework based on stakeholder categories. The identified stakeholder groups are as follows:

- members/consumers;
- employees;
- environment;
- local community.

The relationships with other stakeholder groups are also analyzed in the report: they are suppliers, the Coop system, unions, the cooperative movement and public authorities. In Coop Adriatica the sustainability report supports the decision-making process and allows the company to deeply involve the stakeholders and especially the different local communities in the assessment of past results and in the definition of future goals of the social/societal strategy.

Source: Coop Adriatica, 2004

For example, the indicators could be organized according to a three-level framework (World Business Council for Sustainable

Development, 2000, p. 8; Global Reporting Initiative, 2002, pp. 36-37):

- categories: Stakeholder groups which are specifically affected by clusters of indicators;
- aspects: Thematic areas monitored by groups of performance indicators related to a given category of stakeholders;
- indicators: Measurements that supply information related to a given aspect. They can be used to check and demonstrate organizational performance. The information can be qualitative, quantitative (physical and technical) or economic-monetary.

The stakeholder categories adopted could be as follows (Tencati et al., 2004):

- Employees;
- Members/Shareholders, Financial Community;
- Clients/Customers;
- Suppliers;
- Financial Partners;
- State, Local Authorities and Public Administration;
- Community;
- Environment.

Especially the small and medium-sized enterprises could use this proposal as a starting point to build their own shared map, through a specific stakeholder engagement process, in order to assess and communicate the corporate performance.

In chapter 8 the Italian situation with regard to the CSR policies fostered and implemented by different players at different levels will be described in detail.

In chapter 9 the CSR-SC (Corporate Social Responsibility – Social Commitment) Project, promoted and developed by the Italian Government with the technical contribution by Bocconi University, will be presented. In this Project a complete set of key performance indicators according to the stakeholder framework has been developed in order to support companies in their efforts towards sustainability.

In the Appendix the complete set of key indicators and the related social statement will be examined.

7.3 NEW PERSPECTIVES IN SUSTAINABILITY PERFORMANCE MANAGEMENT

Nowadays, and more and more in the future, one of the keys for a successful strategic management is the availability of sustainability performance management tools capable of monitoring and tracking from a qualitative and quantitative viewpoint the overall corporate performance and, in particular, the state, i.e. the sustainability, of the different stakeholder relationships. Thus, there is an urgent call for new systems of measuring the corporate outcomes according to a stakeholder framework in line with a more suitable and correct strategic approach.

In this chapter we have presented SERS, a Sustainability Evaluation and Reporting System, based on a stakeholder view of the firm and therefore really aimed at balancing and integrating financial and non-financial performance indicators, supporting planning, implementation and control activities of a sustainability-oriented and responsive organization.

Our proposal provides a reliable tool in order to help companies to understand stakeholder requirements and assess their own performance. This framework, through an integrated perspective, aims:

- to aggregate different management tools (e.g. social reporting, environmental reporting, and KPIs) into a comprehensive model – methodological integration;
- to map and monitor the entire set of a company's stakeholder relationships – integration of different perspectives into the sustainability accounting system towards a *multiple bottom line* approach;
- to supply information, which can be qualitative, quantitative (physical and technical) and economic-monetary, through the performance measurements – integration of data/information. These indicators build a sort of dashboard of sustainability, that is, an effective Tableau de Bord, which goes beyond the traditional financial data. Moreover, the availability of this broad range of measures allows a company to build integrated performance indicators by relating physical and technical quantities to financial ones. The environmental

intensity ratio presented in the previous section is only an example of a methodology that can be applied by every firm. Companies could develop many other measures according to their specific information needs: e.g., in the occupational health and safety management field, an indicator could relate the trend of the injury rate during the last three years to the costs connected with the projects implemented to improve the work conditions; with regard to R&D policies, another indicator could relate the achieved results in terms of new patents, launch of new products, introduction of new labeling schemes and so on to the investments in this area borne during a specific period of time identified on the basis of the industry competitive dynamics. These comparisons help management to assess the effectiveness of its choices and to review its strategies and define next steps by using a suitable informational support.

In this way, according to a relational view of the firm, the SERS methodology enables a company and its management to manage the stakeholder relationships and address the information needs and the economic, social and environmental concerns of various stakeholder groups. This point is crucial for every kind of firm and especially for SMEs, whose success is deeply rooted in stakeholder networks (Lipparini, 2002).

Moreover, the SERS structure, composed of different modules (the Overall Reporting System, the Integrated Information System and the Key Performance Indicators) is flexible enough to be used by businesses of different sizes operating in different sectors and countries.

However, further steps in the field of sustainability accounting are expected: if stakeholder relationships are the essential assets to create sustainable wealth, not only the company-centered, but also the stakeholder-centered performance should be measured. This means that, for example, the degree of stakeholder trust, the stakeholder satisfaction generated by the corporate strategy and behavior should be carefully evaluated (Ghoshal and Bartlett, 1999; Lev, 2001; Castaldo, 2002; Nelli and Bensi, 2003). This calls for the development of further methodologies that could broaden the available set of measures, but also make more difficult the use of specific performance indicators.

Therefore, if we adopt a stakeholder view of the firm in order to design sustainability accounting systems, we should also understand how the stakeholder relationships and the related engagement processes could impact the quantity and quality of performance indicators aimed at monitoring the corporate sustainability. This perspective could dramatically change the way managers and stakeholders assess firms, their success and their role in the society.

NOTE

1. During the last years other approaches and guidelines have been developed in order to support SMEs in their managerial efforts. Initiatives such as The Corporate Social Responsibility Monitor (Rayner and Raven, 2002), the CSR Europe's SME Key (described at http://www.smekey.org), the 'Responsible Entrepreneurship for SMEs' Program and the 'Corporate Social Responsibility for SMEs' Awareness Raising Campaign (presented at http://europa.eu.int/comm /enterprise/csr/index_en.htm) fostered by the Directorate-General for 'Enterprise and Industry' of the European Commission, the UNIDO Business Partnership Programme (United Nations Industrial Development Organization, 2002; Deloitte Touche Tohmatsu Emerging Markets, 2004) are important steps towards a greater engagement of small and medium companies. However, they did not provide solutions which have become reference point in the management of sustainability.

8. CSR in Italy: situation and company models

8.1 INTRODUCTION

This chapter reviews CSR in Italy by means of a wide-ranging examination of the principal initiatives achieved in the last few years, at both the private and public levels, involving firms, institutions, and local communities. The goal is an updated picture of the dynamics of this topic to describe attitudes towards CSR and the various private and public approaches that reflect the complex nature of the Italian economic and social system.

Part of the chapter explores the results of two surveys carried out between 2002 and 2003 to provide an overview of CSR awareness in Italian companies and a reference framework for interpreting CSR features and behavior.

The forerunner of these initiatives is an innovative project developed by the Italian Ministry of Labor and Social Affairs on CSR, called Corporate Social Responsibility – Social Commitment (CSR-SC). Its goal was to promote CSR culture among businesses and to assure private citizens of the accuracy of corporate reports on ethical and social issues. Launched in June 2002 and officially presented to the EU partners at the European Conference on CSR in Venice on 14 November 2004, 'The role of public policies in promoting CSR', this was apparently the most significant project ever developed in Italy at the institutional level on CSR.

Analyzed in the following chapters, this project aims to enhance a CSR promotional campaign developed after the Sustainable Development Strategy for Europe was approved in June 2001 (CEC, 2001b), and after the Green Paper 'Promoting a European framework for CSR' (CEC, 2001d) was presented in July 2001, which provoked an interesting debate among different EU members on the development of national sustainability strategies.

So far, the Italian project defines a general framework for CSR, in terms of both public policies and private initiatives within this general European framework.

Furthermore, with regard to SMEs and network organizations, the Italian economy provides a unique perspective on the relationship between CSR strategies and these policies and initiatives. Some of the features that distinguish the Italian industrial system from that of the other European countries are listed below. First, to compare the average-sized European companies in the industry, services, and infrastructure sectors, the Italian system has an average of 3.9 employees per firm compared to an average of 6 overall for the 15 EU member states. Second, in the industrial sphere, enterprises with over 250 employees account for 19.7 percent of the total in Italy but 34 percent of the total for the EU.

The Italian industrial system is concentrated in industrial districts in northern and central Italy, along the Adriatic coast, and in a few areas of the South (Becattini, 1987; Goodman, Bamford and Saynor, 1989). Some of the traditional and engineering industries in these districts are leaders of the global market; overall, they account for over two-thirds of total national exports.

Finally, the success of Italian SMEs is often related to their capability of acquiring legitimacy and consensus from local stakeholders such as employees, public authorities, financial organizations, banks, suppliers and citizens. These local networks are based on informal and tacit relationships, whose results are often not communicated or simply not measured. In this context it is relevant to introduce the notion of social capital: 'Whereas physical capital refers to physical objects and human capital refers to the properties of individuals, social capital refers to connections among individuals – social networks and the norms of reciprocity and trustworthiness that arise from them' (Putnam, 2000, p. 19). Moreover, 'stocks of social capital, such as trusts, norms, and networks, tend to be self-reinforcing and cumulative. Successful collaboration in one endeavor builds connections and trusts – social assets that facilitate future collaboration in other, unrelated tasks. As with conventional capital, those who have social capital tend to accumulate more' (Putnam, 1993b). From this perspective, the intangible assets of social capital – reputation, trust, legitimacy and consensus – are fundamental to the long-term performance of Italian SMEs and their districts (Lipparini, 2002).

Regarding this diffusion of managerial tools and standards in Italy, as shown and analyzed in a broad range of literature (SPACE, 1993; Azzone, Bianchi and Noci, 1997), a well-known example was the low diffusion rate in our country of the ISO standards on Total Quality Management. In recent years this situation has rapidly changed, due partly to ancillary actions by industrial associations on the Italian soil. Today, in fact, Italy leads Europe in the dissemination of environmental and social management systems. Responsible business practices are vital and hence an embedded element of the Italian model of capitalism centered on SMEs.

This chapter analyzes the different CSR spheres in Italy as well as the ongoing debate among Italian firms as they come to grips with what is becoming an ever-increasing strategic and competitive corporate theme.

8.2 ANALYSIS OF THE IMPACT OF CSR IN ITALY

In Italy, because of historical (the importance of the cooperative movement and trade unions) and structural (the predominance of SMEs and the diffusion of industrial districts) reasons, a remarkable attentiveness to the social relationships of companies has characterized the national economic system.

Furthermore, the increased public attention to environmental protection, product safety and workers' rights has stimulated institutional actors to promote socially responsible behaviors among enterprises. Moreover, the interest of firms in these issues grows through specific initiatives and actions organized at the individual level or in partnership with industrial associations and nongovernmental organizations (NGOs). So far, the Italian industrial landscape is complex and dynamic, embracing both the private and the public dimensions. The following paragraphs explore the uniqueness of the Italian approach to CSR.

8.2.1 Private Sector Experience

With regard to the private sector, for more than a decade Italian firms and other players (that is, NGOs and bank foundations) have shown a considerable interest in sustainability issues, for example, environmental protection, philanthropy, donating to local communities and, more recently, CSR.

Theoretical and empirical studies carried out by international organizations and scholars have tried to comprehensively assess instruments and practices adopted by companies to implement CSR (CEC, 2004). Several taxonomies have been proposed and used in recent years. Here, in order to review the different ongoing initiatives, we divide the various practices into four main groups: reporting and other disclosure actions; adoption of management standards and certification systems; financial experiences (ethical investment funds, rating); and other initiatives (donation and Cause-Related Marketing actions, social awards, and so on).

Reporting and other disclosure actions

The first group consists of reports on environmental, social and sustainability issues. Probably the first significant step in this area, by the Foundation Eni Enrico Mattei (FEEM), is in the domain of eco-reporting. Part of the ENI Corporation, FEEM researches and studies matters such as environmental protection, energy and energy policies, and economic development. In the mid 1990s, FEEM developed a specific framework to support companies in their environmental accounting and reporting experiences which became the reference model for several firms. In more recent years, reporting on CSR has rapidly increased in response to the demand for greater accountability and transparency: stakeholders ask for information on the performance of businesses in different CSR areas. The responses, implemented on a voluntary basis, use manifold reference standards and methods (like Global Reporting Initiative reporting guidelines analyzed in chapter 6). In Italy such information has proliferated also due to the research program established by the Study Group for Social Reporting (Gruppo Bilancio Sociale - GBS). GBS, as examined in chapter 6, is an Italian think-tank involving academics (CELE – Centre for Ethics, Law and Economics, LIUC University, Castellanza, VA), scholars, managers and independent experts committed to developing standard principles and guidelines for social reporting. Another initiative in this area has been developed by the Italian Banking Association (Associazione Bancaria Italiana – ABI). ABI has an operative working group that promotes specific guidelines for social reporting. Finally, Bocconi University developed and proposed the Sustainability Evaluation and Reporting System (see chapter 7) with the goal to aggregate different management tools into a comprehensive model for an overall assessment of corporate sustainability. So far, Italy counts:

- more than one hundred and fifty organizations (firms, non-profit organizations, and so on) that publish social reports;
- more than one hundred organizations (firms, non-profit organizations, and so on) that publish environmental reports;
- more than 50 organizations that publish sustainability/social-environmental reports, in line with the triple-bottom-line approach.

Management standard and certification systems

The second group focuses on the dissemination of all the components of CSR management standards: environment, human resources, supplier, occupational health and safety, quality and certification systems verified by third parties. Environmental labels and quality labels are included in this group. Among management standards, the Q-RES project is noteworthy (see chapter 6). Launched in Italy in 2000 by CELE, the Centre for Ethics, Law and Economics of the LIUC University – Castellanza (VA), the Q-RES project aims at creating a management framework for the ethical and social responsibility of firms, externally certifiable. Several Italian companies in different industrial sectors, professional associations (e.g., Association of Internal Auditors), accounting, and business organizations (e.g., Sodalitas), participate in the project.

To sum up, in the realm of CSR management systems, Italy is one of the leading countries in Europe:

- as of September 2005, 260 facilities are certified with the Social Accountability 8000 (SA 8000) standard, out of 763 global certifications. Further, Italy has the highest number of certified organizations in the world (34.1 percent of total). The large number of applications for this certification can be attributed to three causes. First, the market pressure of the largest Italian retailer, Coop, which pushed a number of suppliers to apply for the certification; second, the role of some policy makers, for example, the regions of Tuscany and

Umbria, which have launched several measures to support the spread of ethical sourcing practices, boosting the adoption of the SA8000 standard; third, two out of the world's eight accredited certifying bodies are located in Italy;

- with regard to environmental, health, and safety-management systems, in the last few years there has been a remarkable increase in ISO 14001 certifications (more than 5,300 as of April 2005), OSHAS 18001 certifications, and EMAS registrations (413 as of December 2005, including both facilities and organizations registered);
- with regard to environmental labels – EU Ecolabel – Italy leads Europe in number of firms certified (82, as of December 2005). Moreover, on the Italian market, 1490 products, equivalent to 12 product groups, are certified. Finally, other types of labels are spreading, pulled by a demand that seems increasingly focused on social issues: biological certifications, social labels (Transfair), and other environmental labels including the Forest Stewardship Council (FSC).

Financial experiences

The third group embraces initiatives and projects that, despite their differences, all relate to the corporate financial area and evaluation processes. In this context, we report the following trends:

- socially responsible managed saving, or ethical finance, is rising in importance: according to Assogestioni (the Italian Association of Investment Funds), the number of ethical mutual funds increased steadily to thirty in 2005. In response to the growing interest in this sector, Assogestioni introduced the category of Ethical Fund among its categories of financing. Furthermore, trading pension funds begin to combine ethical choice with traditional portfolio management systems (Previambiente and Eurofer, for example). In Italy, in December 2005, the total assets managed by ethical funds amounted to 2,768 million euros (1,500 million Euros in September 2003). In Italy, within this framework, we point out the Forum per la Finanza Sostenibile (FFS – Forum for Sustainable Finance) with members like ABI (Italian Banking Association), ANIA (the

Italian Association of Insurance Companies) and other banking, financial and insurance institutions. The FFS was established in 2001 to promote the diffusion of socially responsible investment concepts and tools, raise the level of debate on sustainable development among the representatives of the financial community, and build professional competencies. Moreover, one of the biggest international ethical rating companies, E.Capital Partners SpA, works in Italy. Since 2000, it has launched two stock Indexes – Ethical Index Euro® and Ethical Index Global® – and four bond indexes. Avanzi SRI Research, the Italian member of the SiRi Group network, also works in the field of socially responsible investments;

- finally, another important organization is the Banca Etica. Founded in 1998, it has been fully operational since March 1999. It specializes in non-profit financing, solidarity economics, social and international cooperation, and civil society. Its savings, made up of socially responsible and sustainable investments, amount to 362 million Euros in November 2005.

Other initiatives

Some entrepreneurial associations, for example, the Italian Banking Association (ABI) and Federchimica (the Italian Chemical Industry Federation), have operative working groups on CSR and different research groups, technical committees and institutes, which offer important theoretical and practical advice.

Various spontaneous initiatives to address different CSR-connected issues – training, environmental management systems, supply chain control, and so on – exist in different industrial sectors/districts, for example, Sassuolo-Scandiano, Lecco, Lecce, Prato.

Furthermore, various organizations promoted by companies and entrepreneurial associations – including Gruppo di Frascati/Cittadinanzattiva, Sodalitas, Impronta Etica and Anima – work within the framework of CSR with cultural promotion, best-practice diffusion, stakeholders' engagement programs, and more.

Also in the realm of private initiatives, a remarkable and increasing phenomenon in the Italian context is cause-related marketing activities (CRM).[1] According to Nielsen Italia

Observatory on corporate investments in communication, in 2004, CRM initiatives accounted for an investment of € 82,325,000 (over 8,000 ads), that is, 0.34 percent of the advertising market. In the same year, more than 200 firms invested in CRM initiatives. These data are in line with the 2003 results (€ 85,747,000 invested, 10.612 ads and 190 companies involved), and show an incremental trend, if compared with previous annual results (in 2002, the expenditures for CRM were around € 78,000,000, or 0.3 percent of the market, with 7,800 ads. realized by 120 companies).

In addition, the increasing attention to CSR-related issues is evident in the creation of specific awards. An example is the initiative 'Oscar di Bilancio', established by the Federation of Italian Public Relations, which identified some specific categories for social and environmental reports and then, consistent with the above-mentioned triple-bottom-line approach, created the 'Oscar di Bilancio di Sostenibilità' to meet this new trend. Another example is the 'Sodalitas Social Award', the award granted to those Italian companies that best implemented socially responsible programs. Moreover, we have other initiatives on specific CSR-related issues, like the Best Workplaces Italia organized by Great Places to Work.

Finally, in Italy bank foundations play a significant role in the promotion and support of non-profit organizations and local communities. In 2004, they disbursed 1,267 million euros for social-related actions with over 23,000 initiatives directed to cultural and artistic activities, training, assistance, philanthropy and charity activities, health, research, promotion, local communities, the environment, sports, and international and religious activities.

Given the above-mentioned initiatives, we can therefore assert that the Italian approach to CSR involves a nationally widespread network of interventions and actions that are highly innovative. It is indeed true that many of the voluntary activities carried out by companies, mostly SMEs, despite a strong relationship with the local community, are scarcely systematic; that is, they are not structured into formalized strategic processes, and they have low visibility outside the company. This common approach to CSR, which can be defined as a sort of 'sunk CSR' (Perrini et al., 2006), is a frequent phenomenon that cannot easily be appreciated and enhanced for use by conventionally competitive multinational corporations.

8.2.2 Public Sector Experience

Government, regions, provinces and local authorities play a central role in promoting CSR policies in the country. So far, many initiatives, programs and incentives have been developed within the public sector with the goal of boosting both the awareness and culture of CSR and the adoption of specific managerial practices and tools. As mentioned above, a complete review of governmental intervention will be found in chapter 9, through an in-depth analysis of the CSR-SC project launched by the Ministry of Labour and Social Affairs. Here we offer a detailed examination of the measures developed by public authorities at the local level, starting with the regional measures.

- Since June 2000, the Tuscany region has activated some specific measures to promote the SA 8000 standard among SMEs. On the one hand, the region grants financial support to local firms (SMEs) that want to obtain the SA 8000 certification, covering up to 50 percent of the consulting and certification costs. In addition, in order to spread the knowledge of CSR issues and to raise the awareness of companies and public opinion, Tuscany established a CSR office within the Department of Economic Development, launched the Fabrica Ethica project, with the goal of supporting companies in training and information services, and created a Multi-Stakeholder Committee (Regional Ethical Commission for CSR) within the regional government (Alabreda et al., 2005);
- the Umbria region approved the Regional Act n.20 of 2002, which provides for the creation of the regional Register of SA 8000-certified companies. In addition, the region had already approved the Regional Act n.21 of 12 November 2002 titled 'Measures for the certification of quality, environmental, safety and ethical systems of Umbrian firms';
- in addition to the program 'Chiaro, Sicuro, Regolare' (CSR – Clear, Safe, Regular) about working safety and quality, the Emilia-Romagna region entrusted the Institute for Labour with a research project to specify the conditions that could facilitate voluntary access to the Label of Social Quality for regional companies. Furthermore, in July 2005 the Emilia-Romagna region adopted the Regional Law n.4 in order to

promote employment and quality, as well as compliance with regulations concerning workplace conditions. In this area, CSR is considered to be a critical tool for improving work conditions, fostering a competitive attitude, and promoting sustainable development and social cohesion at the local level;

- the Marche region is a partner in a project carried out by the Training Center of Marche (CFM) – a consortium of Marche's training companies – to conduct a feasibility study for the establishment of an information system on CSR. Moreover, in February 2005, the Marche region adopted the Regional Law n.11 to promote initiatives, managerial tools and schemes in the area of socially responsible practices. Finally, in 2005 the SIRM project (Sistema Impresa Responsabile Regione Marche – Responsible Business System of the Marche region) was launched;
- the Assessorato for Productive Activities of the Campania region started an investigating study on local, national and international CSR patterns and best practices;
- Sicily region carried out the CSR-Vaderegio Project, funded by the European Commission. This project involves four organizations: Agenda-Social Responsibility in Scotland of Edinburgh (Scotland), the Flemish Ministry of Labour (Belgium, Flanders), the Novia Salcedo Foundation di Bilbao (Spain, Basque region) and the Euro Association of Palermo (Sicily). By involving local institutions, the project aims to understand and promote CSR at local levels. Furthermore, the region of Sicily supports the Etiqualitas Project, which involves the Regional Observatory for the Environment (ORSA), the Euro Association and various local bodies and cooperatives.

As far as provinces are concerned, we report some of the most interesting actions:

- the province of Chieti has brought forward a regional draft bill concerning the 'Introduction of quality certification systems on the Environment and corporate social responsibility for the administrative procedures of the region of Abruzzo, local territorial bodies and other public bodies working in the region of Abruzzo'. Industrial associations

working in the region of Abruzzo'. Industrial associations and universities helped draft the document, which aims to encourage companies to adopt more advanced managing tools;
- the province of Lecce, in cooperation with the local University and Assindustria, has promoted a project to support and develop the system of ethical-social certification for the companies of the province;
- the province of Novara launched the Sonar Project, whose goal is to build a management system for incorporating special-needs populations into the labor market. The province of Novara has also launched a project to establish a CQS system (Social Quality Certification).
- finally, many local authorities (more than 300), including municipalities, provinces and regions, lead and foster local Agenda 21 and local forums for sustainable development and for the definition of sustainable and responsible policies.

8.2.3 Entrepreneurial Associations

The last part of this review represents the entrepreneurial associations' stance in promoting CSR. In recent years, several projects on environmental issues, working conditions, sustainability and CSR have been carried out. So far it is difficult to summarize the multitude of experiences that occurred at various levels, among the different industrial sectors. Special attention and sensitivity to CSR issues distinguish the National System of Chambers of Commerce – Unioncamere, which assumed a leading role in promoting CSR among companies working in Italy. Under its coordination, regional and provincial chambers of commerce are progressively activating CSR front offices (in Italian, 'Sportelli') to promote CSR, collect and spread best practices and provide specific consulting services. Other relevant initiatives are listed below:

- the REBUS Project – Relationship between Business and Society, a European Investigation into CSR – funded by the European Commission, and shared by ISTUD (Istituto Studi Direzionali SpA – Milan), SFERA (Servizi Formativi Emiliano Romagnoli Associati, a consortium whose partners are the training bodies of entrepreneurial associations of

Chamber of Commerce of Milan. The project's aim was to investigate how much attention was paid by SME managers to the concept of CSR and to promote the exchange and knowledge of best practices;

• the CISE, Centro per l'Innovazione e lo Sviluppo Economico – Center for Innovation and Economic Development, a special agency of the Chamber of Commerce of Forlì-Cesena, established the Lavoro Etico (Ethical Labor) network to communicate and disseminate the principles and management tools for SA 8000 certification and training of auditors. The CISE is accredited by the Social Accountability International for the certification of the SA 8000 system and the training of auditors.

In conclusion, the sensibility to CSR and the promotion/consolidation of socially responsible behaviors, mostly among SMEs, are the fundamental elements shared by all public initiatives, all over Italy. A shared reference framework, able to integrate and strengthen these efforts, could improve the action of territorial bodies and chambers of commerce and supply a useful tool for the firms involved.

8.3 MODELS OF CSR IN ITALY

When the Ministry of Labour and Social Affairs launched the Corporate Social Responsibility-Social Commitment (CSR-SC) project in June 2002, the need for a clear understanding of Italian entrepreneurs and managers' social orientation – concerning CSR company awareness and related concepts – was evident. Few studies primarily analyzed the topic, and these mainly explored the diffusion of managerial tools as reporting or management systems, or focused on specific features like environmental protection, human resources and labor conditions (SPACE, 1993; Federchimica, 1998; Carnimeo et al., 2002). Descriptive studies providing insight on business reactions to social and environmental pressures or internal/external barriers to the diffusion of CSR in Italy were lacking.

Therefore a new research agenda was identified with the support of academic partners (Bocconi University and ISVI, Istituto per i Valori di Impresa – the Italian institute for company

Istituto per i Valori di Impresa – the Italian institute for company values) and institutional ones (Confindustria, the leading Italian organization for manufacturing and service industries, and Unioncamere, the Italian Union of Chambers of Commerce).

Two quantitative empirical surveys on CSR awareness and practices in business were carried out between September 2002 and November 2003 throughout Italy.

8.3.1 The First Survey on CSR: Goal and Methodology

The first empirical survey has been designed and carried out by Bocconi University within its Ministry of Labour and Social Affairs project.

Based on a sample of 395 firms, the study was started in autumn 2002 to gather descriptive data and information on the perceptions that Italian entrepreneurs and managers had of corporate responsibility and their interpretations of it. Until that time, in fact, little was known about the involvement of the industrial and economic world in managing these issues with the different categories of stakeholders (employees, shareholders, customers, suppliers, community and financial partners and so on). Although there has been much discussion on the topic among firms, industrial organizations, institutions and NGOs, no empirical evidence was found, despite a detailed analysis of the literature.

Therefore, before developing the proposal for a standard to encourage socially responsible behavior among Italian firms (the CSR-SC project), it seemed appropriate to conduct a preliminary descriptive survey on CSR awareness and attitudes among these companies. More specifically, the aim was to explore the following topics:

- the attention paid by firms to CSR issues;
- the social activity promoted by firms within CSR;
- difficulties and obstacles in implementing CSR;
- perceived advantages related to the enforcement of CSR;
- factors that could lead to greater attention to the issue.

To investigate these topics, we decided to define a sample of 'leading companies on CSR' or 'companies sensitive to CSR'. This approach is related to the general goal of the research project developed for the Italian Ministry of Labour and Social Affairs, devoted at first to CSR 'best in class' firms. The sample was chosen with the support of Confindustria, the leading Italian organization for manufacturing and service industries, and comprises 395 enterprises selected on the basis of the parameters of Confindustria's Associating System. So far, the sample represents the overall population of Italian enterprises in terms of size, sector and geographical distribution, but it is not random.

Moreover, the sample has been chosen considering the distribution of the Italian companies in terms of size (number of employees), industrial sector and geographical criteria. Corrections were introduced to weight the relevance of SMEs in the sample.

The questionnaire, based on current European and Italian literature (CEC, 2002a), consisted of two parts: a group of questions on company data (that is, number of employees, turnover, sector, adoption of specific management programs and tools); and eleven close-ended questions on CSR. The questionnaires were sent to board chairpersons, managing directors, chief executive officers and top managers of the sample companies.

In a first phase, all the information collected was organized using simple statistical tools (that is, weighted mean, percentile ranking and frequency distributions). Ninety-one questionnaires were received, representing a response rate of approximately 25 percent. Although the sample was chosen among 'best in class' firms according to the Confindustria's parameters, the response rate of SMEs (< 50 employees) was in any case lower than that of large firms. Finally, all the companies interviewed were in some way familiar with new managerial issues, quality assurance and management systems.

In a second step, data collected were used to carry out a more in-depth statistical analysis in order to define a more complete picture of the relationships and antecedents at the base of corporate behavior in the CSR field. The statistical tools adopted were linear and logistic regression: this choice was related to the type of dependent variables considered, that is, CSR activities in which companies are involved, tools implemented to promote CSR and companies' opinions on the dimensions of CSR. These dependent variables were correlated with size and geographical location. The size of companies was measured as the number of employees; the geographical location was measured looking at the area where companies operate (North-East of Italy, North-West, Centre and South).

8.3.2 Key Findings of the First Survey

Generally speaking, companies' attention to CSR issues and adoption of CSR behavior seem quite high. The majority of the interviewees (84 percent) declared that they were involved and active in the area of CSR. In addition, for 62 percent of the firms the involvement in socially responsible activities is regular and related to business strategy.

In particular, according to the questionnaires collected the initiatives most frequently realized in the sphere of CSR are: training activities (89 percent); safeguarding employees' health (82 percent); activities on behalf of the local community (72 percent); support of cultural activities (70 percent), and control of product safety (67 percent) and environmental impact (around 62 percent). On the other hand, these companies are not heavily engaged in the following activities: on-site child-care facilities (only 2 percent); participation in fair trade (4 percent); equal opportunity policies (13 percent); programs for protected categories (15 percent) and disadvantaged persons (27 percent) and control of the ethical and social aspects of products (17 percent).

With regard to the concrete tools to promote CSR, respondents are involved in either internal or external programs. Programs to benefit employees (83 percent) and regular sponsorship actions (75 percent) are the instruments used by the majority of the firms involved in the study.

In that a wide range of definitions of CSR exist, one survey question was structured to discover top managers' perceptions of the CSR concept: 'In your opinion, which dimensions do CSR include?' In this case a 5-point Likert scale was used (strongly agree with/strongly disagree with). The results indicate that CSR is considered a very broad concept, encompassing many different dimensions. However, some features seem to be more linked to corporate responsibility than others: employee safety, environmental protection, respect for ethical principles and human rights, company reputation, adoption of conduct codes, transparency, attention to the quality of life and promotion of local community initiatives. Out of the remaining choices, philanthropy, donations and marketing (cause-related marketing) were perceived as least relevant to the subject of the survey.

Interestingly, although the sample was selected from 'sensitive to CSR companies', chosen for their leading role inside Confindustria's network, only 45 percent were familiar with the Green Paper on CSR promoted by the EU.

Another important point the survey explored was the factors that encourage a firm to adopt socially responsible behavior. The most frequent advantages indicated were: benefits to company image (90 percent), opportunity to improve relations with the local community (76 percent) and specific motivations of Top Management (56 percent). Meanwhile, investor relations (13 percent) and pressure from local communities (9 percent) seem less relevant in orienting Italian companies towards CSR. Surprisingly, in the sample we observed, only one company (1 percent) indicated pressures from clients and suppliers and from NGOs as a relevant reason to promote socially responsible initiatives.

In addition, the companies were asked to identify obstacles to implementing CSR. The lack of time and severe time pressure (61 percent) and lack of human resources to address CSR issues were the two principal barriers that emerged from the survey. Other difficulties were lack of financial resources and cost constraints (38 percent) and ignorance of the topic (31 percent).

Finally, the survey analyzed which factors could attract more attention to CSR in the future. The main replies were fiscal incentives (48 percent), followed by the spread of information on CSR (47 percent) and benefits for company image (47 percent). In contrast, firms did not consider the possibility of obtaining greater access to financial resources (7 percent) and better relations with Public Authorities (17 percent) as factors likely to increase the involvement in CSR in the future. Moreover, 43 percent of the sample declared their intention to increase their involvement in CSR over the next three years, while 58 percent declared that they would keep it at its current level.

If we consider the more in depth statistical analysis, in order to test the correlation between CSR activities and firms' size and geographical location, a logistic regression has been implemented. The key findings were as follows:

- geographical location is statistically significant ($p < 0.01$) and negatively correlated to the environmental protection activities ($r = -0.493$);
- geographical location is statistically significant ($p < 0.01$) and negatively correlated to initiatives for equal opportunities ($r = -0.647$);
- environmental protection activities are also statistically significant ($p < 0.05$) and negatively correlated to firm size ($r = -0.289$).
- local community involvement is statistically significant ($p < 0.01$) and negatively correlated to firm size ($r = -0.338$);
- support of sports activities and cultural activities are statistically significant ($p < 0.01$) and negatively correlated to firm size (respectively $r = -0.288$ and $r = -0.313$).

In general, data suggest that activities with a direct impact on the welfare of the local community (environmental protection, local community involvement, support of specific activities such as sports and cultural programs) are based on a stronger involvement of the SMEs. This is consistent with the view of social capital as a fundamental asset for the success of the Italian companies: SMEs are crucial parts of the community where they are located and they maintain and strengthen their local trust relationships over time through a relevant social commitment. Furthermore, according to the negative correlation between environmental protection/equal opportunities and geographical location, the social and environmental consciousness and awareness seem to be higher in northern Italy. Many data, with particular regard to environmental policies, confirm these results (APAT and ONR, 2003).

According to the data, companies located in northern Italy are more interested in using advanced tools (corporate campaigning and codes of conduct) to foster socially responsible initiatives. Besides, SMEs seem to be more sensitive to actions (direct investments in the community, employee involvement programs and adoption of codes of conduct), which could directly and positively affect their relationships with the different stakeholder categories, especially at the local level.

In conclusion, as we expected, the findings have generally demonstrated that the definition of the CSR concept (that is, the different CSR dimensions) is independent from the geographical location or the size of the firms. Enterprises located in northern Italy show a greater attention to the issues related to respect for equal opportunities and local community initiatives. As previously underlined, this result could be related to a higher social awareness and to the fact that industrial districts and networks are more developed in northern and central Italy.

8.3.3 Main Conclusions and Further Development

The survey has provided a first set of findings on CSR in Italy. In general, the companies selected had a positive attitude towards CSR. Despite giving unclear definitions of CSR, firms seem to be engaged in socially responsible activities using several tools: specific programs on social issues, sponsorships, donations, direct investments and adoption of codes of conduct.

The main motives at the core of the CSR initiatives are related to company image and relations with local communities. In particular, the relationship between SMEs and local communities seems to be fundamental to understanding the preferences expressed by the companies in this field. As we pointed out previously, this could be explained if we refer to the concept of social capital as key driver of the long-term success of the firms in the Italian context. For this reason it is probably possible to talk about 'sunk CSR' if we consider the traditional behavior (for example local community initiatives and involvement) of companies in their own environment.

The survey also identified internal and external barriers to the diffusion of CSR among firms, and factors that could lead to a deeper engagement in the near future. From a policy perspective, the need for public support is clearly pointed out by respondents as a critical factor in fostering CSR firms' behavior. More specifically, in addition to fiscal incentives, companies need information on corporate social issues (the lack of publicity on CSR is considered one of the main obstacles to CSR activities). Public Authorities have to develop and spread knowledge about CSR in the business community through promotion and communication.

To sum up, the survey provided a first picture of the Italian 'state of the art' related to CSR issues in business. For a broader and more complete view of the Italian situation and further knowledge of some of the topics previously presented, the Italian

Ministry of Labour and Social Affairs promoted a second investigation in light of the results of the first survey, to support the CSR-SC project.

8.3.4 The Second Survey on CSR: Goal and Methodology

In June 2003 the Ministry of Labour and Social Affairs was pleased to accept the proposal of Unioncamere to carry out a second empirical study throughout Italy to add more depth to the results of the above-mentioned first survey and to build some theoretical models to illustrate the fundamental approaches to CSR carried out by Italian companies (Unioncamere and ISVI, 2004).

This survey, based on a sample of 3663 firms interviewed, represents the most extensive CSR study in Italy to date. It was conducted in July 2003 by means of telephone interviews (carried out with the CATI – Computer Aided Telephone Interviews – method). The sample was stratified taking into account three structural features: business size (1-19 employees, 20-49 employees, 50-249 employees, over 249 employees), economic macro-sector (according to the European NACE taxonomy) and geographical areas (11 macro-regions). So far, from a statistical point of view, it represents the whole range of Italian companies with at least one employee. According to these parameters, a systematic random sampling method was used to draw the final sample.

The questionnaire was prepared with the collaboration of experts from the Italian Ministry of Labour and Social Affairs and scholars from ISVI (the Italian Institute for Enterprise Values) and Bocconi University. It is divided into six parts, concerning:

- the degree of knowledge of CSR, explored by analyzing the familiarity of a number of tools (the Green Paper on CRS promoted by the European Commission; the code of conduct; environmental, social and sustainability reports; managerial standards like SA 8000, ISO 14001 and EMAS);
- relations with the community: donations, sponsorships, cause-related marketing, partnership with non-profit organizations, investments in social responsibility-related activities, and so on;
- relations with customers and suppliers: ethical sourcing, product environmental certification, and so on;

- measures and actions adopted – or in the process of adoption – in the health, safety and environmental sectors, going beyond compliance with legal requirements (for example, programs for reduction of energy consumption, development of alternative energy sources, reduction of water consumption, improvement of product recyclability, reduction of polluting emissions, noise reduction and waste treatment and disposal);
- measures to increase team spirit and motivation among employees: flexible hours, organized activities for spare time, internal communication, more training, and so on.

8.3.5 Main Result of the Survey

This survey must be considered unique both in terms of scale (3663 firms interviewed) and scope (the questionnaire explores several CSR dimensions). In this section we provide a brief description of the main findings of the study.

First of all, the research confirmed the hypothesis of a strong relationship between business size and companies' stance towards social responsibility. Middle-sized and large firms have a higher propensity for CSR than do small ones. On the other hand, whereas in very small and small-sized enterprises the commitment to CSR issues is limited, these organizations show some interest in managerial tools such as ISO 14001 environmental certification and EMAS registration as well as in guiding principles. Moreover, a large number of enterprises belonging to the middle-sized and large group are involved in donations and sponsorships on a regular basis. SMEs (mainly with 20-49 employees) are responsive to practices in favor of employees: flexible hours, meetings on a regular basis to present strategies and results achieved, training. Finally, around half of small and medium-sized enterprises require from their suppliers a quality certification of the product/service or adopt it directly.

A second relevant pattern that emerged in the first explorative study is confirmed in this survey: a variation in firms' attitude towards CSR between geographical areas. Even though of minor importance, this can be attributed to two variables: the sociocultural context and legal-institutional context. In the realm of socio-cultural features, a greater attentiveness to CSR was noticed where there is a concentration of services sector and the most advanced industry and where companies with foreign capital and those that are generally more open towards foreign markets are based. In the legal-institutional realm, in certain regions local authorities have launched policies and initiatives to increase the spread of different management systems related to some CSR features (that is, Tuscany and SA 8000 certification).

8.3.6 Models of 'Social' Orientation

One research goal was to understand models of social orientation. In light of the information gathered, five CSR clusters have been identified, which can be referred to Italian firms. In order to segment the five groups outlined below, a neural network approach, known as a Kohonen map, was used (Kohonen, 1984, 1991). This method, also called Self Organizing Maps (SOM), both reduces multidimensional data by producing a bi-dimensional space model, and displays similarities. With this technique firms that are positioned close together in the fuzzy map have similar characteristics, while firms positioned far away from each other are dissimilar (Unioncamere and ISVI, 2004).

Starting from the set of CSR indicators gathered and from the firms' structural features, the SOM method provided for the division of the Italian companies into five groups, as shown in the Figure below (Figure 8.1.). The horizontal axis shows intensity (adoption of socially responsible behaviors) and the vertical axis considers qualitative features related to corporate practices and behaviors.

Important considerations are derived from this research methodology, both in terms of clarifying the relation between firms' structural variables and CSR attitudes, and of understanding the company response to incentives that could increase the diffusion of mature CSR practices.

Cohesive companies

The area at the top right of Figure 8.1 includes mainly firms that consider CSR as a characteristic of their culture. In these enterprises attentiveness to stakeholder expectations – both internal and external – is not accidental and is carried out through a number of specific actions (for example, measures aiming at staff involvement and enhancement; design of socially friendly products; interventions in favor of the community; initiatives in favor of fair trade; staff involvement in forms of voluntary work during working hours; adoption of social reports and codes of conduct).

The behavior of cohesive companies as a whole feeds the wealth of intangible resources at their disposal – high level of staff motivation, reputation among social stakeholders, customer trust for the benefit of future qualitative and quantitative development. In this area of the map there are many large and medium-sized companies. Among macro-sectors, credit-insurance and services for people prevail, whereas the presence of building and construction companies is very limited. With regard to geographical areas, no major differences were noticed, even though greater penetration of Lombardy and the North-East, as well as Emilia-Romagna and Tuscany emerges.

Finally, cohesive companies seem indifferent to incentives to promote CSR culture or disseminate CSR practices since socially responsible strategies are part of their genetic inheritance.

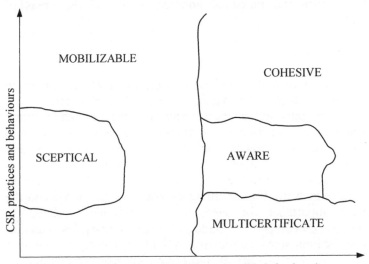

Source: adapted from Unioncamere, 2003

Figure 8.1 Behavior map for CSR in Italian companies

Multi-certificate companies

The nodes at the bottom right of Figure 8.1 represent the second area of special interest, in which many companies are found that require statements and certifications from their suppliers (ISO certifications, product quality certification, and certification of proper waste disposal and code of conduct). At the same time, these companies receive requests for certification from their customers. This second group is more interested in complying with procedures, also with a view to an intensive communication policy. Multi-certificate companies vary in sizes, but the majority are medium-large. With regard to macro-sectors, agroindustrial and manufacturing sectors comprise a significant part. There is also a high percentage of companies belonging to the transport macro-sector. This area attracts mostly companies with foreign or mixed (Italian and foreign) capital.

Moreover, these firms are alert to incentive policies that would speed up the direction already taken. In particular, facilitations could broaden the range of adopted tools and the areas of attention.

Aware companies

The area next to that of cohesive firms includes enterprises in which the exhaustive knowledge of typical CSR practices and tools is not activated as vigorously. On the one hand, these companies are less active in donations compared to cohesive ones and less oriented to openly include social responsibility in their development plans. On the other hand, the nature itself of this sector does not require the recourse to many CSR interventions because of both the limited direct exposure to the public and the reduced importance of environmental problems related to production processes. The area of aware companies includes mainly medium-sized enterprises, belonging mostly to the ICT macro-sector. For this group, incentive measures are of doubtful effect.

Companies that can be mobilized

These companies share a substantially passive position towards CSR matters. They are mainly very small and small enterprises that are usually unfamiliar with CSR topics and tools. This area, defined as low CSR intensity, includes enterprises which recognize that certain economic and relational motivations (cost reduction, business advantages, and relations with trade unions, public subsidies and facilities) may induce them to implement environmental protection programs. These companies are not at all suspicious of any form of CSR promotion; on the contrary, a boost from the external environment may encourage the social evolution of their conduct.

Finally, for this group of firms incentive is crucial to reducing their reticence to virtuous CSR behavior. Policies that disseminate information on CRS can make these issues more familiar, showing the economic effectiveness of socially responsible behavior and reducing the level of expertise and costs related to the implementation of CSR strategies.

Sceptical companies

The central area on the left of Figure 8.1 attracts very small and small enterprises not very familiar with CSR matters, which implement voluntary interventions in a limited way to meet stakeholder expectations and are suspicious of any action for the promotion of a social responsibility culture. Sceptical companies belong to all macro-sectors. By definition, these firms are sceptical about initiatives for the promotion of wider social responsibility. In this case, culture is the main barrier to the diffusion of CSR practices. Changing this culture would require a large amount of time.

NOTE

1. Cause Related Marketing (CRM) is defined as 'the public association of a for-profit company with a non-profit organization, intended to promote the company's product or service and to raise money for the non profit' (Kotler and Lee, 2005, p. 81). CRM can be considered as a promotional strategy that creates a link between social issues and the corporate strategic target and generates a mutually profitable outcome for the business and non-profit.

9. The Italian government proposal: the CSR-SC project

9.1 INTRODUCTION

This chapter presents a careful description of the government proposal on CSR, which represents the first organic and extensive policy developed in Italy on this topic by the public authority. As highlighted in the previous pages, several initiatives on corporate responsibility are ongoing in Italy, spontaneously promoted by local institutions and private parties (industrial associations, non-profit organizations and firms). However, while the European Commission was fostering a new global CSR framework, integrating different perspectives including sustainability, economic competitiveness, environmental protection and social cohesion, the central government in Italy, was operating with a fragmented agenda, without a coherent strategy on CSR.

In this setting, the Italian Ministry of Labour and Social Affairs in June 2002 launched the most significant institutional campaign on social responsibility ever promoted in Italy with the ambitious goal to disseminate a CSR culture and define a CSR standard based on a voluntary approach: the Corporate Social Responsibility-Social Commitment (CSR-SC) project. Since the beginning of the project, Bocconi University was involved by the Italian government as a scientific advisor and technical partner to support the ministry team. The main outcome of this collaboration is the proposal described here, officially presented during the Italian EU Presidency conference on CSR, held in Venice on 14 November 2003. In the following pages we describe the main steps of the CSR-SC project.

9.2 CSR-SC PROJECT: OVERVIEW AND GOALS

From the European strategy on CSR it is possible to infer that being socially responsible means going beyond compliance with regulations in force, 'investing more into human capital, the environment and the relations with stakeholders' (CEC, 2001d).

Starting from these two key principles, in 2002 the Ministry of Labour and Social Affairs launched an innovative project on CSR to pursue some general goals, including:

- promoting a CSR culture and best practices exchange among businesses through communication, dissemination of information, and training;
- guaranteeing citizens and consumers that reporting and communications on corporate social commitment by firms is true and not misleading;
- defining a simple and modular standard – based on a list of key performance indicators – that firms can adopt on a voluntary basis in order to identify socially responsible behavior;
- supporting companies, especially SMEs, in developing CSR strategies and policies;
- fostering experience exchanges among countries in order to identify and trade the best practices at the international level.

Furthermore, specific attention was dedicated to SMEs, in that these firms represent the large majority of the population of Italian companies, and wield a fundamental impact both on the economic and occupational sectors.

Starting from these premises, in order to develop a national standard consistent with the European Union's position on CSR and deeply rooted in the commission documents, a research agenda was established with the scientific advice of Bocconi University. The working methodology that followed was divided into three main phases, characterized by specific research activities (see Figure 9.1).

The first step was dedicated to an in-depth analysis of literature on CSR. The second phase consisted of a detailed and extended benchmark study of the main Italian, European and international standards and initiatives on CSR. The third part of the research project provided a first overview of firms' CSR awareness and behavior through an empirical survey, as described in chapter 8.

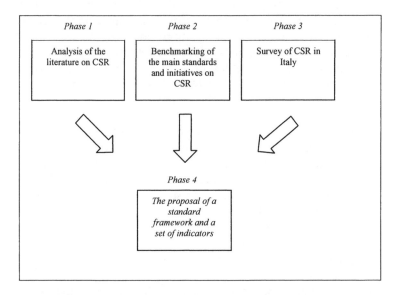

Figure 9.1 CSR-SC project: methodology and scientific approach

On the basis of these three research activities, a first proposal for a CSR-SC standard was presented on 13 December 2002 (Perrini et al, 2002). This first draft was improved during the following months through a stakeholder engagement process, which involved academics from other Italian universities, members of NGOs and entrepreneurial associations and experts from consulting companies and certification bodies.

During the Third European Conference on Corporate Social Responsibility held in Venice on 14 November 2003 and after eighteen months of work, the Ministry of Welfare proposed a two-level standard framework based on Bocconi University research activity, a pilot testing phase and an articulated debate with different stakeholders.

According to the original scheme, a two-level standard framework has been designed to fulfill company needs and the expectations of industrial associations, and to reconcile criticism with different political positions. Common elements of the CSR-SC project are listed below:

- voluntary approach to CSR practices;
- corporate self-assessment;
- no traditional certification mechanisms;
- a set of performance indicators, to support and orient firms.

The first stage of the project (CSR Level) is based on a broad set of performance indicators and on a system of pre-defined guidelines called a Social Statement. The Social Statement allows firms to report on their CSR practices and support them in the self-assessment of their own social performance. The main steps of this level follow:

- a company decides, on a voluntary basis, to participate in the CSR-SC project and draw up the Social Statement according to the set of indicators;
- the Social Statement is based on a specific set of performance indicators, covering a wide range of CSR issues organized according to a stakeholder framework (human resources, shareholders, client, supplier, community, and so on) and covering the economic, social and environmental dimensions according to the Triple Bottom Line model (Elkington, 1997).
- an agency, proposed by the Ministry of Welfare, is expected to be responsible for the final evaluation of Social Statements sent by participating firms;
- a comprehensive database will collect and make available the relevant information on the initiative.

The second stage of the project (SC Level) is based on a proactive role among firms in supporting the welfare policies promoted by the government and local authorities. If a company voluntarily decides to go beyond the CSR Level (presentation of the Social Statement and review carried out by the independent agency), it participates, through its own resources, in the social intervention projects proposed by policy makers financing the Social-Commitment Fund. The underlying principle is to integrate private and public resources according to a modern welfare mix approach and the subsidiary principle.

So far, the goal of the CSR-SC system is to promote socially responsible behavior among firms. In order to guarantee standardization in data presentation and comparable results from different enterprises, the Social Statement, based on a set of performance indicators, will serve as an optimal point of reference in the reporting activity. The set of indicators, as will be fully described below, is designed according to a flexible and modular approach in order to respond to the specific needs of the firms (size, industrial sector, and so on).

To conclude, on the one hand, the CSR-SC standard is intended as a voluntary tool, conceived first of all to lead enterprises towards the improvement of their social behaviors, thus favoring a process of standardization of methods and procedures for assessing, measuring and communicating CSR performances. In this sense, the Social Statement is a document through which enterprises inform the stakeholders about their own social, environmental and sustainability performances. On the other hand, through the circulation of the Social Statement, the Ministry of Labour and Social Affairs aims to increase the degree of enterprises' awareness of social, environmental and sustainability issues, by promoting the spread of a culture of responsibility within the industrial system.

Another goal of the government is to respond to the growing number of requests for information and transparency concerning the CSR and sustainability reporting activities of firms. The definition of a tool, based on a clear and shared reporting model, is intended to guarantee increased credibility of corporate communications, to safeguard consumers and benefit citizens.

There is also a need to adjust the standard to the unique characteristics and aspects of the European orientation toward CSR (see previous chapters), where enterprises have different approaches to subjects in terms of:

- structural characteristics of the national economic and industrial system (for instance, the size of enterprises and the prevailing business model);
- distinctive cultural characteristics of governance and entrepreneurial values;
- influence and control of institutions;
- pressures of demand and, more generally, of markets;
- pressures of public opinion and society in general (mass media, NGOs, local community, and so on);
- training and information activities carried out by trade and professional associations.

Within this framework, the CSR-SC project intends to devote particular attention to SMEs, which represent the fundamental component of the Italian industrial system. Therefore, the CSR-SC project represents an attempt to prepare a tool adaptable to the resources and the needs of various subjects, by offering at the same time new and stimulating management and competitive opportunities.

9.3 CSR-SC PROJECT: GOVERNANCE STRUCTURE AND KEY ELEMENTS

The CSR-SC project structure is based on the actions of three main subjects, with specific roles and responsibilities: firms, the Ministry of Labour and Social Affairs and the CSR Forum. The key elements of the proposal are:

- the Social Statement and the set of indicators;
- the assessment procedure of the Social Statement;
- the benefit-granting system;
- the mechanisms of moral suasion.

A simplified scheme of the architecture of the CSR-SC project is shown in Figure 9.2 below.

9.3.1 Firms

Firms are the driving engine of the system. Their voluntary participation in the CSR-SC project is based on a two-step process: first, the adoption of the Social Statement, consistently with the proposed standard and, second, submission to the CSR Forum of the documents requested for the assessment procedure. The concept of CSR embraced by the proposal, following the European directives, means going beyond the simple fulfillment of legal expectations.

In order to promote participation in the CSR-SC Project, specific guidelines were defined to help companies carrying out their self-assessment procedures and drawing up the Social Statement.

The goal of these guidelines is to support entrepreneurs and managers implementing the system of social performance indicators, to orient decision-making and strategic processes towards CSR and make their activities of communication and information to third parties consistent.

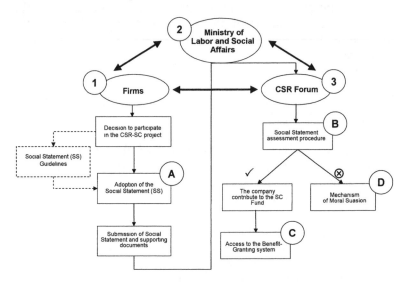

Figure 9.2 CSR-SC project: system structure

Always on a voluntary basis, companies that progress to CSR may decide to fund specific social activities by allocating their financial resources to the above-mentioned SC Fund.

Each element of the Figure 9.2 is explained in the following paragraphs.

9.3.2 The Ministry of Labor and Social Affairs

The first goal of the Ministry of Labor and Social Affairs is to promote the CSR culture among firms and society, by training and communicating. Moreover, in light of the above, the ministry supervises the implementation of the project both at the CSR and CS levels. So far, within governmental priorities, the Ministry of Labor and Social Affairs coordinates the process of identifying the areas of social intervention to be voluntarily funded by corporate resources.

A three-step process based on the Italian policy model is envisaged:

- the Joint Conference (dealing with socio-economic matters and priorities shared by regions, provinces and municipalities) and NGOs are entrusted with the definition of national priorities;
- priorities are transposed in the National Action Plan annually;
- stakeholders – NGOs included – and firms play a leading role in defining action policies. Furthermore, these non-profit organizations submit projects that may be listed among priorities.

Moreover, the roles and responsibilities of the Ministry of Labor and Social Affairs are:

- to promote the establishment of the CSR Forum;
- to select the subjects in charge of the social projects;
- to define the benefit-granting system for those companies that agree to the CSR-SC scheme and decide how to allocate funds (for example, tax incentives);
- to define moral suasion interventions;
- to develop the administrative activity supporting the system.

9.3.3 The CSR Forum

The CSR-SC project introduced into our institutional system a new agency called the CSR Forum. Its job is to interact with the Ministry of Labor and Social Affairs on CSR policies and actions; its goal is to preside over the assessment processes relevant to the Social Statement. The roles and responsibilities of the CSR Forum are:

- to analyze and evaluate the Social Statements (assessment procedure);
- on-site assessment of sample companies participating in the CSR-SC Project;
- to monitor those companies that gained access to the benefit-awarding system;
- to participate in other complementary activities (for example, to discuss strategic issues, mainstream CSR culture, and so on).

Furthermore, the CSR Forum identifies those specific projects that can be funded by the SC Funds in accord with the national priorities that were previously examined.

9.3.4 The Social Statement

The Social Statement (SS) is the key element of the CSR-SC system. Based on a voluntary approach, this tool is mainly conceived to help companies to assess and report their CSR actions and results. The Social Statement is based on a set of performance indicators and organized according to a stakeholder approach. The Social Statement is not intended to replace 'established' public and private CSR initiatives or instruments with an already-defined infrastructure, membership system and widely accepted model; it rather supplements these projects. Furthermore, the CSR-SC proposal is conceived to enhance these tools and practices whose goal is increased transparency for stakeholders and citizens.

As the definition of CSR becomes more refined and applies to a larger number of activities and subjects, a standardization process is simultaneously needed. It is known that tools recognized at the international level (among which are SA 8000, ISO 14001, EMAS, and so on) cover narrow and specific CSR aspects and cannot be considered exhaustive for such a broad issue, involving at the same time a high number of stakeholders. Other instruments like the Global Reporting Initiative (GRI) or AA1000 cover a broader range of issues, but are mainly conceived for the use of large multinational companies, and are difficult to adapt to the resources of a small or medium-size firm. The CSR-SC proposal was conceived to consider a broader range of CSR issues and the specific needs of SMEs. Because of its modularity and flexibility, the Social Statement can integrate other tools already in use. In this regard, for instance, if an enterprise already has SA 8000 certification, it will automatically comply with Social Statement indicators that overlap with SA 8000.

A broader explanation of the specific structure of the Social Statement, namely of its dimensions and social performance indicators, will be given in the next paragraph.

9.3.5 The Assessment Procedure

The purpose of the assessment procedure is to validate the document submitted by a company and the performances achieved in the CSR field. It is based on an external evaluation process by the CSR Forum and on on-site auditing activities of the firms that decide to participate in the CSR-SC Project (see Figure 9.3).

The first step of the assessment process is an internal evaluation, carried out by the CSR Forum, based on the collection of comments, remarks and eventually complaints of social partners and stakeholders in general, which will be examined by this forum (a) as well.

Then the results of the evaluation are announced and, in case of positive response, the company is listed in a special database (b). If the assessment is negative, the enrollment procedure is interrupted and further explanation by the company is required (c).

The purpose of this step is not to penalize those companies that did not meet the evaluation standards of the Social Statement, but rather to start the close examination necessary to improve the CSR reporting and performance measuring processes.

Independent third parties (d) will carry out some on-site post-assessment of sample companies randomly selected. This procedure is designed to guarantee both the firm's commitment to CSR and the quality of the results achieved and submitted through the Social Statement. This evidence-based process further validates the company's activity and increases the stakeholders' trust.

As to the listing of a company in the data-base, the decision can be based on the knowledge and experience acquired at the international level as to other registration/certification practices. Therefore, a three-year period is suggested, with the goal of annually updating the indicators.

If the on-site audits conclude that a company is not complying with the Social Statement requirements and that the problems cannot be immediately solved, moral suasion procedures (f) are suggested.

If the company decides to go beyond the CSR level, by contributing to the SC fund (e) (SC level), then some on-site audits of sample companies (g) are carried out. In the event of non-compliance, the benefits earned by the company for contributing to the SC fund are forfeited and moral suasion is attempted.

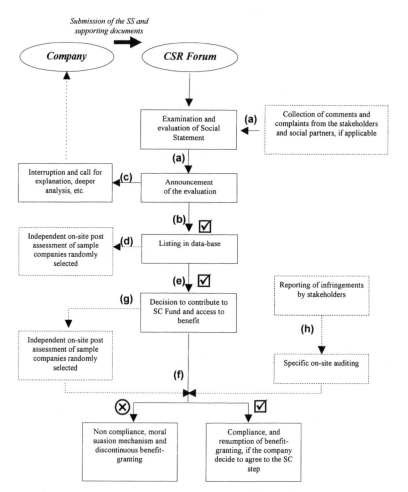

Figure 9.3 CSR-SC project: assessment procedure

The Social Statement procedure permits qualified and accredited stakeholders to report possible infringements of CSR principles. In this case, ad-hoc on-site auditing processes (h) will be activated, to determine whether benefits will continue and/or moral suasion (f) is necessary.

9.3.6 Benefit-Granting System

The CSR-SC scheme offers benefits and incentives to promote its standards and spread the CSR culture among firms.

Firstly, the benefit-granting system envisages the possibility to benefit from tax incentives. They could be structured according to the level of participation in the CSR-SC Project. Specific terms have to be defined in the future. Particularly, as far as allocations to the SC Funds are concerned, the incentives will aim at rewarding those financings that represent a further effort with regard to any other CSR commitments. Indeed, this project is designed to encourage the continuation and the increase of CSR-related actions that companies have already carried out voluntarily.

Secondly, it envisions the promotion of CSR through targeted campaigns supported by the government and high media visibility.

Further, additional incentives may include social security (retirement indemnity allocated to pension funds, including ethical funds); financial rewards (creation of ethical investment funds following the CSR-SC model – an interesting example is the UK's version of this); and streamlining administrative procedures (to be defined).

9.3.7 Mechanisms of Moral Suasion

To protect citizens and consumers and other stakeholder categories, as well as the firms that aim to enhance their CSR-related commitment, cooperative brainstorming with the Ministry of Labour and Social Affairs led to the suggested solution of moral suasion mechanisms. The ultimate goal is to prevent opportunistic, proprietary and non-transparent behaviors by companies.

Comparative analysis with other public policy measures has led to the proposal of two main mechanisms:

- market mechanisms, that is, listing in a data-base the companies that joined the government project, and the activation of procedures to publicly expose infractions;
- incentive-related mechanisms, for example, repealing tax benefits and holding on to monies allocated by companies to the SC Fund.

In conclusion, the governance structure for the CSR-SC standard framework described above is at the proposal stage, and several ideas require further analysis and discussion. For example, the reform of the pension funds and the introduction of new taxation mechanisms/incentives concern the policies of both the Ministry of Economy and Finance and the Ministry of Labour and Social Affairs. So far, key elements of the governance structure, including moral suasion mechanisms and benefit-granting, must cohere with other political measures relevant to other ministries or departments. Though not within the scope of the present project proposal, the ultimate project policies are subject to revision in that they must be integrated with other national policies.

Finally, concerning the assessment procedure suggested for the CSR-SC standard framework, although it still needs some 'fine tuning' and a set of specific procedures and guidelines must be established to regulate various pathways, we explore herein a 'third way' between the classical accountability and reporting frameworks. In fact, the verification and certification processes, normally based on market mechanisms through auditing/consulting companies or on public systems through institutional controls, are replaced with a procedure whereby accredited stakeholders, through a new body called the CSR Forum, play a central role in assessing the credibility of firms' CSR behavior.

9.4 THE SOCIAL STATEMENT

As outlined above, the Social Statement is the key element of the CSR-SC proposal. It is a voluntary tool mainly conceived to help firms reporting their CSR actions and performance, by standardizing the method of information collection and presentation and by enhancing the comparison and evaluation of outcomes. Moreover, the Social Statement is grounded in the two definitions of CSR given by the European Commission in the Green Paper published in 2001 (CEC, 2001d):

- 'a concept whereby companies integrate social and environmental concerns in their business operations and in their interaction with their stakeholders on a voluntary basis'.

- 'being "socially responsible" means not only fulfilling legal expectations, but also going beyond compliance and investing more into human capital, the environment and relations with stakeholders'.

The Social Statement is based on a suitable set of CSR performance indicators. Any process carried out by any organization needs effective and efficient measurement mechanisms and tools. The measurement activity helps decision-makers in defining strategic and tactical objectives, allows for monitoring the efforts made to reach these goals, allows evaluation of the performances obtained and comparison of these performances in time and space. Within this framework, indicators are measures that, through a process of simplification, work to identify and/or describe complex phenomena by balancing two diverging needs: scientific accuracy and the ability to synthesize.

In the CSR-SC Project, the specific goal of the set of indicators is to monitor the commitment to CSR and the activities carried out in its name by enterprises through the support of decision-making and implementing processes.

Toward this end, starting from the first proposal presented at Bocconi University on 13 December 2002, through a series of meetings with the major stakeholders and after a pilot testing phase, a series of indicators were identified and selected.

In the final document, each indicator is organized in a framework divided into three levels, where a stakeholder-oriented approach was preferred to the Triple Bottom Line or to other models. This three-level framework was more familiar and comprehensible to the SMEs – the main target of the CSR-SC project. A structure based on stakeholder categories focuses on the relationships and the related performance that companies, and especially SMEs, develop through their activities and behavior. In particular, as previously mentioned, in the Italian context networks between companies and local stakeholders (community, environment, financial partners, trade unions, and so on) directly affect the overall corporate performance.

Therefore, the set of indicators is divided into:

- *categories*, groups of stakeholders to whom specific clusters of indicators are addressed;

- *aspects*, thematic areas monitored by groups of performance indicators, within a designated category of stakeholders;
- *indicators*, qualitative and quantitative measures that provide information concerning a specific issue. They can be used to control and illustrate the performance of an organization.

The eight categories of indicators are organized as follows:

1. Human Resources;
2. Shareholders/Members and Financial Community;
3. Customers;
4. Suppliers;
5. Financial partners;
6. State, Local Authorities and Public Administration;
7. Community;
8. Environment.

Indicators are organized into qualitative (for instance, in case a description of CSR initiatives carried out by the company is requested) or quantitative categories (in those cases in which the information requested must be expressed in numerical form, or as a percentage, ratio, quotient, or as economic or financial data, and so on).

Moreover, the set of indicators is divided into two main typologies:

- *Common indicators* (C), which must be used by all the enterprises in carrying out the Social Statement (from SMEs to large enterprises);
- *Additional indicators* (A), which can be implemented in the case of large enterprises (with at least 50 employees) on the basis of specific criteria, by supporting and integrating common indicators.

Finally, before the final set was published, a suitable analysis was made of each indicator through stakeholders' meetings and a pilot test initiative. The following elements were analyzed and discussed:

- relevance with reference to the notion of CSR;
- comprehensibility for enterprises;

- availability of information functional to indicator determination (for instance, available documentation);
- collection and measurement procedures;
- enforceability with reference to the different types of enterprises.

The field research and experiment were carried out on twenty-four firms, representative of the Italian population, chosen on the basis of size, sector of activity, geographical location and legal status. All the enterprises joined the initiative voluntarily. So far, the pilot test, which studied the applicability of indicators to different corporate realities, has progressed to the following measured proposal:

- Small-sized companies – with less than 50 employees (see the Recommendation of the EC Commission, 06/05/2003, concerning the definition of micro, small and medium-sized enterprises) intending to agree to the project, shall apply the set of common indicators (C) to the drawing up of the Social Statement;
- Medium-sized companies (between 50 and 250 employees) and big companies (more than 250 employees) shall apply common indicators (C) and specific clusters of additional indicators (A) that are adequately selected and still to be defined;
- Listed companies of any size shall use the complete set of common indicators (C) and additional indicators (A) while drawing up the Social Statement.

As Table 9.1 shows, the CSR-SC proposal is designed to adapt to the different needs and availability of resources that characterize SMEs and big firms. On the other hand, it is clear that those companies that are already able to use a wide number of indicators, out of the set required to participate in the project, can do so by using the other suggested performance measurements and adapting them to their specific size and organizational characteristics.

Finally, the Social Statement is intended as an opportunity to lead enterprises towards excellence in the procedures of social accounting, thus favoring the continuous improvement of corporate performances in this field. In this sense, if any of the additional indicators included were considered as not applicable to the company due to factors related to its structural and/or organizational characteristics (size, trade sector, legal status and corporate structure, complexity of collection and/or measurement of information requested), the reasons for exclusion shall be duly specified and grounded by the company management while drawing the standard.

Finally, the evaluation and reporting system represented by the indicators of the Social Statement is not intended to replace public and/or private acknowledged CSR initiatives, but it must rather be considered as an integration of these projects. The suggested approach is meant to enhance these experiences, with the final objective of allowing a higher transparency and clarity of information to stakeholders.

Table 9.1 Set of indicators and typology of company: a first proposal

	Less than 50 employees	Between 50 and 250 employees	More than 250 employees
Not listed	*Common Indicators* (C)	*Common indicators* (C) and clusters of additional indicators to be defined (A)	*Common indicators* (C) and clusters of additional indicators to be defined (A)
Listed	The complete set of common indicators (C) and all additional indicators (A)		

The complete set of indicators for drawing up the Social Statement follows (see Table 9.2). The Appendix presents a detailed explanation of each of the Social Statement's indicators.

9.5 FURTHER STEPS

As emphasized earlier, through the CSR-SC Project, the Italian Minister of Labour and Social Affairs aims to involve firms in the dissemination of socially responsible behaviors and the development of CSR actions, according to the size, industrial sector, corporate structure, organization model and CSR experience of companies.

Table 9.2. CSR-SC project: complete list of indicators

Categories, aspects and indicators	C/A	X	Y
1. **Human Resources**			
1.1. *Staff composition*			
1.1.1. Category	A		■
1.1.2. Age	A		■
1.1.3. Seniority in grade	A		■
1.1.4. Geographic origin	A		■
1.1.5. Nationality	A		■
1.1.6. Contract type	A		■
1.1.7. Level of education	A		■
1.2. *Turnover*			
1.2.1. Employment policies	A	■	
1.2.2. Permanent employees and non-permanent employees	A		■
1.2.3. Employment termination (by kind of contract)	A		■
1.3. *Equal opportunity*			
1.3.1. Gender ratio (managerial staff and executives)	A		■
1.3.2. Salary by gender (also by category and seniority in grade)	A		■
1.3.3. Policy for people with disabilities and minorities in general	C	■	■
1.4. *Training*			
1.4.1. Training projects (by kind)	A	■	
1.4.2. Training hours by category (net of contractual or legal training hours)	C		■
1.4.3. Internships	A		■
1.5. *Working hours by category*	A		■
1.6. *Schemes of wages*			
1.6.1. Average gross wages	A		■
1.6.2. Career paths	A	■	■
1.6.3. Incentive systems	A	■	■
1.7. *Absence from work*			
1.7.1. Days of absence	A		■
1.7.2. Causes	A	■	
1.8. *Employee benefits*	C	■	■
1.9. *Industrial relations*			
1.9.1. Compliance with the rights of free association and collective bargaining	A	■	■
1.9.2. Percentage of trade union members among employees	A		■
1.9.3. Other considerations (hours of strike, participation in the company's government, and so on)	A	■	■

C = Common indicators; A = Additional indicators
X = Qualitative indicators; Y = Quantitative indicators

Categories, aspects and indicators		C/A	X	Y
1.10.	*In-house communications*	A	■	
1.11.	*Occupational health and safety*			
1.11.1.	Injuries and diseases	C	■	■
1.11.2.	Projects	A	■	
1.12.	*Employee satisfaction*			
1.12.1.	In-house customer satisfaction surveys	A	■	■
1.12.2.	Projects	A	■	
1.13.	*Protection of workers' rights*	C	■	
1.13.1.	Child labor	A	■	■
1.13.2.	Forced labor	A	■	
1.14.	*Disciplinary measures and litigation*	A		■
2.	**Shareholders/Members and Financial Community**			
2.1.	*Capital stock formation*			
2.1.1.	Number of shareholders by share type	A		■
2.1.2.	Segmentation of shareholders by category	A	■	■
2.2.	*Shareholders'/Members' remuneration (share indicators and ratios)*			
2.2.1.	Earning per share	A		■
2.2.2.	Dividends	A		■
2.2.3.	Price/earning per share	A		■
2.2.4.	Others (e.g., allowance, contributions to mutual funds)	A	■	■
2.3.	*Stock price fluctuation*	A		■
2.4.	*Rating*	A	■	■
2.5.	*Shareholders' participation in the government and protection of minorities*	A		
2.5.1.	Existence of independent directors inside the Board of Directors	A	■	■
2.5.2.	Existence of minority shareholders inside the Board of Directors	A	■	■
2.5.3.	Occurrence of Board of Directors' meetings	A	■	■
2.5.4.	Others (e.g., compliance with self-regulatory measures)	A	■	
2.6.	*Benefits and services for shareholders*	A	■	
2.7.	*Investor relations*			
2.7.1	Communication and reporting activities	C	■	
2.7.2.	Institutional presentations and documents	A	■	
2.7.3.	Road show	A	■	■
2.7.4.	One-to-one meetings	A	■	■
2.7.5.	Communications on the Internet	A	■	■
2.7.6.	Others	A	■	■

C = Common indicators; **A** = Additional indicators
X = Qualitative indicators; **Y** = Quantitative indicators

Categories, aspects and indicators	C/A	X	Y
3. **Customers**			
3.1. *General characteristics*			
3.1.1 Division of customers by category	A	■	■
3.1.2. Division of customers by kind of offer	A	■	■
3.2. *Market development*			
3.2.1. New customers	A	■	■
3.2.2. New products/services	A	■	■
3.3. *Customer satisfaction and customer loyalty*			
3.3.1. Customer-satisfaction-oriented initiatives (research, measurement, usability research, call centre and queries, and so on)	A	■	■
3.3.2. Customer loyalty initiatives	A	■	■
3.4. *Product/service information and labeling (safety, Life Cycle Assessment, voluntary initiatives)*	C	■	■
3.5. *Ethical and environmentally friendly products and services (public utility)*	A	■	■
3.6. *Promotional policies (adherence to code of conduct)*	A	■	■
3.7. *Privacy*	A	■	■
4. **Suppliers**			
4.1. *Supplier management policy*	C	■	■
4.1.1. Division of suppliers by category	A	■	■
4.1.2. Supplier selection	A	■	■
4.1.3. Communication, awareness creation and information	A	■	■
4.2. Contractual terms	C	■	■
5. **Financial partners**			
5.1. *Relations with banks*	A	■	
5.2. *Relations with insurance companies*	A	■	
5.3. *Relations with financial institutions (e.g., leasing companies)*	A	■	
6. **State, Local Authorities and Public Administration**			
6.1. *Taxes and duties*			
6.2. *Relations with local authorities*			
6.3. *Codes of conduct and rules for compliance with laws*			
6.3.1. Codes of conduct and rules for compliance with laws and internal auditing systems			
6.3.2 *Conformity verification and inspections*			
6.4 *Contributions, benefits or easy-term financing*			

C = Common indicators; **A** = Additional indicators

X = Qualitative indicators; **Y** = Quantitative indicators

7.	**Community**			
7.1.	*Corporate giving*	C	■	■
7.2.	*Direct contributions in the fields of action*			
7.2.1.	Education and training	C	■	■
7.2.2.	Culture	C	■	■
7.2.3.	Sport	C	■	■
7.2.4.	Research and innovation	C	■	■
7.2.5.	Social solidarity (including international solidarity too)	C	■	■
7.2.6.	Other (volunteering, community daycare, and so on)	C	■	■
7.3.	*Communications and engagement of the community (stakeholder engagement)*	C	■	
7.4.	*Relations with the media*	A	■	■
7.5.	*Virtual community*			
7.5.1.	Contacts (characteristics and analysis)	A	■	■
7.5.2.	Security	A	■	
7.5.3.	Relation management systems	A	■	■
7.6.	*Corruption prevention*	C	■	
8.	**Environment**			
8.1.	*Energy and materials consumption, emissions*	C	■	■
8.1.1.	Energy consumption	A	■	■
8.1.2.	Water consumption	A	■	■
8.1.3.	Raw materials, maintenance, repair and operations (MRO) and packaging	A	■	■
8.1.4.	Athmospheric emissions	A	■	■
8.1.5.	Water emission	A	■	■
8.1.6.	Waste management	A	■	■
8.2.	*Environmental strategy and community relations*	A	■	■

C = Common indicators; **A** = Additional indicators
X = Qualitative indicators; **Y** = Quantitative indicators

If, indeed, it is true that many considerations prove the increasing attention paid to social and environmental issues by large corporations, it is also true that European and Italian studies indicate less awareness of CSR among SMEs.

In particular, some surveys carried out in Italy (see chapter 8) also show that among SMEs, the CSR-related activities are not organized according to a formal strategy, are not systematic and are not disseminated with adequate tools, thus remaining sunk and invisible.

In light of the above, the proposal for a simple, flexible and modular standard is based on a set of CSR performance indicators that have been carefully identified and selected. Its goal is to promote a wide dissemination of the Social Statement in the business community, mobilizing firms towards CSR-committed initiatives.

Within this framework, the policy maker especially intends to involve SMEs, by highlighting already-existing virtuous behaviors on the one hand and promoting the adoption of a homogenous reporting model, on the other, to support the internal processes of performance measurements and communications to external stakeholders.

The proposal presented in Venice during the Italian EU Presidency conference on CSR, on 14 November 2003, ended the first part of the CSR-SC project. A considerable amount of political, technical and administrative elements, which included (1) the CSR Forum internal governance role, organizational structure and mechanisms, (2) the role of the Ministry of Labour and Social Affairs, (3) the definition of the procedures required to assess the Social Statement, (4) the incentive-granting system and (5) moral suasion mechanisms had to be analyzed and reviewed further. Moreover, specific improvement of the set of indicators proposed above were needed in order to better adapt the information requirements to the specific financial, size and industry characteristics of the firms interested in the project.

So far, in subsequent years a broad number of initiatives have been carried out by the Ministry of Labour and Social Affairs in order to implement the CSR-SC proposal, always with Bocconi University scholars advising. First of all, due to a general lack of consensus among social parties and stakeholders, the Social Commitment level of the project has been 'frozen' and not yet implemented. According to the authors, a misunderstanding of the project's goals, mainly related to politics and specific interests, stimulated the controversy over this part of the standard. However, the purpose of the SC level was to facilitate partnership among businesses, public authorities and NGOs, whose purpose in turn was to address the most important national priorities in the field of welfare policies (e.g., protection and improvement of working conditions, assistance to aged and disabled people, and so on).

With regard to the promotion of CSR awareness, in the last two years the Ministry of Welfare and Social Affairs organized some public campaigns. Among these initiatives was a communication campaign launched in 2004-2005 through TV and newspapers with the goal of promoting the concept of CSR and its meaning among citizens. Furthermore, Italian public institutions launched several award initiatives to involve firms in the Social Statement implementation mechanism (e.g., the National Award for CSR, City of Rovigo – December 2005 and Annual Unioncamere Award for Social Responsibility). Finally, on 14 July 2005, Ferrari hosted the event 'CSR in pole position' in Maranello. During this conference thirty Italian best practices were presented to increase CSR awareness among firms and to open dialogues with stakeholders.

In order to promote the proliferation of CSR practices and behavior, several public-private partnership agreements were signed between the ministry and other business-based institutions. Among them: Assolombarda, the association of firms operating in Lombardia; Unioncamere; Confapi, the National Association of Small and Medium-sized Enterprises; Federambiente, the National Association of Public Utilities and companies whose concern is the environment.

With regard to CSR level, probably the most important initiative has been the establishment of the Italian CSR Multi-Stakeholder Forum. This new organization, previewed in the CSR-SC proposal, drew inspiration from the European Multi-Stakeholder Forum in which social partners (companies, trade unions), the government and non-profit organizations are represented.

The Italian CSR Multi-Stakeholder Forum is composed of fifty stakeholders, representing national-level employers, trade unions, institutions, civil society, under the leadership of the Minister of Labour and Social Affairs. The forum has directed its activity toward two kinds of goals:

- high-level meetings to evaluate and discuss strategic objectives and analyze results;
- four roundtables with specific targets: mainstreaming CSR culture among firms and establishing best practices, mainstreaming CSR among SMEs, promoting transparency and assessing CSR practices; and analyzing the relationship between CSR and sustainable development, especially from the environmental standpoint.

Another critical step towards the implementation of the CSR-SC proposal is the partnership established with Unioncamere, which is very concerned with the promotion of CSR among firms operating in Italy. Under its leadership, regional and provincial Chambers of Commerce started to activate CSR front offices with the goal of mainstreaming the CSR culture among firms, spreading best practices and providing specific consulting services. Moreover, Unioncamere, through its territorial network, might become the supporting structure to collect Social Statements and monitor companies' activities.

To conclude, the last noteworthy initiative is the establishment, according to the Finance Act 2005 (Art. 1 paragraph 160 of the Law 30 December 2004, n.311), of the Foundation for Corporate Social Responsibility 'Italian Centre for Social Responsibility (I-CSR)'. This organization, funded by the Ministry of Labour and Social Affairs, Bocconi University, INAIL (the Italian Workers' Compensation Authority) and Unioncamere, intends to spread the knowledge of CSR and develop scientific research with specific attention to the needs of the national economy, based mainly on SMEs.

10. The future of CSR in Europe

On 22 March 2006 the European Commission published a new communication entitled 'Implementing the Partnership for Growth and Jobs: Making Europe a Pole of Excellence on Corporate Social Responsibility'. In this document the Commission underlines the strong relationship between corporate social responsibility (henceforth CSR), globalization, competitiveness and sustainability (CEC, 2006, p. 1):

> The Commission is committed to promoting the competitiveness of the European economy in the context of the relaunched Lisbon Partnership for Growth and Jobs. In turn it calls on the European business community to publicly demonstrate its commitment to sustainable development, economic growth and more and better jobs, and to step up its commitment to CSR, including cooperation with other stakeholders.

According to the Commission, sustainable growth and more and better jobs are the two main related challenges the European Union must face in a context of global competition and ageing population to safeguard the European model of society, based on equal opportunities, high quality of life, social inclusion and a healthy environment. In this perspective (CEC, 2006, p. 8):

> CSR can contribute to sustainable development, while enhancing Europe's innovative potential and competitiveness, thereby also contributing to employability and job creation. Further promoting CSR is central to the new partnership for 'growth and jobs' as well as for implementing sustainable development objectives.

Therefore, this communication is the last step of a process begun in February 2005 when the Commission fostered a new start for the Lisbon Agenda by launching a Partnership for Growth and

Jobs and continued in December 2005 by revising the Sustainable Development Strategy (CEC, 2005).

The communication confirms that CSR is fundamentally about voluntary business behavior: an approach entailing additional obligations and administrative burdens for companies is considered counter-productive and contrary to the principles of better regulation.

Thus, the Commission acknowledges that enterprises are the primary actors in CSR, supports a closer collaboration with European business and announces backing for a European Alliance for CSR. This is an open, voluntary alliance of European enterprises, which share the same ambition: to make Europe a pole of excellence on CSR. The Alliance is a political umbrella for new or existing initiatives carried out by large and small- and medium-sized companies, and their stakeholders. It is not a legal instrument and it is not to be signed by firms, the Commission or public authorities. The crucial concept underlying this initiative is partnership. So, the Alliance is intended as a vehicle for mobilizing the resources and capacities of European companies and their stakeholders to promote CSR.

In line with the final results of the European Multi Stakeholder Forum on Corporate Social Responsibility (2004), activities of the Alliance cover the following three areas:

- raising awareness and improving knowledge on CSR and reporting on its achievements;
- helping to mainstream and develop open coalitions of cooperation;
- ensuring an enabling environment for CSR.

The partners of the Alliance (32 European enterprises and 26 associations on 22 March 2006) identified some priority areas for action (CEC, 2006, p. 11):

- fostering innovation and entrepreneurship in sustainable technologies, products and services which address societal needs;
- helping SMEs to flourish and grow;
- assisting enterprises to integrate social and environmental considerations in their business operations, especially those in the supply chain;

- improving and developing skills for employability;
- better responding to diversity and the challenge of equal opportunities, taking into account the demographic changes alongside the rapid aging of the European population;
- improving working conditions, also in cooperation with the supply chain;
- innovating in the environment field with a special focus on integrating eco-efficiency and energy savings in the product and service creation process;
- enhancing pro-active dialogue and engagement with all relevant stakeholders;
- further addressing the transparency and communication challenge to make the nonfinancial performance of companies and organizations more understandable for all stakeholders and better integrated with their financial performance;
- operating outside the borders of the EU in a socially and environmentally responsible way as companies do inside the EU.

To improve the transparency, visibility and credibility of CSR practices, the Commission encourages enterprises that support the Alliance to be accountable and make CSR information available to all stakeholders. In particular, large companies should try to present CSR strategies, initiatives and their results or best practices in a way that is easily accessible to the public. This attention paid by the Commission to the corporate accountability towards stakeholder groups is in line with the focus of the SERS framework and the CSR-SC Project: improving the corporate performance evaluation and reporting systems in order to support companies in enhancing their decision-making processes and in meeting the information needs of stakeholders.

Moreover, the Commission will continue to support stakeholders in developing their capacity to assess and evaluate CSR practices.

In fact, even if the Commission promotes this Alliance and, according to a strategic view of CSR, considers enterprises primary interlocutors in this field, it 'continues to attach utmost importance to dialogue with and between all stakeholders' (CEC, 2006, p. 2) and recognizes that 'without active support and constructive criticism of non-business stakeholders, CSR will not flourish. The Commission's backing of the Alliance is not a substitute for further dialogue with all stakeholders. The Commission remains committed to facilitating such dialogue, including through regular review meetings of the Multistakeholder Forum' (CEC, 2006, p. 5).

Finally, the Commission identifies the following areas to further promote CSR practices:

- awareness-raising and best practice exchange;
- support to multi-stakeholder initiatives;
- cooperation with member states;
- consumer information and transparency;
- research;
- education;
- SMEs;
- the international dimension of CSR.

In this framework the Commission stresses the strategic role played by SMEs: 'The collective impact of CSR as practiced by SMEs is critical if the potential of CSR to contribute to growth and jobs and sustainable development in Europe is to be fully harnessed' (CEC, 2006, p. 7). Therefore, it is necessary to recognize what many SMEs already do in the field of CSR. Furthermore, some other research on SMEs is needed: 'CSR as practiced by SMEs is an important research topic in its own right, but should also be adequately reflected in other areas of CSR research' (CEC, 2006, p. 6). The research activities carried out by Bocconi University are consistent with the Commission's priorities and will be continued in future years, in particular with regard to the study of the relationships between CSR and European competitiveness and of the partnerships ('open coalitions of cooperation') that could be activated to boost local communities' development.

To sum up, the publication of this new communication four years after the previous one emphasizes that, even if through long and controversial processes, the European Commission confirms its approach to CSR, seen as a business contribution to sustainable development (CEC, 2002b). The 'EU's vision of long-term prosperity, solidarity and security' (CEC, 2006, p. 4) encompasses a fundamental role for companies, called to carry on voluntary and innovative efforts on CSR by considering the requests of, and cooperating with, different stakeholders (employees, trade unions, NGOs, consumers, investors, public authorities, local communities, people in other parts of the world, future generations) thanks to evolving partnerships.

'Europe does not need just business but socially responsible business' (CEC, 2006, p. 2). The European strategy on CSR and sustainable development, which has been analyzed in this book, tries to reconcile economic growth, social cohesion and environmental protection, and could give an interesting perspective for other countries and other regions.

Bibliography

Abt, C.C. (1977), The Social Audit for Management, New York: Amacom.

AccountAbility (1999), *AccountAbility 1000 (AA1000) framework. Standard, guidelines and professional qualification*, London: Isea.

AccountAbility (2003), *AA1000 Assurance Standard*, London: Isea, http://www.accountability.org.uk.

AccountAbility (2005), *AA1000 Stakeholder Engagement Standard. Exposure Draft*, London: Isea, http://www.acc ountability.org.uk.

Acea (2004), *2003 Sustainability Report*, Milan: Acea, http://www.aceaspa.it.

Ackerman, R.W. (1975), *The Social Challenge to Business*, Cambridge: Harvard University Press.

Adams, C.A. (2002), 'Internal organizational factors influencing corporate social and ethical reporting. Beyond current theorising', *Accounting, Auditing & Accountability Journal*, **15**(2), 223-250.

Adler, P.S. and S.W. Kwon (2002), 'Social capital: Prospects for a new concept', *Academy of Management Review*, **27**(1), 17-40.

Alabreda, L., A. Tencati, J.M. Lozano and F. Perrini (2005), 'The role of government in promoting corporate responsibility. A comparative analysis of Italy and the United Kingdom from the relational state perspective', Paper presented at the *4th EABIS Annual Colloquium*, Warsaw: Leon Kozmiski Academy, December 5-6.

Andriof, J. and M. McIntosh (eds) (2001), *Perspectives on Corporate Citizenship*, Sheffield, UK: Greenleaf.

Ansoff, H.I. (1979), 'The Changing Shape of the Strategic Problem', in D.E. Schendel and C.W. Hofer (eds), *Strategic management: A new view of business policy and planning*, Boston: Little, Brown, & Company, 30-44.

APAT and ONR (2003), Rapporto Rifiuti 2003, Roma. Retrieved April 20, 2004, http://www.sinanet.apat.it

Assopiastrelle and Snam (1998), *Rapporto Integrato Ambiente, Energia, Sicurezza-Salute, Qualità. L'industria italiana delle piastrelle di ceramica e dei materiali refrattari verso uno sviluppo sostenibile*, Sassuolo: Assopiastrelle, http://www.asso piastrelle.it.

Aupperle, K.E., A.B. Carroll, and J.D. Hatfield (1985), 'An empirical examination of the relationship between corporate social responsibility and profitability', *Academy of Management Journal*, **28**, 446-463.

Azzone G., M. Brophy, G. Noci, R. Welford and W. Young (1997), 'A stakeholders' view of environmental reporting', *Long Range Planning*, **30**(5), 699-709.

Azzone, G., R. Bianchi, and G. Noci (1997), 'Implementing environmental certification in Italy: Managerial and competitive implications for firms', *Eco-management and auditing*, **4**, 98-108.

Bakan J. (2004), *The Corporation: The Pathological Pursuit of Profit and Power*, New York: Free Press.

Banca Lombarda (2005), *Company Profile, History*. http://www.bancalombarda.it.

Bandura, A., G. Caprara, and L. Zsolnai (2002), 'Corporate Transgressions', in L. Zsolnai (ed.), *Ethics in the Economy.* *Handbook of Business Ethics*, Oxford and Bern: Peter Lang Academic Publisher, 151-164.

Barber, B. (1983), *The Logic and Limits of Trust*, New Brunswick (NJ): Rutgers University Press.

Bartolomeo, M., R. Malaman, M. Pavan, and G. Sammarco (1995), *Il Bilancio Ambientale d'Impresa*, Milano: Il Sole 24 Ore.

Becattini, G. (1987), *Mercato e Forze Locali: Il Distretto Industriale*, Bologna: Il Mulino.

Beck, M. (ed.) (1993), *Ökobilanzierung im betrieblichen Management*, Würzburg: Vogel Buchverlag.

Bennett, M. and P. James (1999), 'Key themes in environmental, social and sustainability performance evaluation and reporting', in M. Bennett and P. James (eds), *Sustainable Measures. Evaluation and Reporting of Environmental and Social Performance*, Sheffield: Greenleaf Publishing, pp. 29-74.

Blacconiere, W.G. and D.M. Patten (1994), 'Environmental disclosure, regulatory costs, and changes in firm value', *Journal of Ac-counting and Economics*, **18**, 357-377.

Blomqvist, K. (1997), 'The many faces of trust', *Scandinavian Journal of Management*, **13**(3), 271-286.

Bonal et al. (1981), *Responsabilità Sociale e Bilancio Sociale d'Impresa*, Milan: Franco Angeli.

Bowen, H.R. (1953), *Social Responsibilities of the Businessman*, New York: Harper and Brothers.

Brophy, M. and R. Starkey (1996), 'Environmental reporting', in R. Welford (ed.), *Corporate Environmental Management*, London: Earthscan, 177-198.

Bundesumweltministerium and Umweltbundesamt (eds) (1995), *Handbuch Umweltcontrolling*, Munich: Verlag Franz Vahlen.

Burritt, R.L. (1997), 'Corporate environmental performance indicators: Cost allocation – boon or bane?', *Greener Management International*, **17**(Spring), 89-100.

Burritt, R.L., T. Hahn and S. Schaltegger (2002), 'Towards a comprehensive framework for environmental management accounting: Links between business actors and environmental management accounting tools', *Australian Accounting Review*, **12**(2), 39-50.

Calcaterra, M. and F. Perrini (2002), 'La costruzione degli indici etici in Italia e alcune prime evidenze empiriche sulla relazione tra Corporate Social Resposibility e Financial Performance', in D. Masciandaro and G. Bracchi (eds), *Banche: Le Nuove Frontiere della Concorrenza. VII Rapporto Fondazione Rosselli*, Rome: Edibank, pp. 251-286.

Calcaterra, M., A. Giorgieri, and F. Perrini (2002), 'Rating etico', *Economia & Management*, **2**, 103-120.

Carnimeo, G., M. Frey, and F. Iraldo (2002), *Gestione del Prodotto e Sostenibilità. Le Imprese di fronte alle Nuove Prospettive delle Politiche Ambientali Comunitarie e della IPP (Integrated Product Policy)*, Milan: Franco Angeli.

Carroll, A.B. (1979), 'A three-dimensional model of corporate social performance', *Academy of Management Review*, **4**(4), 497-505.

Carroll, A.B. (1991), 'The pyramid of corporate social responsibility: towards the moral management of organizational stakeholders', *Business Horizons* (July/August), 39-48.

Carroll, A.B. (1994), 'Social issues in management research', *Business and Society*, **33**(1), 5-25.

Carroll, A.B. (1999), 'Corporate social responsibility. Evolution of a definitional construct', *Business & Society*, **38**(3), 268-295.

Carroll, A.B. and A. K. Buchholtz (2002). *Business & Society: Ethics and Stakeholder Management, 5th edition*. Mason: Thomson - South Western.

Castaldo, S. (2002), *Fiducia e Relazioni di Mercato*, Bologna: Il Mulino.

Cerin, P. (2002a), 'Communication in corporate environmental reports', *Corporate Social Responsibility and Environmental Management*, **9**(1), 46-66. DOI: 10.1002/csr.6.

Cerin, P. (2002b), 'Characteristics of environmental reporters on the OM Stockholm Exchange', *Business Strategy and the Environment*, **11**(5), 298-311. DOI: 10.1002/bse.336.

Cerin, P. (2004), 'Where is corporate social responsibility actually heading?', *Progress in Industrial Ecology*, **1**(1/2/3), 307-330.

Clark, J.M. (1939), *Social Control of Business*, New York: McGraw-Hill.

Clarkson, M.B.E. (1995), 'A stakeholder framework for analyzing and evaluating corporate social performance', *Academy of Management Review*, **20**(1), 92-117.

Cohen, D. (1998), 'Toward a knowledge context: Report on the first annual U.C. Berkeley forum on knowledge and the firm', *California Management Review*, **40**(3), 22-39.

Commission of the European Communities (CEC) (2001a), *The Sixth European Community Environmental Action Programme 'Environment 2010: Our Future, Our Choice'*, Brussels: COM(2001) 31 final.

Commission of the European Communities (CEC) (2001b), *Ten years after Rio: Preparing for the World Summit on Sustainable Development in 2002*, Brussels: COM(2001) 53 final.

Commission of the European Communities (CEC) (2001c), *A Sustainable Europe for a Better World: A European Union Strategy for Sustainable Development*, Brussels: COM(2001) 264 final.

Commission of the European Communities (CEC) (2001d), *Green Paper 'Promoting a European framework for Corporate Social Responsibility'*, Brussels: COM(2001) 366 final,

Commission of the European Communities (CEC) (2001e), *Commission Recommendation of 30 May 2001 on the recognition, measurement and disclosure of environmental issues in the annual accounts and annual reports of companies,* Official Journal of the European Communities L 156 (June 13), 33-42.

Commission of the European Communities (CEC) (2002a), *Towards a global partnership for sustainable development,* Brussels: COM(2002) 82 final.

Commission of the European Communities (CEC) (2002b), *Corporate Social Responsibility: A business contribution to Sustainable Development.* Brussels: COM(2002) 347 final.

Commission of the European Communities (CEC) (2002c), *European SMEs and social and environmental responsibility,* Luxembourg: Observatory of European SMEs, No. 4.

Commission of the European Communities (CEC) (2004), *Public consultation. Review of the EU Sustainable development strategy,* Brussels: SEC(2004) 1042.

Commission of the European Communities (CEC) (2005), *On the review of the Sustainable Development Strategy. A platform for action,* Brussels: COM(2005) 658 final.

Commission of the European Communities (CEC) (2006), *Implementing the Partnership for Growth and Jobs: Making Europe a Pole of Excellence on Corporate Social Responsibility,* Brussels: COM(2006) 136 final.

Commission of the European Communities. Directorate-General for Employment and Social Affairs (2003), *Mapping Instruments for Corporate Social Responsibility,* http://europa. eu.int/comm/employment_social/publications/2004/ke1103002_ en.pdf

Commission of the European Communities. Directorate-General for Employment and Social Affairs (2004), *ABC of the main instruments of Corporate Social Responsibility,* http://europa. eu.int/comm/employment_social/publications/2005/ke1103004_ en.pdf.

Commission on the Private Sector and Development (2003), *Unleashing Entrepreneurship. Making Business Work for the Poor,* New York: United Nations Development Programme.

Conai (2004), *Programma generale di prevenzione e gestione degli imballaggi e dei rifiuti d'imballaggio,* http://www. conai.org.

Coop Adriatica (2004), *03 Bilancio di Sostenibilità.* Villanova di Castenaso – Bologna: Coop Adriatica:. http://www.e-coop.it.

Copenhagen Centre (1998), *The Vision Behind The Copenhagen Center*, http://www.copenhagencentre.org.

Copenhagen Centre (2003), *CSR Europe and International Business Leaders Forum, It Simply Works Better!*, http://www.copenhagencentre.org.

Crane, A. and D. Matten (2003), *Business Ethics. A European Perspective*, Oxford: Oxford University Press.

Cummings, J.L. and J.P. Doh (2000), 'Identifying who matters: Mapping key players in multiple environments', *California Management Review*, **42**(2), 83-104.

Das, T.K. and B.S. Teng (1998), 'Between trust and control: Developing confidence in partner cooperation in alliances', *Academy of Management Review*, **23**, 491–513.

Das, T.K. and B.S. Teng (2001), 'Trust, control, and risk in strategic alliances: An integrated framework' *Organization Studies*, **22**, 251–283.

Davis, K. (1960), 'Can business afford to ignore corporate social responsibilities?', *California Management Review*, **2**, 60-76.

Davis, K. (1973), 'The case for and against business assumption of social responsibilities', *Academy of Management Journal*, **16**, 312-322.

De Bettignies, H.C. (2002), 'Reviewing Meanings and Contexts of the Role of Business in Society', Paper presented during the Launch of the European Academy of Business in Society, Fontainebleau: INSEAD, July 5.

De Silvio M. and A. Tencati (2002), 'I costi della gestione ecologica. Il caso della Centrale termoelettrica ENEL di La Casella', *Economia & Management*, **3**, 107-122.

Deegan, C. and B. Gordon (1996), 'A study of the environmental disclosure practices of Australian corporations', *Accounting & Business Research*, **26**(3), 187-199.

Deloitte Touche Tohmatsu Emerging Markets (2004), *Partnerships for Small Enterprise Development*. New York: United Nations Development Programme (UNDP), http ://www.unido.org/doc/4364 (13 November 2005).

Demattè C., (2002), 'L'impresa schiacciata fra la pressione dei mercati e la responsabilità sociale', *Economia & Management*, n. 4.

Donaldson, T. (1982), *Corporations and Morality*, Englewood Cliff (NJ): Prentice-Hall Inc.

Donaldson, T. (1989), *The Ethics of International Business*, New York: Oxford University Press.

Donaldson, T. (1992), 'The language of international corporate ethics', *Business Ethics Quarterly*, **2**(3), 271-281.

Donaldson, T. and L. Preston (1995), 'The stakeholder theory of the corporation: Concepts, evidence and implications', *Academy of Management Review*, **20**(1), 65-91.

Donaldson, T. and R.E. Freeman (1994), *Business as a humanity*, New York: Oxford University Press.

Donaldson, T. and T.W. Dunfee (1994), 'Towards a unified conception of business ethics: Integrative social contracts theory', *Academy of Management Review*, **19**(2), 252-284.

Donaldson, T. and T.W. Dunfee (1995), 'Integrative social contracts theory: A communitarian conception of economic ethics', *Economics and Philosophy*, **11**(1), 85-112.

Donaldson, T. and T.W. Dunfee (1999a), *Ties that Bind: A Social Contracts Approach to Business Ethics*, Cambridge: Harvard Business School Press.

Donaldson, T. and T.W. Dunfee (1999b), 'Social contract approaches to business ethics: Bridging the 'is-ought' gap', in R.E. Frederick (ed.), *A Companion to Business Ethics*, Blackwell, pp. 38-55.

Dunfee, T.W. (1991), 'Business Ethics and Extant Social Contracts', *Business Ethics Quarterly*, **1**(1), 23-51.

Dwyer, R., Schurr, P. and S. Oh (1987), 'Developing buyer-seller relationships', *Journal of Marketing*, **51**, 11-27.

E.Capital Partners (2004), *Sri Fundwatcher*, www.ecpartners.com, Milan.

Elkington, J. (1994), 'Towards the sustainable corporation: Win-win-win business strategies for sustainable development', *California Management Review*, **36**(2), 90-100.

Elkington, J. (1997), *Cannibals with Forks. The Triple Bottom Line of 21st Century Business*, Oxford: Capstone Publishing.

Elkington, J. (2004), 'Enter the triple bottom line', in A. Henriques and J. Richardson (eds), *The Triple Bottom Line: Does it All Add Up? Assessing the Sustainability of Business and CSR*, London: Earthscan, 1-16.

Elkington, J. and F. van Dijk (1999), 'Socially challenged: Trends in social reporting', in M. Bennett and P. James (eds), *Sustainable Measures. Evaluation and Reporting of*

Environmental and Social Performance, Sheffield: Greenleaf Publishing, 496-508.

Emblemsvåg, J. and B. Bras (2001), *Activity-Based Cost and Environmental Management: A Different Approach to the ISO 14000 Compliance*, Norwell (USA): Kluwer Academic Publishers.

Epstein, M.J. and M. Roy (2001), 'Sustainability in action: identifying and measuring the key performance drivers', *Long Range Planning*, **34**(5), 585-604.

Ethical Investment Association (2004), *2004 EIA Benchmarking Survey*. http://www.eia.org.au.

European Community (1993), *Towards Sustainability. A European Community programme of policy and action in relation to the environment and sustainable development*, Official Journal of the European Communities, No. C 138/5.

European Environment Agency (EEA) (2002), *Environmental signals 2002. Benchmarking the Millennium*, Luxembourg: Office for Official Publications of the European Communities.

European Environment Agency (EEA) (2003), *Europe's Environment: the third assessment*, Luxembourg: Office for Official Publications of the European Communities.

European Multi Stakeholder Forum on Corporate Social Responsibility (2004), *Results – June 2004. Final Forum Report*, http://europa.eu.int.

Eurosif (2003), *Socially Responsible Investment among European Institutional Investors 2003*, http://www.eurosif.org.

Eurostat (2001a), *Environmental pressure indicators for the EU*, Luxembourg: Eurostat.

Eurostat (2001b), *Measuring progress towards a more sustainable Europe*, Luxembourg: Eurostat.

Eurostat (2005), *Sustainable Development Indicators*, http://epp.eurostat.cec.eu.int.

Federchimica and Iefe (1998), *La Gestione Integrata di Salute, Sicurezza e Ambiente: Indicazioni Operative per le Piccole e Medie Imprese del Settore Chimico*, Ed. SC-Sviluppo Chimica.

Figge F., T. Hahn, S. Schaltegger and M. Wagner (2002), 'The sustainability balanced scorecard: Linking sustainability management to business strategy', *Business Strategy and the Environment*, **11**(5), 269-284. DOI 10.1002/bse.339.

Figge, F. and S. Schaltegger (2000), *What Is 'Stakeholder Value'? Developing a Catchphrase into a Benchmarking Tool*, Lüneburg, Universität Lüneburg, Pictet & Cie, UNEP.

Frederick, W.C. (1960), 'The growing concern over business responsibility', *California Management Review*, **2**(4), 54-62.

Frederick, W.C. (1986), 'Toward CSR3: why ethical analysis is indispensable and unavoidable in corporate affairs', *California Management Review*, **28**(2), 126-132.

Frederick, W.C. (1998), 'Moving to CSR4', *Business and Society*, **37**(1), 40-60.

Freeman, R.E. (1984), *Strategic Management: A Stakeholder Approach*, Boston: Pitman Publishing.

Freeman, R.E. and S.R. Velamuri (2006), 'A New Approach to CSR: Company Stakeholder Responsibility', in A. Kakabadse and M. Morsing (eds), *Corporate Social Responsibility. Reconciling Aspiration with Application*, London, UK: Palgrave Macmillan Ltd.

Freeman, R.E., A. Wicks, B. Parmar, and J. McVea (2004), 'Stakeholder Theory: the State of the Art and Future Perspectives', *Politeia*, **74**, 9-22.

Friedman, M. (1962). *Capitalism and Freedom*, Chicago: University of Chicago Press.

Friedman, M. (1970), 'The social responsibility of business is to increase its profits', *New York Times Magazine*, September 13th.

Frosch, R. A. and N. E. Gallopoulos (1989), 'Strategies for Manufacturing', *Scientific American*, September, 94-103.

Garriga, E. and D. Melé (2004), 'Corporate social responsibility theories: Mapping the territory', *Journal of Business Ethics*, **53**, 51-71.

Ghoshal, S. and C.A. Bartlett (1999), *The Individualized Corporation: A Fundamentally New Approach to Management*, New York: HarperBusiness.

Gilardoni, A., S. Pogutz and A. Tencati (1995), 'Innovazione tecnologica, variabile ambientale e sviluppo d'impresa', *SPACE*, Bocconi University, Milan, March.

Glazer, R. (1998), 'Measuring the knower: Towards a theory of knowledge equity', *California Management Review*, **40**(3), 175-194.

Global Reporting Initiative (GRI) (2002), *2002 Sustainability Reporting Guidelines*, http://www.globalreporting.org.

Global Reporting Initiative (2004), *High 5!*, Amsterdam: Global Reporting Initiative.

Global Reporting Initiative (2006), *G3 Sustainability Reporting Guidelines. Version for Public Comment*, 2 January 2006 – 31 March 2006, Amsterdam: Global Reporting Initiative, http://www.grig3.org.

Gonella C., A. Pilling and S. Zadek (1998), *Making Values Count: Contemporary Experience in Social and Ethical Accounting, Auditing, and Reporting*, Research rep. No. 57. London: Association of Chartered Certified Accountants/The New Economics Foundation.

Goodman, E., J. Bamford, and J. Saynor (eds) (1989), *Small Firms and Industrial Districts in Italy*, London: Routledge.

Göteborg European Council (2001), *Presidency Conclusions. A Strategy for Sustainable Development*, 15-16 June, http://europa.eu.int.

Grant, R.M. (2002), *Contemporary Strategy Analysis. Concepts, Techniques, Applications* (4th ed.), Oxford: Blackwell Publishers.

Gray, R., R. Kouhy, and S. Lavers (1995), 'Methodological themes. Constructing a research database of social and environmental reporting by UK companies', *Accounting, Auditing and Accountability Journal*, **8**(2), 78-101.

Greening, D.W. and D.B. Turban (2000), 'Corporate social performance as a competitive advantage in attracting a quality workforce', *Business & Society*, **39**(3), 254-280.

Gruppo per il Bilancio Sociale (GBS) (Study Group for Social Reporting) (2001), *Social Reporting Standards*, Milan: GBS.

Guatri, L. (1991), *La Teoria di Creazione del Valore. Una Via Europea*, Milan: Egea.

Guthrie, J.E. and L.D. Parker (1990), 'Corporate social disclosure practices: a comparative international analysis', *Advances in Public Interest Accounting*, **3**, 159-176.

Hagen, J. M. and S. Choe (1998), 'Trust in Japanese interfirm relations: Institutional sanctions matter', *Academy of Management Review*, **23**(3), 589-600.

Hallay, H., (ed.) (1990), *Die Ökobilanz. Ein betriebliches Informationssystem*, Berlin: Schriftenreihe des IÖW.

Hallay, H., and R. Pfriem (1992), *Öko-Controlling: Umweltschutz in mittelständischen Unternehmen*, Frankfurt: Campus Verlag.

Hasnas, J. (1998), 'The normative theories of business ethics: A guide for the perplexed', *Business Ethics Quarterly*, **8**(1), 19-42.

Hertz, N. (2001), *The Silent Takeover: Global Capitalism and the Death of Democracy*, London: Heinemann.

Hillman, A.J. and G.D. Keim (2001), 'Shareholder value, stakeholder management, and social issue: What's the bottom line?', *Strategic Management Journal*, **22**, 125-139.

Hutton, W. (2002), *The World We're In*, London: Little, Brown.

International Institute for Sustainable Development (IISD) (2001), *The Dashboard of Sustainability*. http://www.iisd.org.

ISO Advisory Group on Corporate Social Responsibility (2003), *Technical Report (TR) Terms of Reference (TOR)*, Geneva: ISO.

Italian Ministry of Labour and Social Affairs (2003), *Project CSR-SC. The Italian contribution to CSR promoting campaign developed at European level*, Rome: Italian Ministry of Labour and Social Affairs, http://www.welfare.gov.it.

Italian Ministry of Labour and Social Affairs (2006), *Corporate Social Responsibility. Italian examples of good practice*, Rome, July 14, www.welfar.gov.it.

Jarboe, K.P. (2001), 'Knowledge management as an economic development strategy: A review', *Reviews of Economic Development Literature and Practice*, U.S. Economic Development Administration, 7.

Jensen, M.C. (2001), 'Value maximization, stakeholder theory, and the corporate objective function', *Journal of Applied Corporate Finance*, **14**(3), 8-21.

Jones, R. and A.J. Murrell (2001), 'Signaling positive corporate so-cial performance. An event study of family-friendly firms', *Busi-ness & Society*, **40**(1), 59-78.

Jones, T.M. (1980), 'Corporate social responsibility revisited, redefined', *California Management Review*, **22**(2), 59-67.

Joyner, B. E. and D. Payne (2002), 'Evolution and Implementation: A Study of Values, Business Ethics and Corporate Social Responsibility', *Journal of Business Ethics*, **41**, 297-311.

Kaplan R.S. and D.P. Norton (1992), 'The balanced scorecard: Measures that drive performance', *Harvard Business Review*, **70**(1), 71-79.

Kaplan, R.S. and D.P. Norton (1996), 'Linking the balanced scorecard to strategy', *California Management Review*, **39**, 53-79.

Kaplan, R.S. and D.P. Norton (2000), 'Having trouble with your strategy? Then map it', *Harvard Business Review*, September-October, 167-176.

Kaplan, R.S. and D.P. Norton (2004), *Strategy Maps: Converting Intangible Assets into Tangible Outcomes*, Boston: Harvard Business School Press.

Kay, J. (2004a), 'Forget how the Crow Flies', *Financial Times*, January 16, http://www.johnkay.com.

Kay, J. (2004b), *Everlasting Light Bulbs. How Economics Illuminates the World*, London: The Erasmus Press.

Kelly, K. (1994), *Out of Control. The New Biology of Machines, Social Systems, and the Economic World*, Boston: Addison-Wesley Publishing Company.

Kennedy, A.A. (2000), *The End of Shareholder Value: The Real Effects of the Shareholder Value Phenomenon and the Crisis it is bringing to Business*, London: Orion Business Books.

Klein, N. (2000), *No Logo: Taking Aim at the Brand Bullies*, Toronto: Knopf-Random House of Canada.

Kohonen, T. (1984), *Organization and Associative Memory*, Berlin: Springer-Verlag.

Kohonen, T. (1991), 'Unsupervised learning algorithms', *Metodologia, Società di Cultura Metodologico-operativa*, **5**.

Kotler, P. and N. Lee (2005), *Corporate Social Responsibility: Doing the Most Good for Your Company and Your Cause. Best practices*, New Jersey: Wiley.

Kreps, T.J. (1940), *Measurement of the social performance of business*, Washington, Government Printing Office.

Lanza, S., M. Calcaterra and F. Perrini (eds) (2002), *Etica, Finanza e Valore d'Impresa*, Milano: Egea.

Lev, B. (2001), *Intangibles: Management, Measurement, and Reporting*, Washington DC: Brookings Institution Press.

Lewicki, R.J., and B.B. Bunker (1996), 'Developing and maintaining trust in work relationships', in R. M. Kramer and T. R. Tyler (eds), *Trust in Organizations: Frontiers of Theory and Research*, Thousand Oaks, CA: Sage Publications, pp.114-139.

Lipparini, A. (2002), *La Gestione Strategica del Capitale Intellettuale e del Capitale Sociale*, Bologna: il Mulino.

Maglioli, R. (2001), *Reti Sociali e Valori Aziendali*, Milan: Franco Angeli.

Manne, H.G. and H.C. Wallich (1972), *The modern corporation and social responsibility*, Washington D.C.: American Enterprise Institute for Public Policy Research.

Margolis, J.D. and J.P. Walsh (2003), 'Misery loves companies: Rethinking social initiatives by business', *Administrative Science Quarterly*, **48**, 268-305.

Marstrander, R. (1996), 'Industrial ecology: A practical framework for environmental management', in R. Welford and R. Starkey (eds), *Business and the Environment*, London: Earthscan.

Matten, D. and A. Crane (2004), 'Corporate citizenship: Towards an extended theoretical conceptualization', *Academy of Management Review*, **30**(1), 166-179.

McGuire, J.W. (1963), *Business and Society*, New York: McGraw Hill.

McWilliams, A. and D. Siegel (2001), 'Corporate social responsibility: A theory of the firm perspective', *Academy of Management Review*, **26**, 117-127.

Miles, R., C. Snow, J. Mathews, G. Miles and H. Coleman Jr. (1997), 'Organizing in the knowledge age: Anticipating the cellular form', *Academy of Management Executive*, **11**(4), 7-24.

Mills, R. W. and B. Weinstein (2000), 'Beyond shareholder value: Reconciling the shareholder and stakeholder perspectives' *Journal of General Management*, **25**(3), 79-93.

Ministry of Labour and Social Affairs (2003), 'SABAF case', in *Developing CSR in Italy and in UK*, Rome, April 29, 2003: 5-8, www.welfar.gov.it.

Monti, M. (2003), 'Politica della concorrenza e responsabilità sociale delle imprese', *Third European Conference on CSR: The role of Public Policies in promoting CSR*, Venice, 14th November 2003 organised in the framework of EU Presidency by Italian Ministry of Welfare and EU Commission.

Moorman, C., G. Zaltman, and R. Deshpandé (1992), 'Relationships between providers and users of market research: The dynamics of trust within and between organizations', *Journal of Marketing Research*, **29**, August, 314-328.

Nelli, R.P. and P. Bensi (2003), *L'Impresa e la sua Reputazione. L'Evoluzione della Media Coverage Analysis*, Milan: Vita e Pensiero.

Norman, W. and C. MacDonald (2004), 'Getting to the bottom of "triple bottom line"', *Business Ethics Quarterly*, **14**(2), 243-262.

O'Higgins, E. (2002), 'The stakeholder corporation', in L. Zsolnai (ed.), *Ethics in the Economy. Handbook of Business Ethics*, Oxford and Bern: Peter Lang Academic Publisher, 105-133.

Oliver, R.L. (1999), 'Whence consumer loyalty', *Journal of Marketing*, Special Issue, 33-44.

Orlitzky, M. and J.D. Benjamin (2001), 'Corporate social performance and firm risk: A meta-analytic review', *Business & Society*, **40**(4), 369-396.

Paine, L.S. (2003), *Value shift: Why companies must merge social and financial imperatives to achieve superior performance?*, New York: McGraw-Hill

Parker, C. (2000), 'Performance measurement', *Work Study*, **49**(2), 63-66.

Patten, D.M. (2002), 'The relation between environmental performance and environmental disclosure: A research note', *Accounting, Organizations and Society*, **27**, 763-773.

Pearce, D., A. Markandya, and E. Barbier (1989), *Blueprint for a Green Economy*, London: Earthscan Publications.

Pélouas, A. (2004), 'L'industrie minière révise sa "responsabilità" vis-à-vis des pays émergentes', *Le Monde Economie*, **21**, September 21, VIII.

Perrini, F. (ed.) (2002), *Responsabilità Sociale dell'Impresa e Finanza Etica*, Milano: Egea.

Perrini, F. (2003), 'La responsabilità sociale dell'impresa, Interview to Roberto Maroni', *Economia & Management*, **5**, 31-42.

Perrini F. (2005), 'Building a Portrait of Corporate Social Responsibility Reporting', *European Management Journal*, **23** (6), 611–627.

Perrini F. (2006a), Strategies for Corporate Social Responsibility. 'The Practitioner's Perspective on Non-Financial Reporting.', *California Management Review*, **48** (2), 73-103.

Perrini F. (2006b), 'Corporate Social Responsibility: nuovi equilibri nella gestione d'impresa', *Economia & Management*, Etaslibri, Milan, **2**, 7-11.

Perrini F., M. Calcaterra, S. Pogutz and A. Tencati, (2002), 'Research Project for the Italian Ministry of Welfare. Proposal for a CSR-SC Standard', in Proceedings of the Conference

'L'impegno Sociale delle Imprese per un Nuovo Welfare', Bocconi University, Milan, http://www.welfare.gov.it.

Perrini, F. and A. Tencati (2003), 'Corporate social responsibility and firm performance: Managing sustainability and the need of a new corporate evaluation and reporting system in a knowledge economy', Paper presented at the 2003 Academy of Management Conference, Seattle, Washington.

Perrini, F., S. Pogutz and A. Tencati (2002), 'Project CSR-SC for the Italian Ministry of Welfare. Ricerca: la CSR in Italia', Bocconi University, with Confindustria, Milan, http://www.welfare.gov.it.

Perrini, F., S.Pogutz and A. Tencati (2006), 'Corporate social responsibility in Italy: State of the art', *Journal of Business Strategies*, **23**(1): forthcoming.

Perrini, F. and C. Vurro (2005), 'Teoría y práctica en la innovación y el cambio social', *Initiativa Emprendadora*, 48, 8-21.

Perrini F. and C. Vurro (2006), 'Social Entrepreneurship: Innovation and Social Change across Theory and Practice', in J. Mair, J. Robinson and K. Hockerts (eds) *Social Entrepreneurship*, London, UK: Palgrave Macmillan Ltd, forthcoming.

Peteraf, M. (1993), 'The cornerstones of competitive advantage: A resource-based view', *Strategic Management Journal*, **14**(3), 179-191.

Petrella, R. (ed.) (1995), *Gruppo di Lisbona. I Limiti della Competitività*, Rome: Manifestolibri.

Pfeffer, J. (1994), 'Competitive advantage through people', *California Management Review*, **36**(2), 9-28.

Pivato, S. and A. Gilardoni (1997), *Elementi di Economia e Gestione delle Imprese*, Milan: Egea.

Pivato S., N. Misani, A. Ordanini and F. Perrini (2004), *Economia e Gestione delle Imprese*, Milan: Egea.

Pogutz, S. and A. Tencati (1997), *Ambiente, Competitività e Innovazione: Teoria e Casi*, Milano: Egea.

Pogutz, S. and A. Tencati (1998), *Il bilancio ambientale: strumento di controllo e comunicazione*, Meeting on Environment and Competitiveness. Milan: Bocconi University.

Porter, M. (1990), *The Competitive Advantage of Nations*, New York: The Free Press.

Porter, M.E. and M.R. Kramer (2002), 'The competitive advantage of corporate philanthropy', *Harvard Business Review*, December, 5-16.

Post, J.E., L.E. Preston and S. Sachs (2002a), *Redefining the Corporation: Stakeholder Management and Organizational Wealth*, Palo Alto: Stanford University Press.

Post, J.E., L.E. Preston and S. Sachs (2002b), 'Managing the extended enterprise: The new stakeholder view', *California Management Review*, **45**(1), 6-27.

Pozza, L. (1999), *Le Risorse Immateriali. Profili di Rilievo nelle Determinazioni Quantitative d'Azienda*, Milan: Egea.

Preston, L. and D.P. O'Bannon (1997), 'The corporate social-financial performance relationship', *Business & Society*, **36**, 419-429.

Preston, L.E. and J.L. Post (1975), *Private management and public policy: the principle of public responsibility*, Englewood Cliffs, NJ: Prentice Hall.

Putnam, R. D. (1993a), *Making Democracy Work. Civic Traditions in Modern Italy*, Princeton: Princeton University Press.

Putnam R.D. (1993b), 'The prosperous community', *American Prospect*, **13**, 35-42.

Putnam, R.D. (2000), *Bowling Alone. The Collapse and Revival of American Community*, New York: Simon and Schuster.

Q-RES (2002), *The Q-RES Project: The Quality of the Social and Ethical Responsibility of Corporations*, http://www.qres.it.

Q-RES (2004), *Q-RES Standard and Guidelines for the improvement of the ethical and social performances of the organisation*, http://www.qres.it.

Q-RES (2005), *Contributing to the convergence of CSR management standards in Italy, Germany, France and the UK by developing and promoting a common CSR framework, terminology and management tools*, http://www.qres.it.

Rajan, R.J. and L. Zingales (1998), 'Power in a theory of the firm', *The Quarterly Journal of Economics*, **113**(2), 387-432.

Rappaport, A. (1986), *Creating Shareholder Value. The New Standard for Business Performance*, New York: The Free Press.

Rayner, J. and W. Raven (eds) (2002), *Corporate Social Responsibility Monitor*, London: GEE.

Reich, R.B. (2006), *Don't Blame Wal-Mart: Making Sense of Corporate Social Responsibility*, ASE Plenary, Annual Meeting Allied Social Science Associations, 5 January, Boston, MA.

Ring, P.S. and A.H. Van de Ven (1992), 'Structuring cooperative relationships between organizations', *Strategic Management Journal*, **13**(7), 483-498.

Ring, P.S. and A.H. Van de Ven (1994), 'Developmental processes of cooperative interorganizational relationships', *Academy of Management Review*, **19**(1), 90-118.

Roberts, R.W. (1992), 'Determinants of corporate social responsibility disclosure: An application of stakeholder theory', *Accounting, Organizations and Society*, **17**(6), 595-612.

Rotter, J.B. (1971), 'Generalized Expectancies for Interpersonal Trust', *American Psychologist*, **26**, 443-452.

Ruggles, R. (1998) 'The state of the notion: Knowledge management in practice', *California Management Review*, **40**(3), 80-89.

Rusconi, G. (1988), *Il Bilancio Sociale d'Impresa. Problemi e Prospettive*, Milan: Giuffrè Editore.

Salzmann, O., A. Ionescu-Somers, and U. Steger (2004) 'The business case for corporate sustainability: Literature review and research options', *European Management Journal* **23**(1), 27-36.

Sancassiani, W. (ed.) (2004), *Agenda 21 Locale in Italia 2004. Indagine sull'attuazione dei processi di Agenda 21. Partecipazione e progetti per lo sviluppo sostenibile*, http://www.a21italy.net.

Schaltegger S. and R. Burritt (2005), 'Corporate sustainability', in H. Folmer and T. Tietenberg (eds), *The International Yearbook of Environmental and Resource Economics 2005/2006*, Cheltenham, UK: Edward Elgar, pp. 185-222.

Schaltegger S., C. Herzig, O. Kleiber, and J. Müller (2002), *Sustainability Management in Business Enterprises. Concepts and Instruments for Sustainable Organisation Development*, Bonn: Federal Ministry for the Environment, Nature Conservation and Nuclear Safety (BMU).

Schaltegger S. and M. Wagner (2006), 'Integrative management of sustainability performance, measurement and reporting', *International Journal of Accounting, Auditing and Performance Evaluation*, **3**(1).

Schwartz, M.S. and A.B. Carroll (2003), 'Corporate Social Responsibility: A three-domain approach', *Business Ethics Quarterly*, **13**(4), 503-530.

SIGMA Project (2003), *The SIGMA Guidelines. Putting Sustainable Development into Practice: A Guide for Organisations*, London: BSI, http://www.projectsigma.com.

Snell, S., M. Youndt and P. Wright (1996), 'Establishing a framework for research in strategic human resource management: Merging resource theory and organizational learning', *Research and Human Resources Management*, **14**, 61-90.

Social Investment Forum (2004), *Report on Responsible Investing Trends in the U.S. 2003*, http://www.socialinvest.org.

Social Investment Organization (2003), *Canadian Social Investment Review 2002*, http://www.socialinvestment.ca.

SPACE (1993), *Le Politiche Ambientali delle Prime Cento Imprese Italiane*, Milan: Bocconi University.

Stakeholder Research Associates Canada, United Nations Environment Programme and AccountAbility (2005), *The Stakeholder Engagement Manual*, Canada, Cobourg: Stakeholder Research Associates, http://www.uneptie.org.

Stewart, G.B. (1991), *The Quest for Value: A Guide for Senior Managers*, New York: HarperCollins Publishers.

Stiglitz, J.E. (2003), *The Roaring Nineties*, New York: W.W. Norton & Company.

Stroup, M.A. and R.L. Neubert (1987), 'The Evolution of Social Responsibility', *Business Horizons*, **30** (March-April), 22–24.

SustainAbility (2004), *Risk & Opportunity, Best Practice in Non-Financial Reporting*, London: SustainAbility, http://www.acc ountability.com

Teece, D. (1998), 'Capturing value from knowledge assets: the new economy, markets for know-how and intangible assets', *California Management Review*, **40**(3), 55-79.

Tencati, A. (1999), 'Etica e responsabilità ambientale dell'impresa. La misurazione della performance ecologica dell'azienda: il bilancio sociale e il bilancio ambientale', in L. M. Alfieri and M. L. Fornaciari Davoli (eds), *Etica ed Economia*, Modena: Mucchi, 297-319.

Tencati, A. (2002a), *Sostenibilità, Impresa e Performance. Un Nuovo Modello di Evaluation and Reporting*, Milan: Egea.

Tencati, A. (2002b), 'Managing Sustainability', in L. Zsolnai (ed), *Ethics in the Economy. Handbook of Business Ethics*, Oxford and Bern: Peter Lang Academic Publisher, 187-209.

Tencati, A. (2005), 'SERS-SPACE: un nuovo modello di evaluation and reporting della sostenibilità d'impresa', in G. Rusconi and M. Dorigatti (eds), *Modelli di Rendicontazione Etico-Sociale e Applicazioni Pratiche*, Milan: Franco Angeli, pp. 73-94.

Tencati, A. and F. Perrini, (2006), 'The Sustainability Perspective: A New Governance Model', in A. Kakabadse and M. Morsing (eds), *Corporate Social Responsibility. Reconciling Aspiration with Application*, London, UK: Palgrave Macmillan Ltd, pp. 94-111

Tencati, A., F. Perrini and S. Pogutz (2004), 'New tools to foster corporate socially responsible behaviour', *Journal of Business Ethics*, **53**, 173-190.

Ullmann, A.A. (1985), 'Data in search of a theory: A critical examination of the relationship among social performance, social disclosure, and economic performance of U.S. firms', *Academy of Management Review*, **10**(3), 540-557.

Ulrich, H. and W. Krieg (1973), *Das St. Galler Management-Modell*, Bern: Verlag Paul Haupt.

UNCTAD secretariat on the Consultations on Social Indicators (2004), *Review of the Comparability and Relevance of Existing Indicators on Corporate Social Responsibility*, United Nations Conference on Trade and Development (UNCTAD), Trade and Development Board, Commission on Investment, Technology and Related Financial Issues, Intergovernmental Working Group of Experts on International Standards of Accounting and Reporting, http://www.unctad.org.

Unioncamere and ISVI (2004), *I modelli di Responsabilità sociale nelle imprese italiane*, Milan: Franco Angeli.

United Nations (1993), *Integrated Environmental and Economic Accounting*, New York: United Nations.

United Nations, European Commission, International Monetary Fund, Organisation for Economic Co-operation and Development, World Bank (2003), *Integrated Environmental and Economic Accounting 2003. Handbook of National Accounting*, New York: United Nations.

United Nations Industrial Development Organization (UNIDO) (2002), *Corporate Social Responsibility. Implications for Small and Medium Enterprises in Developing Countries*, Vienna: UNIDO.

United States Environmental Protection Agency (EPA) (1995), *An Introduction to Environmental Accounting as a Business Management Tool: Key Concepts and Terms*, Washington DC: US EPA Office of Pollution, Prevention and Toxics, http://www.epa.gov.

Van Buren III, H.J. (2001), 'If fairness is the problem, is consent the solution? Integrating ISCT and Stakeholder Theory', *Business Ethics Quarterly*, **11**(3), 481-500.

van Marrewjik, M. (2003), 'Concepts and definitions of CSR and corporate sustainability: Between agency and communion', *Journal of Business Ethics*, **44**(2-3), 95-105.

Vanderbilt, T. (1998), *The Sneaker Book: Anatomy of an Industry and an Icon*, New York: The New Press.

Vicari, S. (ed.) (1995), *Brand Equity. Il potenziale generativo della fiducia*, Milan: Egea.

Vicari, S., G. Bertoli and B. Busacca (2000), 'Il valore delle relazioni di mercato. Nuove prospettive nell'analisi delle performance aziendali', *Finanza Marketing e Produzione*, **3**, 7-54.

Vogel, D. (2005), *The Market for Virtue: The Potential and Limits of Corporate Social Responsibility*, Brookings Institution Press.

Waddock, S.A. and S.B. Graves (1997), 'The corporate social performance: Financial performance link', *Strategic Management Journal*, **18**, 303-319.

Wagner M. and S. Schaltegger (2003), 'How does sustainability performance relate to business competitiveness?', *Greener Management International*, **44**(Winter): 5-16.

Walsh, J.P, K. Weber, and J.D. Margolis (2003), 'Social issues and management: Our lost cause found', *Journal of Management*, **29**, 859-881.

Wartick, S.L. and P.L. Cochran (1985), 'The evolution of corporate social performance model', *Academy of Management Review*, **10**(4), 758-769.

Weiser, J. and S. Zadek (2000), *Conversations with Disbelievers. Persuading Companies to Address Social Challenges*, New York: The Ford Foundation.

Wheeler, D. and J. Elkington (2001), 'The end of corporate environmental report? Or, the advent of cybernetic sustainability reporting', *Business Strategy and the Environment*, **10**, 1-14.

Willis, A. (2003), 'The role of the Global Reporting Initiative's Sustainability Reporting Guidelines in the social screening of in-vestments', *Journal of Business Ethics*, **43**(3), 233-237.

Wood, D.J. (1991), 'Corporate social performance revisited', *Academy of Management Review*, **16**(4), 691-718.

World Business Council for Sustainable Development (WBCSD) (1999), *Corporate Social Responsibility. Meeting Changing Expectations*, http://www.wbcsd.org.

World Business Council for Sustainable Development (WBCSD) (2000), *Measuring Eco-efficiency. A guide to reporting company performance*, Geneva: WBCSD, http://www.wbc sd.ch.

World Business Council for Sustainable Development (WBCSD) (2003), *Sustainable development reporting. Striking the balance*, Geneva: WBCSD, http://www.wbcsd.ch.

World Commission on Environment and Development (WCED) (1987), *Our common future*, Oxford University Press.

World Commission on the Social Dimension of Globalization (2004), *A Fair Globalization: Creating Opportunities for All*, Geneva: International Labour Office (ILO).

World Summit on Sustainable Development (WSSD) (2002a), *Johannesburg Declaration on Sustainable Development*, http://www.un.org.

World Summit on Sustainable Development (WSSD) (2002b), *Plan of Implementation of the World Summit on Sustainable Development*, http://www.un.org.

Yoo, B. and N. Donthu (2001), 'Developing and validating a multidimensional consumer-based brand equity scale', *Journal of Business Research*, **52**, 1-14.

Zadek S. (2002), *Mapping Instruments for Corporate Social Responsibility*. European Commission, Directorate-General for Employment and Social Affairs, http://europa.eu.int/comm /employment_social/publications/2004/ke1103002_en.pdf

Zadek, S., P. Pruzan and R. Evans (eds) (1997), *Building corporate AccountAbility: Emerging Practices in Social and Ethical Accounting, Auditing and Reporting*, London: Earthscan.

Zaheer, A. and N. Venkatraman (1995), 'Relational governance as an interorganizational strategy: An empirical test of the role of trust in economic exchange', *Strategic Management Journal*, **16**(5), 373-392.

Zaheer, A., B. McEvily and V. Perrone (1998), 'Does trust matter? Exploring the Effects of Inteorganizational and Interpersonal Trust and Performance', *Organization Science*, **9**(2), 141, 159.

Zingales F. and K. Hockerts (2003), *Balanced Scorecard and Sustainability: Examples from Literature and Practice*, Fontainebleau: INSEAD.

Zsolnai, L. (ed.), (2002), *Ethics in the Economy. Handbook of Business Ethics*, Oxford and Bern: Peter Lang Academic Publisher.

Zsolnai, L. (2002), 'New agenda for business ethics', in L. Zsolnai (ed.), *Ethics in the Economy. Handbook of Business Ethics*, Oxford and Bern: Peter Lang Academic Publisher, 1-7.

Appendix – Social Statement: key performance indicators

To conclude this broad review of the different CSR-related activities carried out in Italy, this chapter offers an in-depth examination of the Social Statement, focusing on Bocconi University's analysis of the set of indicators developed within the CSR-SC project.

As previously examined, the Social Statement (SS) is a voluntary tool mainly conceived to support companies reporting their CSR actions and performance, by standardizing the methods of data collection and presentation and by enhancing the comparison and evaluation of results. Furthermore, this instrument is designed to provide an answer to the rising number of requests for information from many stakeholders on CSR. Based on a clear and consolidated reporting model, the SS aims to ensure higher transparency in corporate communication by protecting consumers and thereby benefiting all citizens.

Starting from these assumptions, the Social Statement is organized into two main sections:

- the company profile;
- the set of indicators.

A.1 THE COMPANY PROFILE

The company profile focuses on the general features of the firm that intends to adopt the Social Statement:

- name;
- legal status of the company (Ltd or PLC, public company, cooperative, and so on);

- core business (or operating sectors);
- turnover;
- headquarters;
- branches;
- reference markets;
- number of employees.

The company profile also includes a request for more specific information about the company's commitment to CSR: the adoption of Codes of Conduct, Management Systems (for example, quality systems, environmental and safety management systems, ethical sourcing systems), certifications and social, environmental and sustainability reports. These documents may be attached to the Social Statement to prove the company's commitment to these categories.

A.2 THE SET OF INDICATORS

The set of indicators is divided into three levels:

- *categories*, groups of stakeholders to whom specific clusters of indicators are addressed;
- *aspects*, thematic areas considered according to groups of performance indicators, in the framework of a determined category of stakeholders;
- *indicators*, that is, qualitative and quantitative measures that provide information about a specific aspect. They can be used to control and show the performance of an organization.

The indicators are divided into eight categories, on the basis of the different groups of stakeholders:

1. Human Resources;
2. Shareholders/Members and Financial Community;
3. Customers;
4. Suppliers;
5. Financial Partners;
6. State, Local Authorities and Public Administration;
7. Community;
8. Environment.

The set of indicators is divided into two main typologies:

- Common indicators (C), that must be used by all the enterprises to conform to the Social Statement (from SMEs to large enterprises);
- Additional indicators (A), which can be implemented in case of large enterprises (with at least 50 employees) on the basis of specific criteria, by supporting and integrating common indicators.

Finally, indicators can be either qualitative (for instance, in case the description of a project or of an initiative carried out by the company is requested) or quantitative (in those cases in which the information requested must be expressed in numerical form: percentage, ratio, quotient, economic or financial data, and so on).

The complete set of indicators – according to triple-bottom-line (see table below) – found necessary for the CSR-SC Project is listed below. For each indicator an explanatory guide is provided, containing the following information:

- a progressive code articulated according to the eight stakeholders' categories and the three-level framework;
- the name of the indicator;
- the relevance for firms (common indicator or additional indicator);
- the qualitative or quantitative nature of the information;
- explanatory remarks, describing the indicator and the goals;
- a description of some suggested measurement procedures/methods.

Table A.1 Pillars for the sustainable development of socially responsible corporations

	ECONOMIC	SOCIAL		ENVIRONMENTAL
STAKEHOLDER GROUPS	2.*Shareholders/members and financial community* 3. *Customers* 4. *Suppliers* 5. *Financial partners* 6. *State, local authorities and public administration*	*1. Human resources*	*7. Community*	*8. Environment*
AREAS	3.1 General characteristics 3.2 Development of the market 3.3 Customer satisfaction and customer loyalty 3.4 Product/service information and labeling (safety, Life Cycle Assessment, voluntary initiatives) 3.5 Ethical/environmentally friendly products/services (public utility) 3.6 Promotional policies (adherence to code of conduct) 3.7 Privacy 4.1 Supplier management policy 4.1.1 Division of suppliers by category 4.1.2 Selection of suppliers 4.1.3 Communication, awareness creation, and information 4.2 Contractual terms 5.1 Relations with banks 5.2 Relations with insurance companies 5.3 Relations with financial institutions (e.g., leasing firms) 6.1 Taxes and duties 6.2 Relations with local authorities 6.3 Codes of conduct and rules for compliance with legislation 6.4 Contributions, benefits or easy-term financing	1.1 Staff composition 1.2 Turnover 1.3 Equal opportunity 1.4 Training 1.5 Work hours by category 1.6 Schemes of wages 1.7 Absence from work 1.8 Employee benefits 1.9 Industrial relations 1.10 In-house communications 1.11 Occupational health and safety 1.12 Employee satisfaction 1.13 Protection of workers' rights 1.14 Disciplinary measures and litigation	7.1 Corporate giving 7.2 Direct contributions in various fields of action 7.2.1 Education and training 7.2.2 Culture 7.2.3 Sport 7.2.4 Research and innovation 7.2.5 Social solidarity (including international solidarity) 7.2.6 Other (volunteering, community daycare, etc.) 7.3 Stakeholder engagement and dialogue 7.4 Media relations 7.5 Virtual community 7.6 Corruption prevention	8.1 Energy and materials' consumption, emissions 8.1.1 Energy 8.1.2 Water 8.1.3 Raw materials, auxiliary materials, and packaging 8.1.4 Atmospheric emissions 8.1.5 Water emissions 8.1.6 Waste management 8.2 Environmental strategy and community relations

Source: Italian Ministry of Labour and Social Affairs (2006), p.5.

A.3 KEY PERFORMANCE INDICATORS IN DETAIL

1	**Human Resources**
1.1	*Staff composition*
1.1.1	Category
1.1.2	Age
1.1.3	Seniority in grade
1.1.4	Geographic origin
1.1.5	Nationality
1.1.6	Contract type
1.1.7	Level of education
Additional	Quantitative
Explanatory remarks	Description of the company profile in terms of employee composition. Emphasis is on the connections between staff composition and the local community.
Measurement procedure	The percentage of employees (of the grand total) by category, geographic origin (region or municipality according to the size of the company and the social context), nationality, level of education. Average age and seniority of employees (if applicable, divided into specific categories). For complete data for this indicator, refer to the Collective Labor agreement/s with employees. In the event of further labor agreements, please indicate the distribution of employees among the various agreements and the relevant criteria.

1.2	*Turnover*
1.2.1	Employment policies
Additional	Qualitative
Explanatory remarks	Review of the company's employment policies.
Measurement procedure	Description of the company's employment policies (employment, career advancement, improvement in employee loyalty, and so on).
1.2.2	Permanent employees and non-permanent employees
Additional	Quantitative
Explanatory remarks	Quantification of the percentage of permanent and non-permanent employees in the company.

Measurement procedure	Measure the number of non-permanent employees in the company divided into categories (e.g., free lancers, continued employment, temporary workers, other recently introduced forms of employment). Calculate the percentage of permanent and non-permanent employees of the total of both categories of employee. Briefly describe the activities for which companies frequently use non-permanent employees.

1.2.3	Employment termination (by kind of contract)
Additional	Quantitative
Explanatory remarks	Measurement of the methods most often used to terminate the employment relationship.
Measurement procedure	Number of termination cases for each of the last three years out of the average number of employees for each year. Termination of the employment relationship by category (dismissal, resignation, retirement, and so on).

1.3	*Equal opportunity*
1.3.1	Gender ratio (managerial staff and executives)
Additional	Quantitative
Explanatory remarks	Measurement of the extent to which equal opportunity policies are applied by the company.
Measurement procedure	Percentage of men and women according to employment category: manager or executive.
1.3.2	Salary by gender (also by category and seniority in grade)
Additional	Quantitative
Explanatory remarks	Explanation of the correct implementation of the equal treatment policy by focusing on average salaries of women and men.
Measurement procedure	Gross annual salary for managers and executives, gross annual salary for male managers and executives, gross annual salary for female managers and executives in the last three years. These data will be divided into seniority categories, if applicable.
1.3.3	Policy for people with disabilities and minorities in general
Common	Quantitative and qualitative
Explanatory remarks	This broad indicator covers all considerations connected to disabled persons and the protection of minorities, with reference to both in-house personnel (employees, external workers, outsourced personnel), and structural and logistic

	considerations (e.g., elimination of architectural barriers).
Measurement procedure	Number of actions and summary description of them. Total expenses. Total expenses on Value Added (VA). Disabled employees (permanent and non-permanent) or employees belonging to minority groups considered in relation to the total of employees (percentage and absolute value).

1.4	*Training*
1.4.1	Training projects (by kind)
Additional	Qualitative
Explanatory remarks	This indicator monitors the training investment (net of the contractual or legal training hours) implemented by the firm to develop individual professional skills, without gender discrimination (category, sex, and so on).
Measurement procedure	Description of ongoing projects with the number of employees involved, and for terminated projects, the results achieved. Funding or easy terms for each project, if applicable.
1.4.2	Training hours by category (net of contractual or legal training hours)
Common	Quantitative
Explanatory remarks	Monitoring of the company's training investment (net of the contractual or legal training hours) to develop individual professional skills, without gender discrimination (category, sex, and so on).
Measurement procedure	Hours/employee (divided by sex). Expenses borne for external courses on the Added Value. Training hours (in-house and outside) – hours of training that are contractually compulsory/number of employees and assimilated workers.
1.4.3	Internships
Additional	Quantitative
Explanatory remarks	Monitoring whether the company accepts internships and evaluating the effectiveness of this training tool.
Measurement procedure	Number of internships per year. Percentage of employees of the annual total of apprentices.

	Workers coming from internship programs (held in the last three years in the firm) divided according to type of contract (training, fixed-term contract, and so on).

1.5	*Working hours by category*
Additional	Quantitative
Explanatory remarks	Specification of working hours and different shifts scheduled by the firm.
Measurement procedure	Working hours for each category. Average overtime per week, per head, per category. Average overtime per head per category during the busiest week.

1.6	*Schemes of wages*
1.6.1	Average gross wages
Additional	Quantitative
Explanatory remarks	Measurement of wage criteria set by the company.
Measurement procedure	Average gross wage per category. Minimum gross wage for each category of the collective labor agreement enforced.
1.6.2	Career paths
Additional	Quantitative and qualitative
Explanatory remarks	Explanation of career-path and career-advancement policies of the company.
Measurement procedure	Description of the policies on career advancement, career opportunities and personnel evaluation criteria and methods. Number of grade advancements implemented last year. Number of career advancements (e.g., from manager to executive, from employee to manager, and so on) last year. Number of managers coming from in-house career paths.
1.6.3	Incentive systems
Additional	Quantitative and qualitative
Explanatory remarks	Examination of the company's incentive programs.
Measurement procedure	Description of implemented incentive programs. Number of employees who benefited from incentive tools last year. Average per-capita value of implemented incentives

1.7	*Absence from work*
1.7.1	Days of absence
1.7.2.	Causes
Additional	Quantitative and qualitative
Explanatory remarks	Calculation of the occurrence of absences and determination of the most widespread causes.
Measurement procedure	Number of total hours of absence in one year. Number of average per-capita hours of absence in one year. Percentages of causes of absence (disease, trade-union leave, paid holidays, medical examination, paid leave, unpaid leave, and so on).

1.8	*Employee benefits*
Common	Quantitative and qualitative
Explanatory remarks	Definition of different ways to improve the company's ambience and employees quality of life (and that of relevant families). It excludes fringe benefits (e.g., luncheon vouchers, company car, mobile phone). Examples: in-house kindergarten, flexible hours, tax counseling, possibility of accommodations for employees (e.g., near the production site), and so on
Measurement procedure	Number of initiatives. Expenses borne on VA. Number of employees involved in the total.

1.9	*Industrial relations*
1.9.1	Compliance with the rights of free association and collective bargaining
Additional	Quantitative and qualitative
Explanatory remarks	Description of the company's policies for ensuring compliance with ILO Conventions on industrial relations. Specifically, measurement of actions concerning the company's branching abroad.
Measurement procedure	Description of the relevant actions carried out by the company, with particular attention to the branches abroad. Description of the policies and activities carried out in compliance with ILO Conventions concerning the rights to organize (trade union freedom) and collective bargaining which are not translated into binding local rules.

1.9.2	Percentage of trade union members among employees
Additional	Quantitative
Explanatory remarks	Analysis of the presence of trade unions in the company.
Measurement procedure	Number of trade union members compared with the total number of employees.

1.9.3	Other considerations (hours of strike, participation in the company's government, and so on)
Additional	Quantitative and qualitative
Explanatory remarks	Measurement of interaction between the company and trade unions.
Measurement procedure	Description of initiatives under way promoted by the company or trade union representatives. Hours of strike per year and percentage of strikers among employees.

1.10	*In-house communications*
Additional	Qualitative
Explanatory remarks	Definition of the communication activities implemented by the company (newsletters, intranet, informal communication means for employees to send comments and remarks to managers, and so on).
Measurement procedure	Brief description of initiatives carried out, with information on the employees' satisfaction and amount of media usage.

1.11	*Occupational health and safety*
1.11.1	Injuries and diseases
Common	Quantitative and qualitative
Explanatory remarks	Verification of the company's commitment to the reduction of risk for the workers' safety and health.
Measurement procedure	Injury frequency rate and injury severity rate. (sector benchmarking based on adequately examined national statistics). Projects implemented. Examples: introduction of a real System of Health and Safety Management in the workplace that, beyond ensuring the compliance with law, allows for a better performance.

1.11.2	Projects
Additional	Qualitative
Explanatory remarks	Description of the company's commitment to minimize risks to workers' safety and health.
Measurement procedure	Description of the projects carried out to reduce accidents, beyond the activities to ensure compliance with binding laws.

1.12	*Employee satisfaction*
1.12.1	In-house customer satisfaction surveys
Additional	Quantitative and qualitative
Explanatory remarks	Listing of the initiatives carried out by the company to monitor personnel satisfaction.
Measurement procedure	Description of initiatives adopted. Percentage of answers obtained on the total number of employees involved in each initiative. Summary of results.

1.12.2	Projects
Additional	Qualitative
Explanatory remarks	Description of the company's commitment to enhancing personnel satisfaction.
Measurement procedure	Descriptions of carried-out projects.

1.13	*Protection of workers' rights*
Common	Qualitative
Explanatory remarks	Description of the company's structure at the international level to ensure compliance with ILO Conventions
Measurement procedure	Description of the localization of production and commercial subsidiaries or affiliated companies abroad (joint ventures included). Description of the activities carried out in relation to ILO Conventions that are not translated into binding local laws.

1.13.1	Child labor
Additional	Qualitative and quantitative
Explanatory remarks	Description of the company's policies for ensuring compliance with ILO Conventions – specifically quantifying

	the number of minors employed. Measurement of company actions, relative to its production and commercial branches abroad, to monitor the hiring of minors in working activities.
Measurement procedure	Number of children employed divided by age. Description of the policies and activities implemented according to ILO Conventions on child labor not translated into binding laws.
1.13.2	Forced labor
Additional	Qualitative
Explanatory remarks	Explanation of the company's policies that ensure compliance with ILO Conventions specifically assessing the actions carried out by the company to fight against forced labor in its branches abroad.
Measurement procedure	Description of the policies and activities implemented by the company to prevent forced labor in its branches abroad. Description of the activities carried out according to ILO Conventions concerning the forced labor that is not legislated against in binding local laws.

1.14	*Disciplinary measures and litigation*
Common	Quantitative
Explanatory remarks	Analysis of the impact of disciplinary measures on the company.
Measurement procedure	Number of disciplinary measures adopted in the last 3 years, divided by kind (written warning, fine, lay-off and so on). Number of appeals to these measures and outcomes. Number of actions brought forward by employees.

2	**Shareholders/Members and Financial Community**
2.1	*Capital stock formation*
2.1.1	Number of shareholders by share type
Additional	Quantitative
Explanatory remarks	Knowing and monitoring the performance over time of the company's assets
Measurement procedure	Historical series, 3 years at least.

2.1.2	Segmentation of shareholders by category
Additional	Quantitative and qualitative
Explanatory remarks	Description of the participation in the share capital by companies and individuals.
Measurement procedure	Annual audit (for 3 years at least) of the company's structure divided by kind of shareholder: kind of companies, their control and location, geographic origin of individuals, and so on

2.2	*Shareholders'/Members' remuneration (share indicators and ratio)*
2.2.1	Earnings per share
2.2.2	Dividends
2.2.3	Price/earnings per share
Additional	Quantitative
Explanatory remarks	Analysis of the behavior and condition of companies, in terms of their capability to create and distribute wealth over time.
Measurement procedure	Historical series, 3 years at least.
2.2.4	Others (e.g., allowance, contributions to mutual funds)
Additional	Quantitative and qualitative
Explanatory remarks	Wide indicator for co-operative companies that should include all the shareholders' payment schemes implemented by co-operative following the mutual approach.
Measurement procedure	Direction of financial resources to shareholders on VA. Presentation of the different shareholders' payment schemes. Example: beyond allowances, large-scale retail traders carry out some initiatives for the shareholders (for example, particular promotions, sale promotions, and so on).

2.3	*Stock price fluctuation*
Additional	Quantitative
Explanatory remarks	In the case of an unlisted company, understanding the degree of investor confidence in the future of the company.
Measurement procedure	Charting, with the monthly closing of the share, of maximum and minimum fluctuations and their relation to the monthly

	closing rating of the reference stock exchange market.

2.4	*Rating*
Additional	Quantitative and qualitative
Explanatory remarks	This indicator is linked to the company's reliability as an investment-receiver. High ratings conferred by an independent third party suggest a low risk level for investors who are attracted to grant credits/capital stocks.
Measurement procedure	Timing of performance (3 years at least) of the rating scale according to previously determined and public criteria.

2.5	*Shareholders' participation in the government and protection of minorities*
2.5.1	Existence of independent directors inside the Board of Directors (BoD)
Additional	Quantitative and qualitative
Explanatory remarks	Verification of the real control power of the BoD in relation to the members holding operational/managerial proxies.
Measurement procedure	Percentage of the number of 'independent' directors relative to the total. List of powers.
2.5.2	Existence of minority shareholders inside the BoD
Additional	Quantitative and qualitative
Explanatory remarks	Description of the protection of minority shareholders through an adequate degree of representation inside the BoD.
Measurement procedure	Percentage of counselors representing minority shareholders relative to the total of the BoD members.
2.5.3	Occurrence of BoD meetings
Additional	Quantitative and qualitative
Explanatory remarks	Monitoring of the real participation of shareholders in the company's management.
Measurement procedure	Number of meetings per year.

2.5.4	Other (e.g., compliance with self-regulatory measures)
Additional	Qualitative
Explanatory remarks	Description of the governance methods that enhance the general participation of shareholders and foster non-discriminatory policies.
Measurement procedure	Initiatives carried-out, self-regulatory codes, ethical codes protecting minorities.

2.6	*Benefits and services for shareholders*
Additional	Qualitative
Explanatory remarks	Description of the involvement practices regarding shareholders beyond the return on investment and economic prospects (e.g., shareholders who are also customers/co-workers).
Measurement procedure	Description of the privileges reserved for shareholders (e.g., discounts, special promotions, reserved products, and so on)

2.7	*Investor relations*
2.7.1	Communication and reporting activities
Common	Qualitative
Explanatory remarks	Description of the regular flow of information to shareholders/members and the collection of remarks, suggestions, and requirements.
Measurement procedure	Description of the number of initiatives implemented each year and methods of implementation.
2.7.2	Institutional presentations and documents
Additional	Qualitative
Explanatory remarks	Controlling for adequate flow of information relevant for investors (financial statements, news on the media, brochures, advertising activities, and so on)
Measurement procedure	Description of the initiatives and their occurrence (on a 3-year basis).
2.7.3	Road show
Additional	Qualitative and quantitative
Explanatory remarks	Open days with stakeholders to enhance their commitment to the firms' activities

Measurement procedure	Number of initiatives, their occurrence and coverage of national/international territory.

2.7.4	One-to-one meetings
Additional	Qualitative and quantitative
Explanatory remarks	Measurement of the company's attendance at investors' meetings so as to obtain direct feedback, listen to their expectations, address any dissatisfaction.
Measurement procedure	Number of meetings\number of shareholders.

2.7.5	Communications on the Internet
Additional	Qualitative and quantitative
Explanatory remarks	Measurement of the importance of Internet communications with investors.
Measurement procedure	Description of the initiatives on the company's website and their development with time, and of user areas for shareholders and members in which information, economic performances, forecasts and comparisons relevant to budgets are listed.

2.7.6	Others
Additional	Qualitative and quantitative
Explanatory remarks	Description of communications specifically confined to shareholders and investors who are put into contact with other stakeholders during one or more open days to find out their expectations, degree of satisfaction and worries related to risks.
Measurement procedure	Number of initiatives and their description.

3	**Customers**
3.1	*General characteristics*
3.1.1	Division of customers by category
Additional	Qualitative and quantitative
Explanatory remarks	Provision of more detailed information on the company's customers, to improve the efficiency and effectiveness of customer management and to better detect needs and priorities. Analysis of customers and their division into categories.

Measurement procedure	Number of customers by category. Table of customers divided into categories, including the most recent occasions of updating and testing/updating.

3.1.2	Division of customers by kind of offer
Additional	Qualitative and quantitative
Explanatory remarks	Provision of information about management of customers to better measure their needs/expectations and priorities.
Measurement procedure	Number of customers according to type of product/service. Table of customers categorized according to kind of offer, last instance of updating and testing/updating.

3.2	*Market development*
3.2.1	New customers
Additional	Qualitative and quantitative
Explanatory remarks	Completion of the profile of the company's activities and reference market by requiring the measurement and description of new customers (new customers on the market and/or customers of competitors), by offering to help measure new market niches and planning strategies to increase already launched activities and/or develop new initiatives.
Measurement procedure	Measurement of the number and quality of new customers acquired, with remarks and comments.

3.2.2	New products/services
Additional	Qualitative and quantitative
Explanatory remarks	Measurement of the company's readiness to 'read and listen to' customer and market needs and to translate these needs/expectations into plans and developments for new products/services. Monitoring of the improvement/renewal/evolution process of the company over time.
Measurement procedure	Expense on VA (divided into market research, development, production). Number of projects related to new products/services.

3.3	*Customer satisfaction and customer loyalty*
3.3.1	Customer satisfaction initiatives (e.g., research, measurement, call centre and queries)

Additional	Qualitative and quantitative
Explanatory Remarks	Evaluation of the company's follow-up activities while analyzing and measuring the degree of customer satisfaction, with the goal of meeting customer expectations, identifying and solving problems of dissatisfaction, creating stronger relationships and developing new market opportunities.
Measurement procedure	Number of actions to measure customer satisfaction/perception. Number of customer actions/requests. Number of customer actions/queries Benchmark

3.3.2	Customer loyalty initiatives
Additional	Qualitative and quantitative
Explanatory remarks	Measurement of how the company interacts with customers and listens to/answers their requests/expectations by finding ways to consolidate and increase their loyalty.
Measurement procedure	Loyalty curve according to client/category with distinction between: repeated requests for services/products and requests for other products/services that differ from those generally purchased. Term of contracts. Expenses for customer loyalty initiatives.

3.4	*Product/service information and labeling (safety, Life Cycle Assessment, voluntary initiatives)*
Common	Qualitative and quantitative
Explanatory remarks	Evaluation of the company's commitment to creating products/services that protect customer and consumer interests and to ensuring transparent communications on quality, environmental impact and safety of products. Reference is made to the methods used to study and describe the products, to communicate their correct usage, to voluntary initiatives (e.g., Ecolabel, Environmental Product Declaration, mark of conformity of organic food, social labels like Fair Trade, and so on) that go beyond simple compliance with the laws in force.
Measurement procedure	List of the products/services with the above-mentioned characteristics. Percentage, for 'labeled' products/service, of the total turnover. Examples: in the case of banks, one could refer to particular products (ethical funds, bank charges or interest partially allocated to charity).

3.5	*Ethical and environmentally friendly products and services (public utility)*
Additional	Qualitative and quantitative
Explanatory remarks	Focus on the detailed attention paid to the supply of services/products with clear and measurable ethical and environmental value.
Measurement procedure	Number of ethical/environmental products and services/total of products and services. Expense for research, production, maintenance of ethical/environmental products and services/overhead. Profits from ethical/environmental products and services/total of products and services.

3.6	*Promotional policies (adherence to code of conduct)*
Additional	Qualitative and quantitative
Explanatory remarks	Measurement of company methods of promoting its products/services with detailed attention to the thoroughness of information, respect for existing or potential customers, ethical/environmental principles
Measurement procedure	Expenses for/profits from promotional activities.

3.7	*Privacy*
Additional	Qualitative and quantitative
Explanatory remarks	Analysis of the activities to protect privacy, with reference to customer data and behaviors that go beyond simple compliance with the laws in force. Companies are therefore asked to activate tools/procedures that meet this requirement and also to inform customers (or whoever asks customers for authorization to use the data with a detailed description of the usage aims and methods) of products/services to which laws do not make specific reference (e.g., loyalty cards, etc).
Measurement procedure	Investments in privacy protection actions. Number of products/services subject to privacy protection laws /total number.

4	**Suppliers**
4.1	*Supplier management policy*
Common	Qualitative and quantitative
Explanatory remarks	Description of direct suppliers (particularly suppliers relevant to the company's core business) and of the company's policies to inform them about and involve them in CSR, environmental and safety issues (e.g., location of the production activities and compliance with ILO conventions by direct suppliers).
Measurement procedure	Selection criteria for direct suppliers and others connected with the company's core business, aimed at involving them in and informing them about the company's CSR environmental and safety issues. Initiatives to involve them in and inform them about CSR, environmental and safety issues.
4.1.1	Division of suppliers by category
Additional	Qualitative and quantitative
Explanatory remarks	Evaluation of the company's actions to detect, select and manage in the most effective and efficient way its suppliers, and also to better detect supplier needs and requests.
Measurement procedure	Number of suppliers by category.
4.1.2	Supplier selection
Additional	Qualitative and quantitative
Explanatory remarks	Evaluation of research activities and selection of suppliers, also considering the management and implementation systems of company products and services (e.g., quality system management, environment, safety, social responsibility) and/or signed procedures and policies. Specific attention is paid to suppliers that have the most impact on the characteristics (quality, environment, safety, ethical-social considerations) of the company's products/services. Non-EU suppliers are requested to carry out a detailed analysis and careful management, particularly of sites in developing countries: specifically, suppliers are requested to check for the existence of and compliance with ILO and international-convention-protection policies.
Measurement procedure	Number of suppliers by category with management system/total. Number of suppliers with non-EU sites by category.

4.1.3	Communication, awareness creation and information
Additional	Qualitative and quantitative
Explanatory remarks	Focus on the company's policies and activities aimed at: • Informing suppliers about the policies, principles and procedures adopted by the company to protect quality, sustainability, respect for environment and ethical-social principles; • Creation of awareness among suppliers of the need to respect these principles and implement parallel procedures and policies.
Measurement procedure	Number of suppliers that actively comply with these principles/total suppliers. Number of educational activities.

4.2	*Contractual terms*
Common	Qualitative and quantitative
Explanatory remarks	Evaluation of company's procedures for paying suppliers. This could be divided into the categories of invoice amounts and terms of payment (deadlines), to precisely highlight company policies.
Measurement procedure	Payment terms and relevant national benchmarking.

5	**Financial partners**
5.1	*Relations with banks*
Additional	Qualitative
Explanatory remarks	Specification of criteria used to select the partner (e.g., ethical behaviors, employment schemes, profit sharing) and the ways in which the company's risk profile is communicated.
Measurement procedure	Certified evaluation of the partner, company's risk information. Description of selection criteria.

5.2	Relations with insurance companies
Additional	Qualitative
Explanatory remarks	Specification of the criteria used to select the partner (e.g., ethical behaviors, employment schemes, profit sharing) and the ways in which the company's risk profile is communicated.
Measurement procedure	Insurance company's rating, information on the financial statement, company's criteria for analysis of the business and financial risks.

5.3	Relations with financial institutions (e.g., leasing companies)
Additional	Qualitative
Explanatory remarks	Description of the company's proactive behaviors in the stakeholder category (e.g., preliminary evaluation of ethical behaviors, profits allocation and management policies).
Measurement procedure	Adopted evaluation procedures.

6	**State, Local Authorities and Public Administration**
6.1	Taxes and duties
Additional	Qualitative and quantitative
Explanatory remarks	Measurement of the wealth produced and allocated by the company, in different forms and to public subjects, to better understand the company's contribution to territorial development.
Measurement procedure	Quantification of different taxes (regional tax on productive activities, corporate income tax, local property tax, stamps and duties) as absolute values and as a percentage of the AV.

6.2	Relations with local authorities
Additional	Qualitative
Explanatory remarks	Analysis of the existing relationships between the company and public institutions, by describing involvement and/or partnership activities. For example, compliance with voluntary or program agreements on specific initiatives of economic (territorial development), environmental and social value.

Measurement procedure	Description of initiatives, relevant targets and state of implementation (on a 3-year basis).

6.3	*Codes of conduct and rules for compliance with laws*
6.3.1	Codes of conduct and rules for compliance with laws and internal auditing systems
Common	Qualitative
Explanatory remarks	Evaluation of explicit policies and in-house auditing systems (adopted on a voluntary basis) to ensure compliance with laws.
Measurement procedure	Adoption of codes of conduct and in-house rules and implementation of relative control systems.
6.3.2	Conformity verification and inspections
Additional	Qualitative and quantitative
Explanatory remarks	Measurement of the company's compliance with the laws in force so as to verify the consistency of declared behaviors (codes of conduct, ethical codes, policies, and so on) with implemented behaviors.
Measurement procedure	Number and kind of inspections by authorities and challenging of failures to comply.

6.4	*Contributions, benefits or easy-term financing*
Additional	Qualitative and quantitative
Explanatory remarks	Checking of whether the company was granted various kinds of public benefits and financing.
Measurement procedure	Description of the procedures to apply for funds, to plan funded activities, to implement activities and report them (on a 3-year basis). Description of funded projects and results achieved.

7	**Community**
7.1	*Corporate giving*
Common	Qualitative and quantitative
Explanatory remarks	Review of the company's commitment to the communities (for example, with reference to solidarity, culture, education,

	and environmental regeneration) through donations and other gifts.
Measurement procedure	Expenses on VA. Description of beneficiary institutions and relative initiatives.

7.2	*Direct contributions in various fields of actions*
7.2.1	Education and training
7.2.2	Culture
7.2.3	Sport
Common	Qualitative and quantitative
Explanatory remarks	Measurement of activities carried out in the fields of education (e.g., organization or promotion of courses on social/environmental issues or for training skilled professionals), culture (organization of cultural events) and/or sport (sponsoring of sports events with positive social impact on the community, for example, through involvement of a large youth population).
Measurement procedure	Expenses on VA or turnover. Description of initiatives implemented.

7.2.4	Research and innovation
Common	Qualitative and quantitative
Explanatory remarks	Evaluation of the company's commitment in the field of research and innovation. In particular, innovation may concern production processes (operations, logistics, information handling, and so on) and products. It is clear that this commitment positively affects the company's competitiveness and its value, that is, the value of its economic capital. However, innovation also has a wider value: the company's efforts in this direction aim to ensure its sustainability, that is, its endurance, by creating values for stakeholders and the community in general, thus contributing to the development of the country. Comparison with national (and European) statistics by homogeneous-size categories.
Measurement procedure	Expenses on VA or turnover. Description of research projects.

7.2.5	Social solidarity (including international solidarity)
Common	Qualitative and quantitative
Explanatory remarks	Measurement of the company's commitment in the field of social support (assistance, health, interventions in favor of groups and/or disadvantaged groups, and so on), including at the international level. For example, direct investment in developing countries (hospitals, nursery schools, schools or other interventions for local economic development) or, still at the local level, actively sponsoring activities in home help programs for the elderly, or recovery programs for drug addicts, and so on.
Measurement procedure	Expenses on VA or turnover. Initiatives carried out.

7.2.6	Other (e.g., volunteering, community daycare, etc.)
Common	Qualitative and quantitative
Explanatory remarks	Measurement of the company's commitment in the field of social responsibility through initiatives different from those above. Examples: voluntary charity services promoted by companies, start-up of refugees, kindergartens.
Measurement procedure	Expenses on VA or turnover. Number of hours devoted to the activity.

7.3	*Stakeholder engagement and dialogue*
Common	Qualitative
Explanatory remarks	Measurement of communication activities and involvement of stakeholders, particularly of those in the community (citizens, NGOs, media, and so on). Examples could be 'Open Factories and Plants', public presentations of social reports or sustainability reports, structured dialogues with stakeholders to select the indicators to measure the company's performance, and so on.
Measurement procedure	Description of the activity of communication/dialogue and involvement carried out by the companies for the sake of the stakeholders.

7.4	Relations with the media
Additional	Qualitative and quantitative
Explanatory remarks	Analysis of the relationships between the company and the media (press, television, radio). Measurement of the company's degree of disclosure and the amount of attention paid to requests from the media.
Measurement procedure	Number of press conferences held and object of the initiatives. Costs/investment in the relationship with the media on the VA and the turnover. Existence of organizational units for the management of media relations.

7.5	Virtual community
7.5.1	Contacts (characteristics and analysis)
Additional	Qualitative and quantitative
Explanatory remarks	In light of the increasing importance of the Internet and digital technologies, examination of the number, profile and characteristics of the subjects who address the company by using the Web.
Measurement procedure	Existence of a company's portal/site (kind and characteristics). Number of average daily contacts. Monitoring of the characteristics of users who visit the company's site.

7.5.2	Security
Additional	Qualitative
Explanatory remarks	Methods to protect sensible information (personal data, payment terms and references, and so on) beyond that provided by the privacy act.
Measurement procedure	Description of the projects carried out by the company to protect the interests of users (customers, suppliers, other stakeholders) who interact with the company on the Internet.

7.5.3	Relation management systems
Additional	Qualitative and quantitative
Explanatory remarks	Monitoring of the systems that manage the relationships with stakeholders carried out through the Internet (e.g., on-line forum, informative campaigns, targeted services, and so on)

Measurement procedure	Descriptions of initiatives carried out and results achieved.

7.6	*Corruption prevention*
Common	Qualitative
Explanatory remarks	Evaluation of explicit in-house control policies and systems to avoid corrupt practices and, in general, unethical behaviors.
Measurement procedure	Adoption of self-regulatory codes and in-house rules.

8	**Environment**
8.1	*Energy and materials consumption, emissions*
Common	Qualitative and quantitative
Explanatory remarks	Measurement of the company's commitment to environmental sustainability in terms of reduction, beyond the limits imposed by applicable laws, of the consumption of raw materials (input) and pollutants (output, that is, air emissions, water dumping, noise, waste, and so on).
Measurement procedure	Number of initiatives developed to minimize the company's environmental impact (processes, products, etc) and relevant targets for improvement. Description of the activities to train and sensitize the personnel. Examples: Investments in a system of water return to reduce the usage of water resources in the plant, or replacement of hazardous raw materials with lower-impact products.
8.1.1	Energy
Additional	Qualitative and quantitative
Explanatory remarks	Measurement of the quantity of energy resources used by the company for different purposes (energy efficiency) and of the use of renewable sources of energy, if applicable. Data on a 3-year basis.
Measurement procedure	TOEs directly used for organizational activities: total in absolute values and indexed according to productive or economic standards, based on the kind of organization, for example: • TOEs/tons of output x manufacturing sector • TOEs/number of employees x utility and service

	companies
	TOEs directly used for related activities (travel, transport of goods, product life-cycle, usage of high-intensity energy raw materials), represented as above.
	Number of initiatives and brief description of them as a further specification of the above in the set of common indicators, aimed at:
	• Use of renewable resources (wind, waste to energy, biomass, photovoltaic, geothermal systems) • Increase in energy efficiency
	Total investment/VA.

8.1.2	Water
Additional	Qualitative and quantitative
Explanatory remarks	Measurement of the quantity of water resources used by the company for different purposes according to the source. Data on a 3-year basis.
Measurement procedure	Cubic meters used for the organization's activities: total in absolute value and indexed according to productive and economic standards based on the kind of organization, for example: • m^3/tons of output x manufacturing sector • m^3/number of employees x utility and service companies • % of re-used/recycled water resources calculated as a recycled quantity/(collected quantity + recycled quantity) Total m^3 used divided by kind of source Number of re-usage/recycle initiatives and brief description of them. Total investment/VA.

8.1.3	Raw materials, auxiliary materials and packaging
Additional	Qualitative and quantitative
Explanatory remarks	Measurement of the quantity of raw materials and packaging used by the company for its output divided by macro-class (if applicable, to show the environmental friendliness). Data on a 3-year basis.
Measurement procedure	• % of raw materials, consumable materials and packaging derived from recycled material/total

	consumed
	• % of raw materials, consumable materials and packaging with eco-labeling /total consumed.
	• total consumption/output.
	Number of initiatives to save raw materials and packaging and use of environmentally friendly raw materials and packaging; brief description of them
	Total investment/VA.
8.1.4.	Atmospheric emissions
Additional	Qualitative and quantitative
Explanatory remarks	Measurement of the quantity of air emissions (from pollutants and widespread substances) divided by kind of effect on the environment (for example, green house effect, detrimental for the ozone layer). Data on a 3-year basis.
Measurement procedure	Total emitted tons of NO_x, SO_2, dusts, VOC and other meaningful emissions and characteristics of the processes. Total emitted tons of CO_2, CH_4, N_2O, HFCs, PFCs, SF_6 and total tons expressed in CO_2 equivalent. Total emitted tons for each group of pollutant (in case of green house gases) or for single pollutant indexed on productive or economic standards according to the kind of organization, for example:
	• tons of VOC equivalent/tons of output x manufacturing sector
	• tons of CO_2 equivalent/number of employees x utility and services companies
	Tons of hazardous substances for the ozone layer and total tons emitted into the atmosphere (CFCs, trichloroethane, and so on). Emissions deriving from direct activities (e.g., production) and indirect activities (e.g., transport) shall be considered. Number of initiatives aimed at reducing air emissions or at compensation (e.g., reforestation initiatives); brief description of them.
	Total investment/VA.
8.1.5	Water emissions
Additional	Qualitative and quantitative
Explanatory remarks	Measurement of the quantity of substances dumped into water or into the municipal or syndicated sewage system, divided by kind. Data on a 3-year basis.

Measurement procedure	Total dumped kg of total nitrogen, phosphor, chlorides, BOD, COD, metals and other significant substances and characteristics of the processes.
	Total dumped kg for each group of pollutant or for single pollutant indexed on productive or economic standards according to the kind of organization, for example:
	• kg of COD/tons of output x manufacturing sector • kg of BOD/number of employees x utility and services companies
	Number of initiatives aimed at reducing waste dumping and the relevant pollutant concentration; brief description. Total investment/VA.
8.1.6.	Waste management
Additional	Qualitative and quantitative
Explanatory remarks	Measurement of the quantity of waste produced by the organization divided according to kind (at least assimilated to urban, special and hazardous waste) and destination (disposal, recovery, recycling). Data on a 3-year basis.
Measurement procedure	kg of waste produced by category (assimilated to urban, special, hazardous waste) and indexed based on productive or economic standards according to the kind of organization, for example:
	• kg produced/tons of output x manufacturing sector • kg produced/number of employees x utility and services companies.
	Percentage (%) of waste sent to re-usage/recycle by category Kg of waste sent to disposal by kind of disposal. Number of initiatives aimed at reducing and recovering/recycling waste; brief description of them. Total investment/VA.

8.2	*Environmental strategy and community relations*
Additional	Qualitative and quantitative
Explanatory remarks	Evaluation of the definition of an environmental strategy and of activities to inform and involve the stakeholders, as well as the policies adopted to implement the best environmental standards/tools. Some examples could be initiatives of dialogue with

	environmental associations, the organization of public presentation of the environmental report, structured communication with stakeholders to formulate the indicators to measure the company's environmental performance, etc.
Measurement procedure	Description of the adopted environmental strategy and the activities of communication/dialogue and involvement carried out by the companies and aimed at the stakeholders. Description of environmental tools adopted. Description of the environmental strategy adopted in developing countries.

Index